WORD OF WISDOM HELPS

FOOD

WORD OF WISDOM HELPS

FOOD

By Mildred Nelson Smith

Herald Publishing House, Independence, Missouri

COPYRIGHT © 1979
MILDRED NELSON SMITH

All rights in this book are reserved. No part of the text
may be reproduced in any form without written permission
of the publishers, except brief quotations used in
connection with reviews in magazines or newspapers.

Library of Congress Cataloging in Publication Data

Smith, Mildred Nelson.
  Word of Wisdom Helps: Food
  1. Cookery. I. Title.
TX652.S57   641.5   78-16735
ISBN 0-8309-0221-X

Printed in the United States of America

CONTENTS

Acknowledgments	7
Introduction	8
Facts About Certain Popular Foods	35
Facts About Recipes	55
Helps for Making 100 Percent Whole Wheat Products	61
Quick Breads	78
Cakes	96
Cookies	113
Pastries	123
Fruit Desserts	136
Milk Desserts	149
Main Dishes	157
Vegetables	193
Soups and Salads	212
Beverages	226
Confections	236
Recipe Index	240

ACKNOWLEDGMENTS

I deeply appreciate the assistance of all the people who have, through the years, contributed to the happiness and well-being of our family by sharing their knowledge and skill in the fields of food and nutrition. I am indebted to numerous unnamed family members and friends who may recognize in this work a recipe or an adaptation of one they once shared with me. I have borrowed liberally from knowledge imparted to me and from recipes (some of which I helped develop) provided me by Iowa State University and the United States Department of Agriculture Cooperative Extension Service.

Special thanks must go to the Nauvoo millers, Lee and Carmen Ourth, and to their predecessors, Harold and Mildred Smith, for allowing me to share many of the recipes they developed through the years and have printed in their own recipe book.

I want to thank Pamela and Duane Duff for permitting me to borrow from their cookbook, and Marvel Riley who spent many hours making her recipes available to me.

I appreciate the helpful suggestions of those who read the manuscript at the request of the First Presidency of the Reorganized Church of Jesus Christ of Latter Day Saints.

Calculations of nutritive values given in fact sheets and in recipes are from data contained in these United States Department of Agriculture publications:

Agriculture Handbook No. 8, Composition of Foods, Raw, Processed, Prepared, 1975.

Agriculture Handbook No. 8-1, Composition of Foods, Dairy and Egg Products, Raw, Processed, Prepared, Nov. 1976.

Agriculture Handbook No. 456, Nutritive Value of Foods in Common Units, 1975.

Home and Garden Bulletin No. 72, Nutritive Value of Foods, 1971.

Home Economics Research Report No. 36, Pantothenic Acid, Vitamin B6 and Vitamin B12 in Foods, 1969.

INTRODUCTION

This is not just a cookbook. It is a book to be *read* for practical helps in the selection, preparation, and serving of good, plain basic foods in a manner designed to preserve their beauty and wholesomeness. Recipes are included to illustrate a variety of ways in which foods may be prepared and served, but no attempt is made to supplant all cookbooks. Standard works will still be needed to supply information not included here, and specialty items or equipment will require their own instructions. Meats and gourmet foods receive little attention in this work except for a few family favorites not readily available from most other sources.

The purpose of the book is to make observing the "Word of Wisdom" (Doctrine and Covenants 86) easy, economical, and enjoyable. Its suggestions are based on the premise that

1. Whole grains are meant to be the staff of life.

2. Whole grains need to be supplemented by other proteins. Animal proteins are excellent choices. Eggs, milk, and fish are especially helpful because of their availability, efficient use of primary foods in their production, and comparative low cost.

3. Meats (flesh of beasts and fowls) are to be used sparingly and in times of winter, cold, famine, and excess of hunger (especial nutritional need).[1]

4. Vegetables and fruits are vital to healthful living, especially green leafy vegetables and fruits with fairly certain supplies of vitamin C.

5. Excessive use of sweets should be avoided.

6. Calories and protein should fit individual need.[2]

7. Beverages should be free of harmful drugs and excessive sweets and should provide needed nutrients commensurate with their cost.

8. Food choices should be on the basis of current facts, not on unfounded claims of nutritional value.[3]

9. Food is meant to be enjoyed.

Because I expect the recipes contained in the book to be used by many inexperienced cooks, I have been very explicit in giving instructions.

Since accurate measurement contributes to happy results in food preparation, some helps with measuring—including conversion to metric measurements—are included.

The use of whole wheat flour made from many varieties of wheat, each with its own unique characteristics, ground by varying methods to varying consistencies, poses problems in the formulation of good whole wheat recipes. Before you attempt any recipe using whole wheat flour, read the section titled *"Very Important Information."* It will help you adjust the recipes to fit your flour and ultimately to have good results.

Suggested meal plans and recipes are obviously designed largely for use in the United States and Canada with adaptations of some Oriental and Mexican dishes. It is hoped that the suggestions will stimulate ideas for adapting available food supplies in other cultural settings to good nutrition practices. There is no effort to proscribe individual tastes or national dishes.

PLANNING MAKES ALL THE DIFFERENCE

Planning is the key to good nutrition at prices consistent with good stewardship. Wise planning will be needed if the right foods are to be available at the right time, waste avoided, bargains capitalized on, the level of nutrition kept high and the level of expenditure kept low. A few suggestions may be helpful.

Plan for Good Nutrition

The Daily Food Plan designed by modern nutritionists calls for the following:

1. Four or more servings of fruits and vegetables, including at least one fruit or vegetable important for vitamin C daily and a dark green or dark yellow vegetable at least every other day, plus fruits and vegetables including potatoes. Count as one serving, ½ cup vegetable or one whole or half fruit as usually served.

2. Four or more servings whole grain, enriched or restored cereals or bread daily. Count a one oz. slice of bread or 1 oz. dry cereal or ½ to ¾ cup cooked cereal, noodles, etc., as one serving.

3. Two or more servings of foods rich in protein as are meats, fish, poultry, eggs, dry beans and peas, nuts, peanut butter. Count as one serving, 2 to 3 oz. cooked boneless meat, poultry, or fish; 2 eggs; 1 cup cooked dry beans, peas, or lentils; or 4 Tbsp. peanut butter. Smaller portions may be combined with whole grains and milk or milk products to supply the need safely.

4. Milk or milk products to equal:
> 2 to 3 cups for children under 9 years
> 3 cups or more for children 9 to 12 years
> 4 cups or more for teen-agers
> 2 cups or more for adults (3 or more for pregnant women and 4 or more for nursing mothers)

"Cups" as used here are 8 oz. ones; ½ cup cottage cheese, ice cream, or ice milk may be substituted for ⅓ c. milk. A 1-inch cube (17 g.- 0.6 oz.) cheddar cheese may be substituted for ½ c. milk.

(See M. N. Smith, *Word of Wisdom, Principle with Promise*, chapters 4, 5, 6 for details of nutrients supplied and correlation with the Word of Wisdom. Consult extension service materials for specific helps in meal planning.)

Calorie and Protein Needs

Many of us are so aware of 1200 and 1500 Calorie diets for weight reduction that we tend to think these values are normal for all dietaries. More nearly adequate average intakes to assure efficient utilization of protein and adequate intake of other nutrients run something like this:

Years	Calories per day[4]
Children 1 through 10	1300 to 2400
Males 11 through 22	2800 to 3000
Males 23 through 50	About 2700
Males 51 or older	About 2400
Females 11 through 14	About 2400
Females 15 through 22	About 2100
Females 23 through 50	About 2000
Females 51 or older	About 1800

For pregnancy add 300 Calories; for lactation add 500 Calories. Persons of both sexes over 51 will need less food than indicated if activity is reduced. It is better for them to keep activity up and eat the food.

These figures are for "reference" persons. Children who grow faster or adults who grow bigger will need more food for the same amount of activity. Those who work really hard (such as lumberjacks and athletes) may increase their need by several hundred Calories. Those who are very sedentary may need less.

Recommended Daily Dietary Allowances for protein run like this. Variations in need for body growth and repair and quality of protein in the average diet should be taken into consideration, of course.

Children 1 to 10, weights up to 66 lb. (30 kg.)	23-36 grams
Boys and girls 11 to 14, weights up to 97 lb. (44 kg.)	44 grams
Girls ages 15-18 years, weights up to 119 lb. (54 kg.)	48 grams
Females 19 years to life, weight 128 lb. (58kg.)	46 grams
Females 19 years to life, weight 154 lb. (70 kg.)	56 grams
Boys ages 15-22, weight up to 147 lb. (67 kg.)	54 grams
Males 23 years to life, weight 154 lbs. (70 kg.)	56 grams
Males 23 years to life, weight 198 lbs. (90 kg.)	72 grams

(For pregnancy add 30 grams protein; for lactation add 20 grams protein.) (RDA for nonobese adults is 0.8 grams protein per kilogram of weight. One kg. = weight in pounds divided by 2.2. There are 2.2 lb. per kg.)

Buying Hints

1. Plan menus at least a week ahead. Make plans flexible enough to take advantage of specials in the stores. Include snacks if needed.

2. Study the grocery ads. Plan menus with specials in mind.

3. Go to the store with a list. Buy only what is on the list *plus* unexpected bargains you can adequately substitute, use, or store.

4. Stock up on staples when they are on sale.

5. Keep an eye on markdowns. Often good quality foods are available at a bargain because of outdating, marred packaging, and the like. "Overripe" fruit may be enjoyed most, and grapes are no less good if they have fallen off the stems. Some outdated foods to look for are bread, eggs, cheeses, jams and jellies, meats, and salad dressings. Be certain those you buy are still good quality. Spoiled food is no bargain.

Overripe or blemished fruit and vegetables are often real bargains. Foods that may not keep for another day on the grocery shelves may keep for long periods of time if made into soup, gelatin salad, a casserole to be frozen or just refrigerated. If there is a bargain in ripe bananas, for example, buy enough for a fruit plate for lunch, a snack for the children, and a gelatin dessert with pineapple or orange juice to be served later. Some could be sliced on the next morning's cereal, and—if any remain—they might be mashed with a bit of vitamin C (to keep them bright) and frozen for a banana loaf in the future. And bananas *can* be refrigerated for days; this is not done at the store because refrigeration causes the skins to darken, but the food value remains the same.

6. Locate markets other than the grocery store that may have foods at bargain prices. Farmer's markets often offer bonanzas of price and flavor. Bakery discount outlets fre-

quently have fresh bread at one third the regular price. Some "warehouse" markets may have food in case lots at a bargain. Even the grocery store may offer a good discount on quantity purchases.

7. Adjust your buying to the season. There are times during the year when fresh grapefruit or oranges or broccoli or beans are far cheaper than processed foods; there are other times when they are poor in quality and out of sight in price. Just before the new crop comes in is often a time when processed fruits and vegetables are put on special and may be purchased at bargain prices.

8. Take advantage of available storage facilities to freeze or can your own food when it is available and inexpensive.

9. Leave junk foods off your list and in the store, but be sure to have enough nutritious goodies around the home that family members will not be tempted to patronize the store for the junk. Early training and a bit of self-discipline helps. Who knows, if enough junk foods are left in the market, they might just disappear from the shelves! They are there only because people buy them.

10. Avoid the use of a lot of prepared foods and mixes. With little more effort you can make your own and have them tastier, cheaper, and more nutritious. Cereals are a good case in point. Hot cereals are really very easy to make and may be made ahead of time and warmed quickly for breakfast. Or you may make your own dry cereal. (There are recipes in the breakfast section.) Of course yours will not have 100 percent of the USRDA of 10 vitamins and 7 minerals, but if you need them, you can purchase them more cheaply in a pill than in breakfast cereals—and yours may have a few vitamins and minerals the commercial ones never thought of. The balance of vitamins and minerals can be easily obtained in other meals and snacks of the day—if menus are properly planned.

11. Read the labels. Most of them will not tell all they ought to tell, but there is some important information on them. In the U.S.A. look for:

(1) The name of the product. It must have a common or usual name that clearly identifies what it is. If it is made to

look like a more nutritious product or is represented as a substitute for such a food, it must be labeled "imitation." If it is a nutritious substance that is similar to another, it can bear a different name and not have to be so labeled. "Eggbeaters," for example, are eggless but do not have to be labeled "Imitation."

(2) The weight. Unfortunately, the net weight includes the water, oil, or syrup in which a product is packed. It is hard to tell how much actual food is present. Efforts are in process to require the weight of the food to be specified.

(3) The name and place of business of the manufacturer, packer, or distributor. It is there so anyone wanting to comment, complain, or ask for information can contact a responsible person.

(4) The ingredients, if the product is not "standardized." (To learn the ingredients of a standardized product not voluntarily labeled, it is necessary to contact the manufacturer or consult the U. S. Food and Drug Administration food standards.) Ingredients must be listed by weight in descending order. Unfortunately, it is impossible to know the percentage of each ingredient from this. If "wheat flour" is listed before "whole wheat flour" on the label of "whole wheat" bread, it is apparent that more than half the flour used is white, but how much more is not discernible. If a number of grains have been used, and "wheat flour" heads the list, it is apparent that white flour is there in larger proportion than any other.

If more than one form of a product, such as sugar, is used, it is impossible to tell where in the list of ingredients that substance actually belongs. Some products include it as "sugar," "corn sweetener," "corn syrup," "honey," "lactose," "maltose," "dextrose," and other "ose" forms, all of which would need to be added together to show accurately the amount of sweetening actually included. (Chemical terms ending in "ose" usually refer to a sugar.) I have seen honey listed after salt but included to make the product appeal to those who hold honey in high esteem. There are some products in which varying forms of sugar perform needed func-

14

tions. There just needs to be a way to also identify the amount of sugar contained.

(5) Additives used (with a few exceptions). Artificial color does not have to be listed on butter, cheese, and ice cream. In other products the presence of artificial colors and flavors must be noted, but they do not have to be given by name. The Food and Drug Administration is suggesting that some, especially tartrazine, FD&C Yellow No. 5, be listed by name because of the number of persons thought to be allergic to it.

(6) Nutritional labeling. Any product may be voluntarily nutritionally labeled. If a nutrient has been added or a nutritional claim is made for the product, it must be labeled with appropriate information:

a. The number and size of servings.

b. The Calories, amount of protein, carbohydrates, and fat in each serving. You can even tell how many Calories come from each nutrient. Multiply the grams of carbohydrates and protein by four and the grams of fat by nine. Add the figures for the total, which should about equal the amount of Calories given. If alcohol is included, its grams must be multiplied by seven. It is sometimes shocking to discover that some "natural" cereals, for example, have more than half of their Calories from fat.

c. Seven of the 19 vitamins and minerals for which there have been USRDAs[5] established must be listed by percentages of the USRDA contained, or a statement must be made that there is less than 2 percent of the USRDA present. Values for 12 other vitamins and minerals, cholesterol, fatty acids, and sodium may be included optionally.

This information may be helpful, or it can be misleading. Some cereals, for example, may have large amounts of these vitamins and minerals with little other supporting nutrient content. Nutritious home cooked cereals invariably *appear* less nutritious than these highly fortified prepared ones.

d. Protein must also be given as a percentage of the USRDA. These percentages must be given in terms of their protein efficiency rating (PER)[6] when compared to the PER of the casein of milk. If the PER of the protein is equal to or

15

better than that of casein, it is given as a percentage of 45 grams USRDA. If the PER is less than that of the milk protein but not as low as 20 percent of casein for adults and 40 percent for children, it is given as a percentage of 65 grams USRDA. If the PER is lower than that specified, the food cannot be considered a significant source of protein.

e. If fats and cholesterol are given, the fats are usually given as "saturated," "unsaturated," or "polyunsaturated," and the statement is made that the information is for those who have been advised by a physician to modify their total dietary intake of fat and cholesterol.

Saturated fats are those that have no chemical bonds free to accept additional hydrogen. They are usually viscous or solid at normal room temperatures. Their primary use in the diet is for energy. Animal fats often are high in saturates, but some plant fats are also. Coconut oil is highly saturated.

Fats can be saturated by hydrogenation, but most food fats are only partially hydrogenated to obtain desired consistencies and keeping qualities when hydrogenation is employed. Ordinary margarine, for example, has only about 2.2 grams saturated fat per tablespoon margarine and 8.7 to 9.0 grams unsaturated fat, of which 3.1 to 4.4 grams is the essential linoleic. By contrast, butter has about 6.3 grams saturated and 4.1 grams unsaturated fat per tablespoon.

Unsaturated fats are those that do not have all their chemical bonds attached to hydrogen or some other entity. They generally remain fluid at room temperatures unless they are emulsified as they are in margarine or mayonnaise. They may be monounsaturates (with one open bond) as is oleic acid or polyunsaturates (with more than one open bond) as are the essential fatty acids linoleic (from which the others can be made), arachidonic or linolenic. They are likewise found in both plant and animal fats and oils but in larger proportions in plant oils and in some fish fats and oils.

The RDA for the essential fatty acids, linoleic plus linolenic plus arachidonic, varies with the Caloric intake of the individual. For one consuming 2,400 Calories it is 5 grams. For one eating 3,000 Calories it is 6 grams or 54 Calories

16

worth.[7] That can easily be obtained from 2 tablespoons of ordinary margarine, but with salad dressings, whole grains, nuts, vegetables, and baked goods made with margarine or oils in the diet, it is not necessary to get it all from margarine.

The U.S. Select Committee on Nutrition and Human Need has recently recommended that no more than 30 percent of the Calories eaten should be in the form of fat, and that the fat eaten should be about evenly divided between saturated, monounsaturated, and polyunsaturated.[8] Following that recommendation would markedly increase the amount of polyunsaturates over the current RDA.

The American Medical Association has issued a statement, "There is insufficient evidence at this time to assume that benefits will be derived from the adoption of such universal dietary goals," and the American Dietetic Association indicates that while we should continue to examine our dietary habits closely, our practice should probably be somewhere between complete adoption and outright rejection of the goals. See "Dietary Goals; A Statement by the American Dietetic Association," *Journal of the American Dietetic Association*, Vol. 71, Sept. 1977, p. 227.

Increased intake of polyunsaturates is recommended as a method for reducing cholesterol levels in the blood. That it has been effective in so doing is documented.[9] There is also concern, however, for other effects of high polyunsaturate intake. It is well known that increased polyunsaturate intake requires increased vitamin E in the diet.[10] Now high intakes are being suspected of promoting cancer in laboratory animals.[11]

TIME-SAVERS

1. *Plan sequence meals.* That means planned leftovers ("planned-overs"). Here are a couple of examples.
   (1) Prepare a big pot of beans. Serve beans and ham one day. A day or so later serve tacos. Follow the tacos a few days later with chili made from leftover ground

beef, beans, and taco sauce, and if there are still beans left, have a hearty bean soup or bean rabbit (yum!). The beans may be refrigerated for a week without significant loss of nutritive quality, or they may be frozen between times of use. If they are to be frozen, it is best to freeze them in small containers that hold just enough for each meal in which they are to be used.

(2) Another sequence of meals may start with egg foo yung and rice. The extra egg foo yung may go with the youngsters or man of the house for lunch. They're good cold, too. Plan enough rice for breakfast the next morning, a rice pudding for the following day, and finally fried rice on a day in the future.

2. *Make good use of freezer space.*

(1) Have a baking day once a week, or less often. With one bread baking make buns, sweet rolls, pizza crusts, loaves to last, and keep them fresh in the freezer. Make your own pop-up waffles and pancakes of whole wheat, real milk, and eggs.

(2) Do the same for cookies, cakes, muffins, piecrusts, pies, and the like.

(3) Purchase large supplies of bread when it is on special and freeze.

(4) When making foods like meat loaf, lasagna, eggplant Parmesan, taco sauce, chili, whole grain wheat, make enough for several meals and freeze the extra. Foods may be placed in small containers with just enough for one meal or baked in individual baking dishes for attractive, easy service. Not only time but also energy is saved when full use is made of the oven or stove when it is used.

(5) Buy fruits, meats, etc., in large containers when there is a price advantage, divide into amounts to be used at one time and freeze (e.g. 20 oz. cans of pineapple cost much less per ounce than 14 ounce cans, and *sometimes* large cans of tuna cost less per ounce than small. Check to make sure).

Plan to Use It All—No Waste

1. Keep a soup jar handy. If liquid must be drained from vegetables, noodles, or meats, if there are leftover drippings, gravy, bits of vegetables, meats, noodles, or pan scrapings of lasagna, meat loaf, or casseroles, put them in the soup jar, not into the garbage. Even rinse the broiler pan and baking pans for that browned flavor. Use discretion, of course, and you will want to lift off extra fat after the food has cooled. If there isn't enough for a full meal when you are ready to use it, add potatoes, carrots, onions, or open a can of commercial vegetable soup and combine the two.

2. When there are leftover syrups from canned fruit, serve them to sweeten breakfast cereals or put them into a syrup jar and heat to serve on pancakes, French toast, waffles, and the like. They can take the place of a lot of sugar in puddings and cobblers.

3. Plan to use every crumb of breadstuffs.
   (1) Refrigerate whole wheat breads of every kind. Remove enough for each meal and allow to warm or heat in a bun warmer or toaster if desired.
   (2) Use dry breads in dressings, meat or fish loaves, mackerel or salmon patties, bread puddings, French toast, or butter them for casserole toppings.
   (3) Save leftover pancakes, waffles, French toast and rewarm in a toaster, oven, or bunwarmer. Serve as though fresh or spread with butter, brown sugar, and cinnamon, roll up and serve, or use in bread puddings.
   (4) Serve dried cake with stirred custard, fruit sauce, or whipped topping. It may also be folded in with whipped topping and fruit gelatin dessert for a special treat. Or it may be used as short cake, combined with fruit, and drenched with milk or cream.

4. Learn how to store fresh fruits and vegetables to minimize the possibility of spoilage. (Ask your USDA or Canadian Extension Service for information.)

PLANS FOR INDIVIDUAL MEALS

Breakfast—A good breakfast includes:
1. Vitamin C, usually as a fruit or juice. If low vitamin C fruits or juices such as dried fruits, bananas, peaches, apples are occasionally used, a good source of vitamin C should be planned for later in the day.
2. One-fourth to one-third the Calories required for the day in nutritious, unrefined, restored or enriched foods.
3. One-fourth to one-third the protein required for the day.
4. Some fats. These may be naturally in the food (eggs, meats, whole milk).
5. A variety of colors and textures for appetite appeal.

A frequently used menu includes:
1. A fruit or juice.
2. Whole grain cereal with milk and/or whole grain bread with butter or margarine.
3. A protein rich food such as milk, eggs, meat, fish, cheese, nuts.
4. A beverage (milk may double as beverage and protein rich food).

Lunch or Dinner—A good lunch or dinner includes:
1. A protein rich food.
2. A fruit or vegetable or both, for a total of at least four fruits and vegetables for the day - one of them dark green, one high C.
3. A cereal food (bread, rice, spaghetti, etc., . . . may be in the main dish).
4. A beverage (milk may double as beverage and protein rich food). Two to four servings of milk are recommended each day.

Frequently used menus include:
1. A protein rich main dish (may be salad, soup, sandwich, casserole, meat dish, fish, poultry, beans, etc.).
2. One or more vegetables, frequently dark green (may be in salad, soup, sandwich, casserole, or alone).

3. Bread with butter or margarine (may be in main dish or dessert).
4. Fruit, frequently raw, or other dessert as energy needs require or allow.
5. A beverage (milk may double as protein rich food or at least a portion of it).

Breakfasts

Orange or Grapefruit Half or
    Orange Juice or Tomato Juice
Whole Wheat Toast or Bread[12]
Butter   Milk[13]
(Optional - Honey or Jam)

Tomato Juice
Butter-Poached or Scrambled or
    Fried or Cooked-in-the-Shell Eggs
Whole Wheat Bread or Toast
Butter   Milk or Cereal Beverage

Cantaloupe Slice or Orange or
Grapefruit Half or Papaya or Other
    Fruit or Juice High in Vitamin C
Whole Grain Wheat (Cooked
    overnight in a slow cooker or
    rewarmed)
Milk   Honey or Brown Sugar
Whole Wheat Toast   Butter   Milk

Tomato Juice or Grapefruit Half
Toaster or Bun Warmer Heated
Pancakes, Waffles or French
    Toast   Butter   Apple, Guava,
    Rhubarb or Other Fruit Sauce
Milk   Syrup if desired

Choice of Breakfast Fruits or Juices
    as above
Reheated Cereal (Rolled Oats,
    Whole Wheat, Mixed Grain,
    Cornmeal, Brown Rice) with
    Raisins added if desired
Cinnamon with Rice and
    Others if desired
Whole Wheat Toast   Butter   Milk

Strawberries or Other Berries,
    Peaches or Bananas on Prepared
    (Dry) Whole Wheat Cereal
Milk   Honey if needed
Whole Wheat Toast   Butter   Milk
Water or Cereal Beverage
(If not Strawberries, have a high
vitamin C food during the day.)

Scandinavian Sweet Soup or
    Prunes or Other Dried Fruit
    (Cooked)
Cottage Cheese
Whole Wheat Toast or
Bread   Butter
Milk or Cereal Beverage

21

Tomato Juice
Whole Wheat French
Toast   Butter
Syrup or Fruit Sauce
Milk or Cereal Beverage or Water

Cantaloupe or Honeydew Slice
   or Half
Cottage Cheese
Whole Wheat Toast   Butter
Milk or Cereal Beverage or Water

Sliced Tomatoes   Cheese Slices
Toast (Whole Wheat)   Butter
Milk or Cereal Beverage

Lunches and Dinners or Supper

Peanut Butter With Lettuce
   Sandwich on Whole Wheat
   Bread
Sliced Tomatoes   Banana
Milk

Potato-Kale or Parsley Soup
Whole Wheat Croutons or Bread
   Butter
Cheese Slices
Carrot and Celery Sticks
Apple Sauce
Milk or Cereal Beverage or Water

Potatoes, Onion and Kale *or*
   Potatoes and Green Beans
Sliced Cold Meats or Cheese
Garden Relishes (Radishes, Green
   Onions, Carrots, Sweet Peppers)
Whole Wheat Bread   Butter
Milk

Cottage Cheese-Sweet Pepper
   Salad in a Tomato Cup on
   Lettuce with Paprika and
   Parsley Garnish
Corn on the Cob   Butter
Peaches
Milk

Hard-Cooked Eggs
Garden Peas and New Potatoes
   in Cream Sauce
Garden Lettuce Salad
Whole Wheat Bread   Butter
Strawberries
Milk

Creamed Asparagus on Whole
   Wheat Toast
Deviled Eggs
Cabbage and Tomato Salad with
   Coleslaw Dressing
Stewed Rhubarb
Milk

Boiled Vegetable Dinner
Cheese Wedges
Whole Wheat Bread   Butter
Tapioca Pudding
Milk or Cereal Beverage or Water

Creamed Tuna, Salmon, Turkey,
   Chicken *or* Hard-Cooked Eggs
   on Whole Wheat Toast
Green Peas, Beans, Broccoli,
   Asparagus, Brussels Sprouts,
   Okra *or* Cabbage
Waldorf Salad
Milk

Cream of Tomato Soup
Grilled Cheese Sandwiches
Carrot Sticks
Strawberry or Other Jam
Milk, Cereal Beverage, or Water

Vegetable Soup
Egg Salad Sandwiches on Whole
　Wheat Bread With Butter
　and Lettuce
or
Peanut Butter Sandwiches with
Lettuce on Whole Wheat Bread
Fresh Fruit
Milk

Scrambled Eggs
Spinach, Kale or Other Greens
Beet Pickles
Whole Wheat Bread   Butter
Fruit Cup   Cowboy Cookies
Milk

Stewed or Canned Tomatoes
Whole Wheat Bread   Butter
Bread or Rice Pudding or Baked
　Custard
Milk

Scandinavian Sweet Soup
Cottage Cheese   Lettuce Wedges
Whole Wheat Bread   Butter
Milk

Mush (Porridge) and Milk or
　Bread and Milk With Sorghum,
　Honey, Jelly, or Jam
Onion Rings if Desired
Fresh Fruit
Cereal Beverage or Water

Omelet with Cheese Cubes and
　Bacon or Soya Bacon Chips
Green Beans or Broccoli Spears
Sliced Tomatoes
Fruit Cup or Fruit Gelatin
Milk

Fried Rice (Leftover Brown Rice
　reheated with table fat or
　bacon drippings with leftover
　vegetables, meats, poultry, etc.,
　with one or more beaten eggs
　added just before removing
　from heat) Soy Sauce
Fruit Cobbler
Milk

Leftover Beans with Ham or
　Butter
Carrot-Raisin Salad or Cabbage
　Slaw
Whole Wheat Bread   Butter
Cottage Cheese with Sorghum,
Pineapple or Scandinavian Sweet
　Soup
Milk

Tuna, Chicken, Turkey, Salmon
　or Ham Salad Served in Lettuce
　Cup Garnished with Tomato
　Wedges and Parsley
Green Soybeans, Limas or
　Succotash
Whole Wheat Bread   Butter
Canned Fruit or Fried Apples
Milk

Tuna, Salmon, Turkey, Chicken, Ham, Roast Beef *or* Cold Cut Sandwiches on Whole Wheat Bread   Butter
Relish Tray of Radishes, Carrots, Celery, Cucumbers, Pickles, Olives
Fruit *or* Melon
Milk

Chicken, Turkey, Mushroom, Bean, *or* Other Soup
Whole Wheat Croutons, Toast *or* Bread   Butter
Stuffed Celery
Ice Cream
Milk, Cereal Beverage or Water

Leftover Stew (Reheated) on Brown Rice (Reheated)
Soy Sauce   Lettuce Salad
Whole Wheat Bread   Butter
Stuffed Dates or Prunes
Milk

Fruit Plate (Cottage Cheese with Mayonnaise Type Dressing and Cherry Garnish surrounded by any array of fruits available reasonably arranged beautifully on lettuce bed)
Whole Wheat Bread
Peanut Butter
Milk

Whole Wheat Pancakes *or* French Toast   Butter
Fruit Sauce or Fresh Fruit
Ham, Sausage, Bacon *or* Butter Poached Eggs
Milk or Cereal Beverage

Chili   Crackers
Carrot and   Celery Sticks
Apple
Milk

Whole Wheat Waffles
Butter   Syrup
Cottage Cheese and Pineapple Ring Salad on lettuce with cherry
Milk

SUGGESTED MENUS FOR SUMMER MEALS

Summer Breakfasts

Orange Juice
Prepared Cereal with Sliced Banana *or* Peaches
Honey   Milk
Whole Wheat Toast
Butter
Milk or Cereal Beverage

Grapefruit Juice
Cooked Whole Wheat Cereal
Honey   Milk
Whole Wheat Cinnamon Toast or Rolls
Milk or Cereal Beverage

Cantaloupe
Rolled Oats (with Raisins
   if desired)
Honey   Top Milk
Biscuits   Butter
Milk or Cereal Beverage

Orange Slices
Brown Rice
Brown Sugar
Cinnamon
Milk
Whole Wheat Toast *or*
   Muffins
Butter   Jam
Milk or Cereal Beverage

Tomato Juice
Whole Wheat Pancakes *or*
   French Toast
Syrup
Butter
Eggs if desired
Milk or Cereal Beverage

Strawberries
Cornmeal Mush
Honey   Top Milk
Whole Wheat Toast
Butter
Milk or Cereal Beverage

Cantaloupe or Tomato
   Juice
Scrambled Eggs *or*
   Butter-Poached Eggs
Whole Wheat Breakfast
   Cake
Butter
Milk or Cereal Beverage

Papaya, Mango *or* Honeydew
   Melon
Cottage Cheese
Whole Wheat Toast
Butter   Sorghum *or* Molasses
Milk or Cereal Beverage

Summer Lunches

Peanut Butter Sandwich
Relish Tray
Watermelon
Milk

Cheese Plate
Buttered Green Beans
   Cooked with Potatoes
   and Onions
Sliced Tomatoes
Whole Wheat Bread   Butter
Fresh Fruit   Oatmeal Cookies
Beverage

Vegetable Soup
Cheese and Crackers
Radishes and Green Onions
Baked Custard
Milk

Egg Foo Yung
Rice
Soy Sauce
Pineapple Chiffon Dessert
or Ice Cream with Brownie
Beverage

25

Tuna Salad in Lettuce
  Cups with Tomato and
  Parsley
Buttered Broccoli
Whole Wheat Rolls
Butter   Jam
Fruit Gelatin
Beverage

Fruit Plate on Lettuce, centered
with dip of Cottage Cheese
  Topped with Salad Dressing
  and Cherry
Triscuits or Whole Wheat Rolls
  or Toast
Peanut Butter
Milk

Souffle or Omelet
Harvard Beets or Seven-Minute
  Cabbage
Garden Relishes (Radishes, Green
  Onions, Carrots)
Whole Wheat Bread   Butter
Stewed Rhubarb   Milk

Cottage Cheese with
  Chopped Green Pepper,
  Onion and Salad Dressing on
  Lettuce with Tomato and Parsley
Buttered Peas
Bread   Butter
German Love Cookies
Beverage

Egg Salad Sandwiches with Black-
  eyed Peas or Soy Beans or
  Pizza Made with Tuna Fish and
  Cheese
Tossed Salad
Rice Pudding
Top Milk
Beverage

Scandinavian Sweet Soup
Cheese   Lettuce
Whole Wheat Bread   Butter
Milk

Summer Dinners or Suppers

Chopstick Tuna
Buttered Peas
Tossed Salad
Whole Wheat Rolls   Butter
Pickles   Jam
Pineapple Upside-down Cake or
  Fresh Pineapple
Beverage

Mackerel Patties
Buttered Limas or Rice with
  Soy Sauce
Cabbage Salad
Whole Wheat Bread
Fruit Cobbler or Stewed Rhubarb
Top Milk
Beverage

Baked Beans
Buttered Kale or Other
  Green
Carrot-Pineapple-Gelatin Salad
Boston Brown Muffins
Butter
Sliced Peaches
Beverage

Macaroni, Cheese, and Egg
  Casserole
Buttered Whole Carrots
  or Beets
Lettuce with French Dressing
Whole Wheat Bread   Butter
Cherry Puffs or Fresh Cherries
Beverage

26

Tacos (Hard-cooked Eggs *or*
  Soya Protein "Meat" Instead
  of Hamburger; Season Beans
  with Butter or Margarine
  Instead of Ham) *or* Beans
  Seasoned with Butter
Spinach, Chard, *or* Other Greens
Corn Bread   Butter
Applesauce or Fresh Berries
Milk or Cereal Beverage

Tuna Noodle Casserole
  or Green Rice with
  Shrimp
Buttered Broccoli
Sliced Tomato Salad with Green
  Pepper
Whole Wheat Bread   Butter
Peach or Apple Crisp with
Milk
Cereal Beverage or Water

Ocean Perch *or* Fish Sticks
  (Baked or Fried)
Tartar Sauce
Parsley Potatoes *or*
  French Fried Potatoes
Buttered Green Beans
Perfection Salad
Whole Wheat Bread   Butter
Fruit Cup   Coco Mints
Milk or Cereal Beverage

Lasagne with Textured Protein
  Instead of Ground Beef *or*
  Whole Wheat Goulash
Green Beans Tossed Salad
Whole Wheat Rolls or Biscuits
Butter
Nut Torte with Cheese
  Topping
Milk or Cereal Beverage
  or Water

SOME SUGGESTED MENUS FOR

Winter Meals[14]
Winter Breakfasts

Orange Juice
Cooked Mixed Grain Cereal
  with Raisins
Honey   Milk
Whole Wheat Toast
Butter   Jam
Milk or Cereal Beverage

Pineapple Juice with
  Vitamin C
Rolled Oats
Honey   Top Milk
Crisp Bacon (if desired)
Whole Wheat Toast
Butter
Milk or Cereal Beverage

Grapefruit Juice
Brown Rice
Brown Sugar
Cinnamon   Top Milk
Whole Wheat Doughnuts
Milk or Cereal Beverage

Orange Slices
French Toast from Whole
  Wheat Bread
Syrup   Butter
Crisp Bacon (if desired)
Milk or Cereal Beverage

27

Grapefruit Half
Cooked Whole Wheat
   Cereal
Brown Sugar or Honey
Top Milk
Cinnamon Toast or Rolls
Milk or Cereal Beverage

Tomato Juice
Scrambled Eggs (Bacon if
   desired)
Whole Wheat Breakfast Cake
Butter
Milk or Cereal Beverage

Tomato Juice
Whole Wheat Pancakes
Sausage (if desired)
Syrup   Butter
Milk or Cereal Beverage

Frozen Strawberries on
   Prepared Whole Grain
   Cereal
Honey   Milk
Whole Wheat Toast   Butter
Milk or Cereal Beverage

Winter Lunches

Tomato Soup
Grilled Cheese Sandwich
Relish Tray
Oatmeal-Date Bars
Water, Fruit Drink, Milk
   or Cereal Beverage

Mackerel Patties *or*
   Salisbury Steak
Rice & Soy Sauce *or* Corn
Sliced Tomato Salad
Whole Wheat Bread
Butter
Banana   Cowboy Cookies
Milk

Tacos *or*
Pinto Beans with Ham Bone
Corn Bread and Butter
Coleslaw
Fruit Gelatin *or* Fresh Fruit
Milk

Chicken Salad (in lettuce
   cup garnished with
   parsley and paprika)
Fried Okra *or* Buttered
   Peas   Butter
Whole Wheat Rolls
Cheese-Apple Crisp with Lemon
   Sauce
Milk

Chili
Crackers, Triscuits,
   or Bread
Butter
Carrot and Celery Sticks
Tapioca Pudding *or*
   Baked Custard
Milk

Leftovers served as
   Sandwiches
or Pizza and Tossed
   Salad
Ice Cream
Milk or Fruit Drink

28

Ham Salad Sandwiches
Chips and Dips if desired
Carrot Strips
Oatmeal Cake
Milk or Fruit Drink

Vegetable Soup
Cold Cuts   Mustard
Whole Wheat Bread   Butter
Fruit Cup
Milk

Winter Suppers or Dinners

Ham with Cherry Sauce
Baked Sweet Potatoes
Buttered Green Beans
Tossed Vegetable Salad
Whole Wheat Rolls
Butter
Angel Food Cake
Milk, Lemonade, or Warm
  Fruit Punch

Pot Roast with Potatoes
  Onions and Carrots
Pineapple and Cottage
  Cheese Salad
Whole Wheat Bread
Butter   Jam
Doughnuts (Whole Wheat)
Cider or Milk

Wieners and Saurkraut
Parsley Potatoes
Carrot-Raisin Salad
Whole Wheat Rolls
Butter
Pumpkin Pie or Pumpkin
  Custard
Milk or Cereal Beverage

Squash Baked with Sausage
or Egg Plant Parmesan
Black-eyed Peas *or*
  Lima Beans
Lettuce with Thousand Island
  Dressing
Hush Puppies, Corn Bread,
  or Whole Wheat Rolls
Butter   Brownies
Milk

Stewed Chicken and
  Noodles *or* Creamed Chicken
Buttered Broccoli
Cranberry-Orange Gelatin
  Salad
Biscuits   Butter
Honey
Milk

Liver and Onions
Boiled Potatoes and Kale
Waldorf Salad (apple,
  celery and nut)
Whole Wheat Bread
Butter
Banana Loaf
Milk

29

Barbecued Beef
Baked Potato *or* Corn on the Cob
Buttered Peas
Cabbage Slaw
French Bread and Garlic
   Butter
Fruit Pie
Milk

Meat Loaf
Scalloped Potatoes
Buttered Beets
Cabbage-Green Pepper Salad
Whole Wheat Bread
Butter
Pineapple Chiffon Dessert
Milk

Good Snacking

(Just a few ideas to stimulate your imagination)

1. Fruits and berries of *every* kind—fresh, dried, frozen, or canned. Include apples, oranges, peaches, pears, grapefruit, papaya, guava, lilikoi, bananas, grapes, pineapple, plums, cherries, tangerines, kumquats, apricots, strawberries, dates, prunes, raisins, raspberries (thimble berries), blackberries, boysenberries, figs, cantaloupe, honeydew, watermelons, star fruit, lychee—whatever you have available, alone or with cheese or peanut butter, milk or nuts, or (your idea).
2. Fruit juices with or without accompanying whole grain breads or crackers, cheese, nuts, and the like, or frozen in molds or paper cups with a stick placed in just before freezing is completed.
3. Raw vegetables—try rutabaga (or other turnip) wedges, cucumbers (rings, sticks, or whole), sweet peppers (green or red), carrots (whole, sticks, grated in salads, curls), cauliflower flowerettes, cabbage wedges, jicama, radishes, onions, celery (plain or stuffed with cheese or peanut butter), kohlrabi, peas (even the pods), lettuce (with or without peanut butter or cheese), broccoli stems or flowerettes, beet slices, parsley, spinach or other greens, tomatoes, all these alone or with dips made by blending cottage cheese with seasonings such as onion, garlic powder, celery salt or a blend of seasonings especially prepared for dips or soup.
4. Vegetable juices (warm or chilled)—tomato and a

mixture of other juices with tomato are the best known. Try liquid drained from cooked vegetables if you have cooked with extra water. Carrots and other nonacid vegetables may be blended into juices but need to be used immediately or heated to stop enzyme action.

5. Green soybeans (a favorite snack among some Hawaiians)—plants are pulled when pods are well filled but beans are still succulent. Dip the beans, still on the stem, into boiling salted water. Boil nine minutes. Cool. Pop the beans from the hulls into the mouth. These are delicious and nutritious.

6. Sweet potatoes baked in their skins (once a favorite snack for homecoming school children in the southern U.S.A.).

7. Nuts of all kinds, in the shell, shelled, roasted, salted (but not too much), "dry" roasted (check the sugar and salt content). Nuts are high Calorie foods—use with discretion.

8. Cheeses with or without whole grain breads or crackers or fruit.

9. Sandwiches—whole grain breads with table fat only or with table fat and fruits or vegetables, (sliced bananas or tomatoes, lettuce leaves, radishes, onions, sweet peppers, shredded carrots mixed with raisins and salad dressing) or with fillings of meat, cheese, eggs, fish, peanut butter (alone or combined with fruit or vegetables), honey, sorghum or molasses, fruit jams or jellies (in small quantities and accompanied by milk).

10. Whole wheat cookies, muffins, biscuits, doughnuts, or cake accompanied by milk, fruit or cereal beverage, used in moderation and only by those who can afford the Calories.

11. Prebaked whole wheat waffles, pancakes, or French toast heated in the toaster or bun warmer and served plain or spread with table fat, peanut butter, and honey, sorghum, molasses, jam, or brown sugar with cinnamon, and served with milk.

12. Popcorn.
13. Soups (warm and nutritious).
14. Milk, sweet or cultured.
15. Pizza, warmed or cold.
16. Tortilla or lefse, plain or with spread.
17. Custard.
18. Kabob—any foods strung on a stick. Chunks of meat, fruit, vegetables, cheese are examples.
19. Whole wheat cream puff filled with leftover tuna, chicken, or other salad.

(Always rinse well or brush teeth after snacking.)

Suggestions for Refreshments at Home, at Church, Or at Community Functions

Buttered Fruit Bread
Assorted Cheeses   Pickles
Pineapple Punch, Water, or
   Cereal Beverage

Ribbon or Open Faced
   Sandwiches Filled with Cheese
   Spread, Peanut Butter, Egg,
   Chicken, Tuna or Salmon
   Salad Spreads
Rhubarb Thirst Quencher or Other
   Fruit Punch, Milk, or Water

Apple and Cheese Wedges
Assorted Crackers or Buttered
   Whole Wheat Buns
Water or Cereal Beverage

Fruit Bowl or Platter Containing
   Berries, Apples, Grapes, Peaches,
   Nectarines, Plums, Pears,
   Mangos, Melons, Oranges,
   Papaya, Tangerines, Kumquats
   (Whatever fruit is available at
   a reasonable price)
Buttered Nut Bread, Banana,
   Pumpkin Carrot, or Zucchini
   Loaf   Water

Warm Fruit Punch
Popcorn, Assorted Nuts, Whole
   Wheat Crackers, or Buttered
   Buns

Popcorn and Apples
Water

Pineapple, Lemon, or other Fluff
Milk, Water, or Cereal Beverage

Fruit Cup
Whole Wheat Crackers or Buttered
   Buns
Milk or Water

Whole Wheat Cream Puffs Filled
   with Chicken, Tuna, Salmon, or
   Ham Salad
Grape Juice or Fruit Punch

Gingerbread with Whipped Cream
Milk, Water, or Cereal Beverage

Carrot Pudding with Sauce
Milk, Water, or Cereal Beverage

Assorted Cookies (Maybe Cowboy Cookies, Brownies, Party Date Rolls, and Carrot Cookies)
Lemonade

Peanut Butter Bars   Bananas
Milk or Water

Watermelon

Cheese Apple Crisp with Lemon Sauce
Milk or Cereal Beverage

Cake and Ice Cream   Water

Celery Sticks Stuffed with Cheese or Peanut Butter   Carrot Sticks
Buttered Whole Wheat Buns or Toast
Tomato Juice

Relish Tray of Carrot Sticks, Celery Sticks or Curls, Radishes, Cauliflower Buds, Sweet Pepper Rings
Cottage Cheese or Guacamole Dip
Pineapple Juice

Sweet Cider and Whole Wheat Donuts (Special for Hallowe'en)

Fruit in Gelatin Dessert with Whipped Topping
Milk, Water or Cereal Beverage

Heavenly Hash   Fudge Brownie
Water

Creamed Cheese and Chopped Walnuts on Whole Wheat Raisin Bread
Milk, Water, or Orange Juice

Nut Torte with Date Cheese Topping
Water or Fruit Juice

Cheese and Crackers with Lemonade

Open-Faced Sandwiches of Peanut Butter and Banana on Whole Wheat Bread
Milk or Water

Assorted Dried Fruits—Raisins, Prunes, Apricots, Pears, Apples, Pineapple, Dates, Figs— with Nuts
Carrot Sticks   Milk or Water

Plain Fruit, fresh, frozen, or canned
Water

Strawberry Shortcake
Milk or Water

Pie or Tarts with Whole Wheat Crust
Milk, Water, or Cereal Beverage

Warm Soup (Saimin a favorite in Hawaii)
Whole Wheat Toast or Crackers
Water

Special for Christmas

"Wassail" bowl of Spiced Sweet Cider or Warm Fruit Punch
Assorted Cookies, Squares, and Nuts

Orange Smoothie (a special eggnog)
Shortbread   Assorted Cookies
Nuts

Easy Christmas Punch   Christmas (fruit) Cake
Buttered Fruit and Nut Breads Milk or Cereal Beverage
Cheese Cubes   Pickles

1. Because abundant information on the preparation of meats is available from standard cookbooks, attention here is focused on the preparation of other main dish foods with which most help is needed.
2. Calorie counts and protein content of servings are given. See section on planning for helps in evaluation needs.
3. Fact sheets are dispersed throughout the book in appropriate places to provide accurate information about some foods. Additional information may be obtained from *Word of Wisdom—Principle with Promise*, Herald House, Independence, Missouri, 1977.
4. National Academy of Sciences, Recommended Dietary Allowances, Washington, D.C., 1974.
5. For USRDAs and their explanation see *Word of Wisdom*, pp. 29-30.
6. See Vernal Packard, Jr., *Processed Foods and the Consumer*, University of Minnesota Press, Minneapolis, Minn., 1976, pp. 185-187, for explanation for PER. See *Word of Wisdom*, pp. 59-62, for explanation of protein utilization.
7. Nevin S. Scrimshaw and Vernon R. Young, "The Requirements of Human Nutrition," *Scientific American*, Sept. 1976, pp. 62; *Word of Wisdom*, pp. 111-112.
8. "Dietary Goals for the United States," prepared by the staff of the Select Committee on Nutrition and Human needs, United States Senate, U.S. Government Printing Office, 1977, p. 12.
9. Antoine J. Vergroesen, "Physiological Effects of Dietary Linoleic Acid," *Nutrition Reviews*, Vol. 35, No. 1, Jan. 1977, p. 1.
10. *World of Wisdom*, pp. 79-82, 110-121.
11. Gio B. Bori, "Diet and Cancer, an Overview for Perspective," *Journal of the American Dietetics Association*, Vol. 71, Oct. 1977, p. 377; S. Dayton, S. Hashimoto, and J. Wollman, "Effects of High Oleic and High Linoleic Safflower Oils on Mammary Tumors Induced in Rats by 7-12 Dimethylbenz (a) Anthracene," *Journal of Nutrition*, Vol. 107, Aug. 1977, p. 1353, and abstracted in the *Journal of the American Dietetics Association*, Vol. 71, No. 6, Dec. 1977, p. 671.
12. *Bread* may be biscuits, muffins, yeast breads, breakfast cake, sweet rolls, or any other whole wheat bread available, butter, or any table fat.
13. *Milk* is essential to these chiefly cereal and fruit breakfasts if optimum nutrition is expected. Other beverages may be added but not substituted. Where egg or milk in some form is a part of the breakfast, other beverages may be substituted.
14. Note that sausage, bacon, doughnuts, breakfast cake, and many desserts need to be used according to the energy needs of those eating. For many adults they should be used sparingly if at all.

FACTS ABOUT CERTAIN POPULAR FOODS

Honey

Honey may be substituted for sugar in sweetening many fruits, puddings, breads, cakes, cookies, meringues, and other foods. It is sweeter than ordinary sugar and contains more calories in an equal measure. Some facts will help you substitute satisfactorily:

1. *Two-thirds cup honey is usually about as sweet as one cup sugar.* Honey sweetness varies with the proportion of sugars contained in the honey. Honey's major sugars are levulose (fructose), glucose (dextrose) and minute amounts of sucrose (ordinary sugar contained in cane or beet products whether raw, brown, or granulated).

Levulose and glucose are simple sugars that also result from the digestion of sucrose. Levulose (fructose) is the part of the sucrose molecule that seems to be involved in raising blood cholesterol levels under some circumstances.

Levulose is about twice as sweet as ordinary sugar, and glucose is about half as sweet. Honey that contains a high proportion of levulose is sweeter than other honey and sweeter than ordinary sugar. Most honey is in this class.

2. *Honey naturally contains water—about three to five tablespoons per cup.* In dry climates honey may have as little as 16 percent moisture by weight, but in damp climates it

may have much more. An average of 20 percent moisture is generally accepted. Honey is hygroscopic and will take on moisture from damp air. If not kept tightly covered it may take on enough water to allow fermentation (spoilage). Because honey is hygroscopic, some recipes may require a reduction of more liquid than is actually in the honey. For the same reason, products made with honey have a tendency to be moist and to remain so over a longer period of time than those made with sugar. They may require special care in storage to prevent dampness and spoilage.

3. *Two-thirds cup honey may, then, be substituted for one cup sugar in many pudding, fruit, meringue, and bread recipes without altering the recipe significantly.*

4. *For cakes, cookies, and the like about two to three tablespoons liquid may need to be removed from the recipe for every two-thirds cup honey substituted for one cup sugar, or the amount of flour may need to be increased.* If one cup honey is substituted for one cup sugar, the product will be very sweet and about four tablespoons (one-fourth cup) liquid may need to be removed. Honey with the highest proportion of levulose and moisture requires the most liquid to be removed.

5. *Reduce oven temperatures by 25 degrees Fahrenheit (unless moderate temperatures are called for) when baking foods prepared with honey,* and baking times may need to be extended slightly for products to be thoroughly baked. Honey browns quickly at high temperatures.

6. *Mild-flavored honey is usually preferable in cooking and baking.* The color, flavor, and composition of honey varies with the source of the bee's food. Generally light colors have mild flavors.

7. *Almost all honeys crystallize on standing and normal cooling.* The glucose in the honey forms most of the crystals. Those honeys with a higher proportion of glucose crystallize more quickly than those with a high proportion of levulose under the same conditions.

Crystals that form quickly are small and those that form

slowly are coarse. For an even, fine-grained product, honey is sometimes "seeded" with small crystals and conditions are controlled to make it rapidly crystallize; or it may be whipped to produce a finely crystallized consistency sometimes called "creamed" honey or "honey butter" (both misnomers). A temperature approximating 57 degrees Fahrenheit (14 degrees C.) promotes crystallization. Rapid freezing and frozen storage may prevent crystallization.

8. *To reliquify honey that has crystallized, heat to temperatures not exceeding 140 degrees F. (60 degrees C.). Place the honey container on a rack or cloth in a container of warm water. Stir occasionally. Heat above 140 degrees F. (the temperature of pasteurization for honey) adversely affects the flavor and color.*

9. *Pasteurized honey has been heated to 140 degrees F. (60 degrees C.) and held there under carefully controlled conditions for 30 minutes,* or to 145 degrees for 10 minutes or to 160 degrees in a "flash" and cooled quickly, to kill wild yeasts in the honey that might cause fermentation and other organisms that might cause spoilage.

10. *In equal measures of honey and sugar, the honey will contain the most Calories.* One tablespoon sugar has 50 Calories. One tablespoon honey has 65 Calories. One cup sugar has 776 Calories. One cup honey has 1,035 Calories.

11. *In sweetening power, honey may give equal sweetness with sugar for fewer Calories.* Two teaspoons honey about equal three teaspoons sugar in sweetness. Two teaspoons honey have 43 Calories. Three teaspoons sugar have 50 Calories. Two-thirds cup honey about equals one cup sugar in sweetness. Two-thirds cup honey has 690 Calories. One cup sugar has 776 Calories.

12. *Nutritionally honey is superior to granulated sugar in every way but is less nutritious than brown sugar in some nutrients. Neither sweet has enough B vitamins to support its own Calories in the dietary.* One pound honey compares with one pound sugar and with Recommended Dietary Allowances of B vitamins for the honey's Calories as follows:

	Calories	Protein	Calcium[1]	Iron	Vit. A	Thiamin (B1)	Riboflavin (B2)	Niacin (B3)	Vit. B6	Vit. B12	Vit. C
Honey	1,379	1.4g	23	2.3	0	0.02	0.20	1.2	.09	0	5
Br. Sug.	1,692	0	386	15.4	0	0.05	0.15	.8	.20	0	0
Wh. Sug.	1,746	0	0	.5	0	0	0	0	.00	0	0
RDA for 1,379 Calories						0.70	0.83	9.1			

13. Meringues made with honey tend to be more tender but hold their shape longer than those made with sugar.

14. Honey may be a luxury item for many. Those who cannot afford to use it should learn to use as little as possible of all sweeteners.

Resource Material

Arnold H. Johnson and Martin S. Peterson, Ph.D., Subject "Honey," *Encyclopedia of Food Technology*, AVI Pub. Co., Inc., Westport, Conn., 1974.

Private Communication dated January 12, 1977, from Joseph F. Perret, Assistant to the Director, Division of Regulatory Guidance, Bureau of Foods, Food and Drug Administration, Department of Health, Education, and Welfare, Washington, D.C. 20204.

United States Department of Agriculture Leaflet No. 113, *Honey and Some of Its Uses.*

Publications of the American Honey Institute, Madison, Wisconsin, *Honey, Old Favorite Honey Recipes, 100 Honey Helpings.*

Meredith Overton and Barbara Lukett, *Clinical Nutrition, a Physiologic Approach*, Yearbook of Med. Pub., Inc., Chicago-London, 1977, p. 105 (fructose may affect triglyceride formation in some individuals).

I. MacDonald and A. Keyser, "Some Effects, in Baboons, of Chronic Ingestion of Glycerol with Sucrose or Glucose," *American Journal of Clinical Nutrition*, Vol. 30, Oct. 1977, 1661. Abstracted in the *Journal of the American Dietetics Association, Vol. 72, Jan., 1978.*

Belle Lowe, Experimental Cookery, 4th Ed., John Wiley and Sons, Inc., N.Y., London, Sydney, 1955, pp. 50-72.

Sprouts and Sprouting

1. *Seeds of many types may be sprouted*—among them wheat, soybeans, mung beans, and alfalfa.

2. *Sprouts can provide variety to dietaries.* They can also provide some vitamin C and A value, and are especially helpful if other fruits and vegetables are not available.

3. *Claims of prodigious amounts of vitamin C and A value in sprouts are unjustified.*

It takes a whole pound (454 grams) of raw soybean sprouts to provide the amount of vitamin C supplied by one small (three to a pound) orange or of ½ pound (227 g.) of raw, immature (green) soybeans. Claims that the vitamin C of seeds is increased 600 to 1,000 times or more by sprouting are accurate, but when you start with practically zero (the quantity of vitamin C found in most seeds) you can multiply numerous times and still come up with a very small quantity.

Vitamin A value of seeds may be increased by sprouting if the sprouts are exposed to the sun on about the third day. It would take 100 pounds of ordinary soybean sprouts (45,400 g.) to provide the vitamin A value of one pound (454 g.) of carrots, and one pound (454 g.) of soybean sprouts provides less vitamin A value than two ounces (56 g.) of raw, immature green soybeans.

4. *Sprouts increase in weight over seeds primarily by absorption of water.* Seeds are about 10 percent water; sprouts are about 87 percent. Seeds cooked in water also absorb it and may provide more food by weight than an equal amount sprouted. For example:

50 grams (scant 2 ounces) wheat sprouted 72 hours (3 days) produced 120 grams (4.3 ounces) sprouts (food).

50 grams (scant 2 ounces) wheat cooked until tender (about 4 hours) in water produced approximately 210 grams (7.5 ounces) drained weight of food.

5. *The proportion of protein to Calories in the sprouts is comparable to that in many fish, young poultry, some organ meats, and very lean meats that are broiled or boiled but the quantity is not outstanding.* A pound of soybean sprouts has 28.1 grams of protein. This is slightly over *half* as much protein as is in an equal weight of green, immature soybeans and about as much as is in ¼ to ⅓ of a pound of raw lean beef. The 28.1 grams of protein comes in 210 Calories of food as sprouts, 130 Calories as tuna packed in water, 245 Calories as *very* lean beef broiled well done to 330 for broiled lean beef.

6. *Minerals* of seeds can be increased by sprouting only by

the amount contributed by the water absorbed unless the sprouting is done in soil or nutrient solution.

7. *A convenient way to sprout seeds is as follows:*

Measure clean seeds into a wide-mouthed quart jar; ¼ cup (about 50 grams which is slightly less than 2 ounces) wheat will fill a quart jar with sprouts.

Cover the seeds with two or three times as much lukewarm (not hot) water as seeds. Allow to soak in a warm, dark, well ventilated place overnight or 8 to 12 hours. Inside a paper bag may be convenient.

Drain thoroughly, saving the water for cooking cereal, making soup or bread, or for some other purpose. To drain, cover the jar with a clean piece of old nylon hose, cheesecloth, or screen held in place by a strong rubber band, or hold a sieve tightly over the mouth of the jar each time it is drained.

Place jar on its side in a warm, dark, well ventilated place.

Rinse seeds to provide moisture and to remove possible organisms such as mold spores three or more times a day for approximately 72 hours (3 days). *Use* sprouts before the roots become dry and threadlike and the sprouts become bitter. Sprouts may be exposed to light the last day if they are to develop vitamin A value. They may be kept refrigerated for a few days but are best if used immediately after sprouting.

8. *Consider this comparison of nutritive values contained in 100 grams (3½ oz.) mung bean sprouts, soybean sprouts and broccoli, raw and cooked.*

100 g. Food	Calories	Protein	Calcium	Iron	A Value	Vitamins B₁	B₂	Niacin	C
		g.	mg	mg.	IU	mg.	mg.	mg.	mg.
RAW:									
Mung sprouts	35	3.8	19	1.3	20	.13	.13	0.8	19
Soy sprouts	46	6.2	48	1.0	80	.23	.20	0.8	13
Broccoli	32	3.6	103	1.1	2,500	.10	.23	0.9	113
COOKED AND DRAINED:									
Mung sprouts	28	3.2	17	.9	20	.09	.10	0.7	6
Soy sprouts	38	5.3	43	.7	80	.16	.15	0.7	4
Broccoli	26	3.1	88	.8	2,500	.09	.20	0.8	90

Note the vast superiority of broccoli (whether raw or cooked) over mung or soy sprouts as a source of vitamins A and C. The high protein content of the soy sprouts is a function of the high protein content of the soybeans, not of the process of sprouting.

Resource Material

All nutrient comparisons are taken from or calculated from data found in USDA publications noted in the acknowledgments of this book.

Sidney Margolius, *Health Foods, Facts and Fakes*, Wallar and Co., N.Y., 1973 (quoting Ruth Leverton, USDA Foods and Nutrition Specialist), p. 53.

Fiber

1. *Fiber is an essential* ingredient of every normal dietary. It helps the body eliminate wastes and may be helpful in preventing a number of diseases.

2. *Fiber should be used in moderation.* No one knows just how much fiber is needed for optimum good health. The amount varies with persons, their sensitivity to it, the kind of fiber used, and the nature of the rest of the diet (e.g. bran is laxative by nature; some fruit and vegetable fiber is not).

3. *Excessively large amounts* of fiber can

(1) *Interfere* with the absorption of important minerals including iron, copper, calcium, magnesium, zinc.

(2) *Cause* frequent and loose bowel movements.

(3) *Cause* disease of the sigmoid colon (volvulus or twisting) that may require surgery.

(4) *Cause* discomfort and embarrassment.

4. *Wood fiber is not comparable* in character or accompanying nutrients to the fiber of bran or of fruits and vegetables. Its long-term effects on health are not yet known. Because it has no food value, its generous use could lead to malnutrition.

5. *Whole wheat* is 2.3 percent fiber. *White flour* is 0.3 percent fiber.

6. *Raw milled bran* is 9.1 percent fiber. Its use in large quantity is not recommended. Bran prepared for breakfast cereals is usually mixed with other ingredients to reduce the

fiber content to 1.9 to 3 percent of the total, providing about 0.5 to 1 gram fiber per serving. One such cereal has 7.5 percent fiber.

7. *Fiber content* is given in recipes in this book because of interest in it, not to recommend its indiscriminate use. For most people, a diet containing whole grains, fruits, and vegetables (with peelings when possible) as suggested by the Daily Food Plan (see "Plan for Good Nutrition" earlier in this book) should provide adequate amounts of fiber.

Resource Material

1. Barbara Harland (Food and Drug Administration Nutritionist) and Annabel Hecht (FDA staff writer), "Grandma Called It Roughage," *FDA Consumer,* July/Aug., 1977, pp. 18-20.

Alastair M. Connell, M.D., "Wheat Bran as an Etiologic Factor in Certain Disease, Some Second Thoughts," *Journal of the American Dietetic Association,* Vol. 71, Sept. 1977, p. 235.

"Fiber Catches Fancy of Nutrition Congress," "Medical News," *Journal of the American Medical Association,* Vol. 238, Oct. 17, 1977, p. 1715; abstracted in *Journal of the American Dietetics Association,* Vol. 72, Jan. 1978, p. 102.

"Fiber, Debated Topic," "News Digest," *Journal of the American Dietetics Association,* Vol. 72, No. 1, January 1978.

Home Dried Fruits and Vegetables

1. Dried fruits and vegetables can add variety to the dietary and require less storage space than fresh or otherwise preserved foods.

2. While minerals are well preserved in the drying process, some vitamins are adversely affected, especially in drying and storing vegetables. Among those most seriously affected are vitamins C, A, E, and B_1.

3. Many fruits and vegetables require treatment with steam, boiling water, sulfur, or other agents to stop enzyme action before drying if nutrients and quality are to be preserved. The use of sulfur aids tremendously in preserving vitamins A and C but adversely affects the B_1.

4. If you plan to dry foods, obtain accurate information on

the proper treatment and procedures from the U.S. Department of Agriculture, Canadian Extension Services, or comparable agencies, and follow the instructions. Some books found in libraries give gross misinformation on the subject.

5. Storage must be carefully planned to prevent infestation by insects, molding (with consequent development of mycotoxins), further loss of nutrients, and deterioration of quality. See Extension publications for advice. Storage at 70 F. or cooler is desirable.

6. Be aware that most dried fruits and vegetables are not good sources of vitamin C. Fruits generally home dried (e.g. apples, peaches, pears, apricots, grapes, plums) are not rich sources of vitamin C when they are fresh. Whereas one pound of apricots may have 42 milligrams of vitamin C when they are fresh, the equivalent in well cared for dried apricots will likely not have more than 10 milligrams of the vitamin.

Vitamin C losses may be even greater in vegetables dried at home or commercially except with freeze drying. Consider fresh red chili peppers that contain 1,273 mg. vitamin C per pound. An equivalent amount freshly dried contains about 154 mg. of the vitamin, according to data in *Agriculture Handbook No. 8, Composition of Foods*, and after storage only 12 mg. Onions, carrots, and cabbage are listed as loosing two-thirds to three-fourths of their vitamin C with good drying procedures.

7. Accurately controlled dehydration destroys less vitamin C and A than sun drying. Sun drying is especially destructive of vitamin A.

Resource Material

All nutritive comparisons are calculated from data found in *Agriculture Handbook No. 8, Composition of Foods.*

USDA Technical Bulletin No. 997, *Flavor, Texture, Color and Ascorbic Acid Content of Home Dehydrated Vegetables and Fruits*, 1950.

Belle Lowe, *Experimental Cookery*, John Wiley and Sons, Inc., N.Y. and London, 1943, pp. 96-99; *ibid.*, 4th Ed., 1955, pp. 132-133.

4. "The Effects of Food Processing on Nutritional Values," a Scientific Status

Summary by the Institute of Food Technologists' Expert Panel on Food Safety and Nutrition and the Committee on Public Information, *Nutrition Reviews*, Vol. 33, No. 4, April 1975, pp. 123-126. (Note reference is to commercial, not home, procedures.)

Choosing Protein Foods

1. Protein Efficiency Ratings (PER) may help you choose those protein foods that can best supply your family's need. Here are some of the ratings.[3]

Food	PER	Food	PER
Eggs	3.92	Sunflower seed	2.10
Fish	3.55	Soy milk	1.96
Nonfat Milk Powder	3.11	Sesame Seed	1.77
Whole Cow's Milk	3.09	Barley	1.66
Wheat Germ	2.53	Nuts (Av.)	1.65
Whole Wheat (fairly high—almost complete relative amino acid content)		Mature Peas	1.57
Oatmeal	2.35	Lima Beans	1.53
Soybeans	2.32	White Beans	1.40
Beef and Veal	2.30	Lentils	0.93
Pumpkin Seed	2.28	White Bread - 6% milk	1.27
Brewers Yeast	2.24	White Bread - No milk	0.90
Polished Rice	2.18	Red Beans	0.88
Mung Beans	2.12	White Flour	0.06
Coconut	2.10	Gelatin	-1.25

(PERs are determined by weight gains per gram of protein intake in laboratory rats. For further explanation see Vernal S. Packard, Jr., *Processed Foods and the Consumer*, U. of Minnesota Press, Minneapolis, Minn., 1976, pp. 186-187.)

The fact that some protein efficiency ratings are very low does not mean that those proteins are not useful. Combined with foods whose amino acids complement theirs, they can help supply the protein needed. Such combinations as beans with whole wheat or brown rice, milk or milk products with whole wheat, other grains, seeds or nuts, fish and rice, meat and potatoes, beans or whole grains are all capable of providing total protein of excellent quality.[4] Foods that have 10 percent of their Calories in the form of protein that is the equivalent of milk or egg protein are considered good sources of protein.[5]

2. Calorie cost of proteins may help you choose wisely. Here are some Calorie values for foods that provide 56 grams protein, the largest amount recommended (RDA) for reference adults who are not pregnant or lactating. Note that those with a low PER would not actually meet the RDA even with these Calories, and no one is suggesting that all the protein for a day come from one food. This is just a comparison.

Food	Calories	Food	Calories
Tuna, water packed	252	Peanuts	1,215
Turkey, roasted skin and flesh	392	Sunflower seeds	1,305
Beef, lean, well done	487	Whole wheat	1,400
Nonfat dry milk	560	Sesame seed	1,697
Eggs	707	Walnuts, English	2,451
Wheat germ	765	Pecans	4,183
Beans	825		
Whole milk	1,042		
Peanut butter	1,170		

3. Costs may help determine good stewardship in the choice of proteins. At regular (not sale) early 1978 St. Charles, Missouri, prices, 56 grams protein cost approximately the following:

Food	Cost	Food	Cost
Beans	$0.25	Turkey	$0.62
Nonfat dry milk	$0.30	Tuna, water pack	0.82
Wheat germ	0.30	Lean beef (varies)	1.01 (med.)
Whole wheat	0.35	Sunflower seeds	1.03
Peanut butter	0.35	Sesame seeds	1.06
Eggs	0.43	Walnuts, English	2.82
Whole milk	0.60		
Peanuts	0.61		

It is apparent that nuts and some seeds, recently popularized as sources of protein, are extremely expensive both in money and in Calories and have relatively low protein efficiency ratings. Used as a source of variety and flavor they are valuable in the dietary of those who can afford them. Their use as staples is a questionable practice.

Soybean Products as Protein

All mature soybeans or their products must be thoroughly cooked to inactivate a substance that interferes with the action of trypsin, a digestive enzyme necessary in the digestion of protein.

Soy Milk. This is made by soaking dried beans, grinding them, straining out the liquid, cooking and seasoning it. One cup soy milk compares with 1 cup cow's milk (skim) as follows:

Food (1 cup)	Calories	Pro. g.	Calcium mg.	Iron mg.	Potassium mg.	B_1 mg.	B_2 mg.	B_3 mg.	B_6 mg.	B_{12} mg.
soy milk	79	8.2	50	1.9	—	.19	.07	.48	.053	0
cow milk (skim)	86	8.6	290	0.1	348	.10	.43	.24	.096	.00096[6]

Soy Flour and Grits. Beans are dried, cleaned, cracked, dehulled, heated, steamed, and flaked. Formerly the flakes were ground into flour at various stages of oil extraction. Since World War II most oil has been extracted by a solvent, hexane; it is cheaper and gets more oil out.

With hexane, the oil is extracted from the flakes, the meal is desolventized, screened, ground; moisture and protein are adjusted; anticaking agents are sometimes introduced to make it handle better; and oil is returned if necessary to make the meal or flour full fat, high fat, low fat, or defatted.

Textured Protein. Soy flour or grits with 30 to 50 percent protein are forced through small holes at high temperature and under great pressure. Color and flavors, spices, etc. are added before or after extrusion.

Protein Concentrate. Soy flour or grits of 70 percent

protein are treated with alcohol or dilute acids to remove nonprotein substances. The protein is then centrifuged or filtered out, washed, dried, and ground.

Protein Isolates. Soy flour or grits of 90 percent protein are treated with mild alkaline solution to make the protein soluble. Nonprotein substances are centrifuged or filtered out. Acid is applied to this protein solution to precipitate the protein as a curd. The curd is recovered, washed, resolubilized, and dried to form powder.

Spun Protein. Protein isolates are resolubilized and forced through very small holes into an acid bath to precipitate the protein into fine fibers.

Soy Lecithin. Small amounts of steam and acidic catalysts are introduced into soy oil to combine with the phosphatides and cause them to precipitate. They are centrifuged from the oil and dried with high temperatures and vacuum. The process is called degumming the oil. Substances removed include lecithin, cephalin, other fat-like phosphorus containing compounds, and some oil.

Pharmaceutical Lecithin. Soy lecithin is further purified by washing in solvent, such as acetone, in which lecithin is insoluble.

Soy Oil (for human food).

(1) *Hexane extracted oil* is desolventized, usually by steam distillation and degummed (see *soy lecithin* above). Activated earth or carbon absorbs color pigments. With high temperature the oil is deodorized and with pressure in the presence of hydrogen, the oil is partially hydrogenated. (If there is no hydrogenation, the oil develops a fishy or painty odor after long storage.) To further prevent flavor changes in the oil, contact with the air is kept to a minimum and some metal sequestrant, such as citric acid, is added to inactivate trace minerals such as iron or copper.

(2) *"Cold Pressed Oil"* is oil expelled by pressure from soybeans or other seeds while the ground or flaked seeds are heated to 275 F. Because hexane is not used for the extraction, desolventizing is not necessary. The oils may then be

otherwise refined by degumming, deodorizing, removing free fatty acids, and removing coloring matter or they may be left crude. If the oil is clear, it has been refined. Crude oil is not recommended for frying foods. (One exception is olive oil which is pressed from fruit instead of from seeds and is used crude.)

Nutritive Values (Oil). Food oils contain varying amounts of vitamin E depending on the source of the oil, the variety of seed from which it was grown, the climactic conditions under which it was grown and harvested, storage conditions, and length of storage. Other vitamin and mineral content is practically nil even in olive oil that is not refined.

Nutritive Value (soy meal and other products). Because vitamins E and A are fat soluble, they are largely removed with the oil. When oil is returned to the meal, some vitamin E is also returned. There is little vitamin A value in seeds or oil, and after the removal of pigments there is little if any of the A value remaining.

Because minerals and the B vitamins are water soluble, they survive much of the processing of soy flour, grits, and textured protein. Further purification of the protein reduces or eliminates these nutrients along with the fat soluble ones. For protein concentrates, isolates, or spun protein to approximate the nutritive values of soybeans other than in protein, it is necessary for them to have vitamins and minerals returned to them in a restoration or enrichment process.

Because textured protein is often substituted for hamburger, note these comparisons of nutritive values of *equal amounts of protein* from lean raw hamburger and defatted soybean flour from which textured protein may be made:

Food	Protein	Calories	Weight	Fat	Calcium	Iron	Potassium	Magnesium	B_1	B_2	B_3	B_6	B_{12}
	g.		g.	g.	mg.	mg.	mg.	mg.	mg.	mg.	mg.	mg.	mcg.
Soy flour	47.0	326	100	0.9	265	11.1	1820	310	1.09	.34	2.6	.724	0
Hamburger	47.0	406	227	22.7	27	7.0	806	48	0.20	.41	11.4	.749	3.178[7]

48

Resource Material

Chemical Technology, Vol. 8, 69-79 and 83-97 (Oils, Fats and Animal Food Products), Barnes and Noble, N.Y., 1975.

McGraw Hill Encyclopedia of Science and Technology, Vol. 5, p. 202 (Fats and Oils) and Vol. 12, p. 614 (Soybeans), McGraw Hill, New York, N.Y., 1971.

USDA publications noted in "Acknowledgments."

Yogurt

1. Yogurt was originally milk curdled by the action of bacteria (cultured).

2. Yogurt may now be either *cultured* or *acidified.*

3. Acidified yogurt is produced by mixing certain acids and additives with heat treated milk to produce the desired flavors and textures. Such yogurt contains

    (1) heat-treated milk (180 F.- 82C. for 30 minutes). There is no incubation period. After mixing, the substance is chilled at refrigeration temperatures.

    (2) Additional nonfat dry-milk solids.

    (3) An acidulant utilizing one or more of the following: lactic, acetic, citric acids.

    (4) A stabilizer utilizing one or more of the following substances, sometimes combined with dextrose (glucose—a simple sugar): vegetable gum carrageen, agar-agar, gum tragacanth, gum arabic, carboxymethyl cellulose, gelatin.

4. Heat treatment of milk for yogurt making is far more severe than heat treatment for pasteurization or homogenization.

Product	Initial Heat Treatment	Subsequent Treatment
Pasteurized milk	Commercial: 161 F. (72 C.) for 15 seconds (continuous) *or* 145 F. (63 C.) for 30 minutes (vat)	Cooled immediately to 40-42 F. (4.4-5 C.) and refrigerated.
	Home: Usually vat temperatures above.	Cooled and refrigerated.

Product	Initial Heat Treatment	Subsequent Treatment
Buttermilk	Commercial: 180 F. (82 C.) for 30 minutes	Cool to 72 F. (22 C.) and inoculate Culture at 70 F. (22 C.) to 0.8 percent acidity Cooled and refrigerated
	Home: Usually fluid poured from churn after butter is removed. No heat.	Refrigerated
Yogurt (Cultured)	Commercial: 180 F. (82 C.) for 30 minutes *or* 205 F. (96 C.) flash process	Cool to 108-115 F. (42-46 C.) Inoculate and incubate to 0.9 percent acidity Cooled and refrigerated.
Yogurt (Acidified)	180 F. (82 C.) for 30 minutes	Ingredients added and cooled to refrigerator temp.
Yogurt	Home: 212 F. (100 C.)—Boiled[9]	Cool to "warm"—100-120 F. (38-48 C.). Inoculate. Culture until desired consistency (maybe several hours, especial- ly if large containers are used. Cool and refrigerate.

5. Vitamin content of yogurt varies with method of preparation and length of storage.

(1) Yogurt cultured with *Streptococcus thermophilus* and *Lactobacillus bulgaricus* may increase the folic acid tenfold over that in the milk. Fresh milk would contain more folacin than canned evaporated to begin with.

(2) Acidified yogurt may have increased folic acid if additives made from seaweed, as carrageen, are used. Some additives do not contain folacin; others increase the folacin more than tenfold.

(3) Pantothenic acid, biotin, and vitamin B_{12} are decreased in quantity during incubation of bacteria to

form yogurt. Acidified yogurt suffers no such loss.

(4) At refrigerator temperatures yogurt loses folic acid and vitamin B_{12}. In eight days' storage, cultured yogurt loses about 14 percent of its folacin and nearly 57 percent of its vitamin B_{12}. Acidified yogurt loses a little over half its B_{12} but nearly 44 percent of its folacin. Milk loses folacin more rapidly and vitamin B_{12} a little less rapidly than yogurt during storage.

6. Yogurt is not necessarily a low Calorie food. Read the label on commercial yogurt. Calculate homemade values from the ingredients.

Food (8 ounces—1 cup)	Calories (Approximate)
Skim milk	85-90
Buttermilk	85-90
Yogurt, commercial:	
Skim milk with added dry milk	123-127
Whole milk—no dry milk	139-152
Low fat milk—added dry milk	144 (av.)
Coffee and vanilla flavors	194 (av.)
Fruit flavors	225-250-260-270 (see containers)
Yogurt, homemade:	
Popular recipe follows	285 plain (add for fruit and sweetener)
Ice cream, regular commercial	235-257
Ice cream, soft serve	266
Ice cream, rich commercial	329
Whole wheat bread, 1 ounce (28 g.) slice	65

Popular Homemade Yogurt Recipe

Combine:
    1 quart warm water
    1 16 oz. can evaporated milk
    3 c. milk powder (nonfat[10])
    Yogurt culture according to instructions *or*
        2 Tbsp. yogurt from a previous batch

Mix thoroughly and place in glass, other appropriate container(s), or yogurt maker. Cover and place in a warm area where it can be kept at approximately 108 F. (42 C.) until desired consistency is reached. Chill. Add pureed fruit, honey, or other flavor as desired. Keep refrigerated until used.

7. The cost of yogurt may limit its use as a source of the nutrients of milk. Compare the cost of 1 pint of food.

(The following are regular St. Charles, Missouri, early 1978 prices.)

Food	Cost per pint
Reconstituted dry skim milk	8.8¢
Low-fat milk (by gallon)	15.5-17¢
Low-fat milk (by quarts)	21¢
Whole milk (by gallons)	18¢
Buttermilk (by half gallons)	22¢
Yogurt (varied with brand and content)	69-79-85¢
Ice cream (supermarket where yogurt was priced by pint container)	52¢
Ice cream (by gallon)	29¢

8. Yogurt may or may not have protein in excess of that found in an equivalent measure of milk. (Culturing increases volume; 1 cup yogurt weighs 227 grams. 1 cup fluid milk or buttermilk weighs 245 grams.)

Food, 1 cup (8 ounces)	Protein (grams)
Whole milk	8.5
Skim milk or buttermilk	8.8
Low-fat milk with added milk solids	10.3
Plain yogurt with no added solids	7.9
Yogurts with added solids (including gelatin)	9.0-13

9. Flavored commercial yogurts usually contain more carbohydrates (mostly sugar) than an equal measure of ice cream.

Food, 1 cup	Carbohydrate (grams)
Vanilla yogurt	31
Fruit flavored yogurt	43
Regular ice cream	28
Rich ice cream	26

Resource Material

Agricultural Research Service, United States Department of Agriculture, Washington D.C., *Agriculture Handbook No. 8-1, Composition of Foods, Dairy and Egg Products, Raw—Processed—Prepared*, Nov. 1976, pp. 4, 5 and Items No. 01-118 to 01-122.

Ibid., Agricultural Handbook No. 456, Nutritive Value of American Foods in Common Units, Nov. 1975, Items Buttermilk, Milk, Yogurt.

Linda Posati, Research Chemist, USDA Science and Education Administration, Personal Communication.

K. P. Reddy, K. M. Shanani, S. M. Kulkarni, Department of Food Science and Technology, University of Nebraska, Lincoln, "B-Complex Vitamins in Cultured and Acidified Yogurt," *Journal of Dairy Sciences*, Vol. 59, No. 2, pp. 191-195. Labels from various yogurts.

Margarine and Butter

Read labels when purchasing margarines to determine whether a premium price actually gives you enough nutritional advantage to justify the expenditure. Corn oil or safflower oil on the label does not mean that the margarine has no saturated fat present. Even these oils are partially hydrogenated to make the margarine spreadable and to keep it from developing undesirable odors and flavors. Generally speaking, if liquid oil is listed as the first ingredient, the proportion of polyunsaturated fatty acids present is higher than if just oil or partially hydrogenated oil is listed first. When lard is listed first, the amount of polyunsaturates present is usually lower than when all vegetable oil is present. Like butter, however, lard does have some unsaturated fats and part of those are the essential arachidonic acid which the body must make from linoleic acid if none is provided in food.

Each tablespoon of regular or soft margarine or butter contains 11.5 grams fat. Whipped margarine averages about 7.6 grams fat per tablespoon. On the average, the fats in a tablespoon of margarine or butter are distributed as follows:

One Tablespoon Table Fat	Grams Fat Total	Grams Fat Saturated	Grams Fat Unsaturated	Grams Fat Linoleic[11]
Regular Margarine	11.5	2.1	9.0	3.1
Soft Margarine	11.5	2.2	8.7	4.4
Whipped Margarine	7.6	1.4	6.0	2.1
(Wgt. = regular)	11.5	2.2	9.0	3.2
Butter	11.5	6.3	4.1	.3[12]

1. All vitamins and minerals are given in milligrams.
2. Vitamin B_6 and B_{12} requirements are not linked to Calories. Daily RDAs for most adults are 2.0 mg vitamin B_6 and 3 micrograms B_{12}. (1 lb. white sugar = 2¼ c., 1 lb. brown sugar = 2 c., 1 lb. honey = 1⅓ c.)
3. Food and Agriculture Organization of the United Nations Nutritional Studies No. 24, "Amino-Acid Content of Foods and Biological Data on Proteins," Rome, 1970, as reported in Sidney Margolius, *Health Foods, Facts and Fakes*, Wallar and Co., N.Y., 1973, pp. 61-62.
4. *Word of Wisdom*, pp. 59-62; Nevin S. Scrimshaw and Vernon R. Young, "The Requirements of Human Nutrition," *Scientific American*, Sept. 1976, pp. 51-64; Frances Moore Lappe, *Diet for a Small Planet*, Ballantine Books, N.Y., 1973.
5. G. H. Beaton, "Protein-Calorie Ratios in Assessment of Protein Quality," *Food Technology*, Vol. 31, June 1977, p. 89, abstracted in *Journal of the American Dietetics Association*, Vol. 71, Sept. 1977, p. 343.
6. The B_{12} in a cup of milk is about one-third the RDA for adults. Only animal products contain the vitamin. This is especially important for vegetarians to note.
7. Note that this amount of vitamin B_{12}, found in 227 grams (one-half pound) hamburger, is enough to fill one adult RDA if cooking losses are not too great. About a 30 percent cooking loss can be expected. No B_{12} is in the soy flour unless it is fortified.
    Three and one-half ounces (100 grams) of defatted soy flour has protein equaling in amount that contained in one-half pound (227 grams) lean raw hamburger. The proteins of the two foods are utilized about equally well. Of all minerals noted and of vitamin B_1, the soy flour is far richer. Of the other B vitamins noted, the most significant differences are in niacin and B_{12}. To make soy flour equal beef in these two nutrients requires enrichment or fortification.
8. Milk for yogurt and for beverage milk is homogenized (fat globules broken up at 3,000 pounds pressure) while warm—140 F. (60 C.).
9. Canned evaporated milk and dry skim milk are already heat treated and do not have to be boiled. Must be warmed to permit bacteria to work.
10. 1 cup regular nonfat dry milk is equivalent to approximately 1⅓ cups instant nonfat dry milk in nutritive value. Instant contains 25 percent more moisture.
11. Linoleic is a part of the total unsaturated fats.
12. Butter also contains arachidonic acid, an essential unsaturated fat. No vegetable oil contains cholesterol. One tablespoon butter contains 35.5 mg. cholesterol.

FACTS ABOUT RECIPES

Altitude

These recipes are formulated for low altitudes. If they are used in the mountains or on high plateaus, they will need more liquid, less leavening, and a higher baking temperature. At very high altitudes they may need to have sugar and shortening reduced.

Abbreviations

To save space, some abbreviations are used. These are as follows:

c = cup (s)
tsp. = teaspoon (s)
Tbsp. = tablespoon (s)
F. = Fahrenheit
C. = Celsius (Centigrade)
pro. = protein
fib. = fiber
butter = butter or margarine

lb. = pound (s)
oz. = ounce (s)
g. = gram (s)
mg. = milligram
RDA = Recommended Dietary Allowance
Cal. = Calories
wh. wh. = whole wheat
egg = one large egg

table fat = butter or margarine. (Other shortenings may be substituted. I use butter or margarine for their flavor and contribution of vitamin A. If lard or cooking oils are used, the amount should be reduced by 2 Tbsp. per cup. Oils frequently give a different texture and are not appropriate in some products.)

Convenient Measures

3 tsp. = 1 Tbsp. = $\frac{1}{32}$ lb. (14 g.) shortening = $\frac{1}{8}$ stick table fat

$\frac{1}{4}$ cup = 4 Tbsp. = $\frac{1}{8}$ lb. (57 g.) shortening = $\frac{1}{2}$ stick table fat

$\frac{1}{3}$ c. = 5$\frac{1}{3}$ Tbsp. = $\frac{1}{6}$ lb. (76 g.) shortening = $\frac{2}{3}$ stick table fat

$\frac{1}{2}$ c. = 8 Tbsp. = $\frac{1}{4}$ lb. (114 g.) shortening = 1 stick table fat

1 cup = 16 Tbsp. = $\frac{1}{2}$ lb. (227 g.) shortening = 2 sticks table fat

2 cups = 32 Tbsp. = 1 lb. (454 g.) shortening = 4 sticks table fat

Conversion to Metric System[1]

Recipes in this book are given in conventional measure. To change to metric, the following information is needed:

Measures (all conversions are approximate)

(1 cup metric = 1 cup *plus* 2½ teaspoons conventional measure.)

1 teaspoon = scant 5 milliliters (actually 4.93)

1 Tablespoon = scant 15 milliliters (actually 14.79)

1 fluid ounce = 2 tablespoons = scant 30 milliliters (actually 29.58)

1 cup = scant 240 milliliters (actually 236.5) = 0.24 liter (actually 0.2365)

1 pint = 2 cups = 480 milliliters *minus* 1⅓ tsp. = 0.47 liter (0.4732)

1 quart = 4 cups = 960 milliliters *minus* 2¾ tsp. = 0.95 liter (0.9464)

1 ounce (weight) = 28 grams (actually 28.35)

1 pound = 454 grams (actually 453.59) = 0.45 kilograms (actually 0.4536)

1 kilogram = 2.2 pounds (actually 2.205)

Temperatures

To change Fahrenheit temperatures to Celsius (Centigrade):

    1. Subtract 32 from the Fahrenheit temperature

    2. Take ⁵⁄₉ of the result

Some converted temperatures are:

Fahrenheit (25 degrees F. = 14 degrees Celsius)	**Celsius** (Centigrade)
212 (Boiling at sea level)	= 100
300	= 149
325	= 163
350	= 177
375	= 191
400	= 205
425	= 219

Stop! Do Not Attempt Any Whole Wheat Recipe in This Book Until You Have Read This Section

VERY IMPORTANT INFORMATION

Measuring

Always sift flour before measuring. If bran sifts out, return it to the flour for measuring. Only if you are measuring by weight instead of by cupfuls can this step be skipped.

Whole wheat is not standardized as most white flour is. It varies in hardness, fineness of grind, percent of protein, and other qualities. You will need to *experiment* with your flour to determine the exact amount you need to use in these recipes.

The recipes in this book are formulated for finely ground (powdery) hard whole wheat flour that, when sifted once, measures approximately four cups to the pound (454 grams).

Sift and measure your flour. If it is made of very hard wheat and is granular instead of powdery, it may measure as little as 3¼ to 3½ cups to the pound. (Many Canadian flours are in this class.) If it is made from soft wheat and is finely ground (powdery), it may measure as much as 5½ to 6 cups to the pound. (Nauvoo cake flour is in this class.)

Soft wheat flours are *not* suitable for bread baking but are the best for cakes, cookies, quick breads, and the like. When soft wheat flours are used in these recipes for cakes, cookies, and quick breads, they may require 4 to 8 tablespoons *more* flour per cup than the recipe calls for.

Hard wheat flours that are granular and measure 3¼ to 3½ cups to the pound may need 2 to 3 tablespoons *less* flour per cup than is called for in these recipes.

Turn Your Own Favorite Recipes into Whole Wheat Recipes

You can with just a little effort. That is the way many of these recipes were developed. Experiment with your flour to learn how much is needed to produce the texture and structure most like your favorite recipe. If your recipe calls for cake flour and you have soft whole wheat flour available, you may not need to change the recipe at all. If your cake, cookie, quick bread, or pastry recipe calls for all-purpose flour and you have soft wheat flour, you may have to add one-third to one-half cup more for each cup called for in a recipe.

If you have only hard whole wheat flour available and the recipe calls for cake flour, you may need as little as two-thirds the flour called for, and you may want to substitute one or two tablespoons cornstarch for an equivalent amount of flour. If all-purpose flour is in your recipe, you may need only to substitute one or two tablespoons cornstarch for an equivalent amount of flour or reduce the amount by one to two tablespoons per cup. In some cases you may not have to change the recipe at all.

Just experiment and record the amount needed; then enjoy your new whole wheat recipe.

To use the recipes in this book you will still need to experiment with *your* flour. Adjustments for kinds of flour used will need to be made *approximately* as follows:

Hard Whole Wheat Flours		Soft Whole Wheat Flours
At 4 cups/pound Recipe calls for	At 3¼-3½ cups/pound You will need	At 6 cups/pound You will need up to
		(Not for yeast breads)
¼ cup	3½ Tbsp.	⅓ cup plus 2 tsp.
⅓ cup	¼ cup plus 2 tsp.	½ cup
½ cup	½ cup minus 1 Tbsp.	¾ cup
¾ cup	⅔ cup	1 cup plus 2 Tbsp.
1 cup minus 2 Tbsp.	¾ cup	1⅓ cups
1 cup	1 cup minus 2 Tbsp.	1½ cups
1¼ cups	1 cup plus 1½ Tbsp.	2 cups minus 2 Tbsp.
1⅓ cups	1 cup plus 2 Tbsp.	2 cups
1½ cups	1⅓ cups (scant)	2¼ cups
1⅔ cups	1½ cups minus 2 tsp.	2½ cups
1¾ cups	1½ cups	2½ cups plus 2 Tbsp
2 cups	1¾ cups	3 cups

When hard whole wheat flours are used for cakes, cookies, quick breads, pastries, and the like, they frequently benefit by having one to two tablespoons cornstarch substituted for an equivalent amount of flour. To substitute cornstarch for flour, measure the cornstarch into the cup and fill the cup with flour.

Some Problems You May Encounter

Hard whole wheat flours, even with cornstarch substituted for part of the flour, will not make products that equal in volume, lightness, and velvety texture those made from soft whole wheat flours and rarely will either equal white flour products in these characteristics.

If your product is too moist or falls, you probably have too little flour, although it is possible that you have not mixed it enough (with more sugar and fat in the recipe and soft flour, more mixing is required) or the product may not be thoroughly baked.

If the product is stiff or crumbly and dry you probably have used too much flour, although it may be that you have overmixed or overbaked it. The amount of mixing allowed depends on the quantity of sugar and fat in the recipe and the hardness of the flour. Overmixing hard flour products develops the gluten and gives the product a bready texture. It is especially critical when hard flours are used without cornstarch in cakes, quick breads, and the like.

In the case of yeast breads, underkneading or allowing them to rise too high for their gluten strength may cause them to fall and be coarse and crumbly. Overkneading, especially if there are large flakes of bran in the flour, may cause gluten strands to break preventing the bread from rising properly. Frequently, however, when they are coarse and crumbly it is because too much flour has been used.

---

1. In general it is recommended that conventional measures continue to be used with conventional recipes and that metric measures be used with recipes written to be used with metric measures. In practice, measures and temperatures will be replaced by easy-to-use quantities, not converted to equivalent amounts.

   Recommended Celsius temperatures will equal approximately one-half the present Fahrenheit figures and will be rounded out to multiples of 10. For example, 200 F. will probably be replaced by 100 C., 300 F. replaced by 150 C., 325 F. replaced by 160 C., etc.

HELPS FOR MAKING 100 PERCENT WHOLE WHEAT PRODUCTS

Flour

1. Select a finely ground hard wheat flour for a fine textured, light bread. Soft wheat flours do not have enough gluten to make light yeast breads. Coarsely ground wheat may make a tasty bread, but generally it cannot be kneaded as much as finely ground flour and will not make as light a loaf.

2. Select cool-ground flour and store it in a cool dark place to retain nutrients. Home ground flour that gets hot in the grinding needs to be used at once or chilled quickly before storing.

3. Allow flour to age at least a week after grinding for best volume and ease of handling the dough, or add gluten from an outside source (i.e. already aged white or gluten flour). Either addition will reduce the nutritive value of the flour slightly.

Gluten flour may be prepared at home by thoroughly kneading a dough of hard wheat flour and water, washing out the starch and other nutrients, leaving only the rubbery gluten. The gluten must then be baked, ground, dried, and reground in a tedious and wasteful process. Commercial gluten is available.

Freshly ground flour may be used alone for yeast breads. The product is usually tasty but heavy and of poor texture.

4. Use the proper amount. Keep the dough soft. It should pull like the pull of a very heavy rubber band when you are kneading it and should hold its shape when put to rise, but it should feel soft, springy, and "alive" when touched. Bread dough is very versatile. If you get it too stiff with flour, *do not* throw it out or resign yourself to dry, crumbly bread. Add a little water until it has the right feel again. If you get too much water, compensate with a little more flour. It is very difficult to ruin bread dough once you learn how it ought to feel.

5. Knead it properly. Gluten which forms the skeleton of light bread, must be developed by mixing and kneading, but some whole wheat flours can be kneaded more than others. Flour that has a low gluten content and that which has large flakes of bran may "break" in less time than other flour needs for developing the gluten. To "break" means that the gluten strands become short and the bread cannot rise properly. Experiment with your flour to see how much kneading it can take. The more it can be kneaded, the nicer the texture of your bread and the greater the volume to which it can safely rise.

Knead in the bowl to avoid getting too much flour into the dough. Only experts can knead whole wheat dough successfully on bread boards. If you do want to knead on a board, use a canvas or heavy fabric covered one. Do not expect the dough to become satiny smooth as white flour dough does.

To knead, reach under the dough with your fingers (use one hand if you knead in the bowl and keep the other hand to turn the bowl). Pull the dough toward you. Then press vigorously with the heel and palm of your hand, pushing the dough against the bowl or board. Turn the bowl or dough a quarter turn and repeat the process. Continue for the time designated by your recipe or determined by you to be sufficient to develop the gluten in your flour. Establish a rhythm for best results.

Allowing the dough to rest occasionally during kneading allows the gluten to tighten up and become stronger. Do not worry if you have to stop to answer the phone or help the children. Just add the minutes out to the kneading period so you knead the specified time.

6. Let the dough *rise* twice. After it has risen, punch your fist into the middle of it. Fold it in from the sides, cover, and let it rise again. The second rising allows more yeast to develop, makes finer cell walls, allows more phytase activity to break down phytates into inositol, phosphorus, and other needed minerals.

Yeast

Dry or compressed yeast may be used equally well. One package of dry yeast is equal to approximately 1 Tablespoon bulk dry yeast, and each is approximately equal to 1 ounce of compressed yeast. Bulk yeast is the cheapest and can be kept refrigerated for long periods of time. Large quantities of yeast produce bread that rises quickly. Smaller amounts rise more slowly but produce equal volume at lower cost if time is not important. Be careful not to kill yeast with too hot water (over 110 F.) or salt.

Liquid

1. *Water.* This allows the flavor of the wheat to be maximized.

2. *Water with nonfat dry milk.* Milk may mask the flavor of the wheat but also adds nutrients including "complete" protein to increase the nutritive value of the bread. When substituting it in a recipe that calls for fluid milk, reduce the amount of fluid by 1 tablespoonful for every ¼ cup dry milk

used, and there is no need to scald and cool.

3. *Milk.* This adds nutrients as dry milk does. Whole milk adds fat, vitamin A, and Calories.

Fresh or pasteurized milk must be scalded and cooled before using in yeast breads unless it is sterile. Bacteria in the milk must be killed or they will multiply during the fermentation periods and develop off flavors. The milk must be cooled or the yeast will be killed. Dry skim milk already has the bacteria killed and can be used with warm (not hot) water.

When fluid milk is substituted for water and dry milk in a recipe, add 1 tablespoon milk for every ¼ cup dry milk called for in the recipe.

4. *Potato Water.* This makes good, tasty bread. It adds some nutrients not found in water alone but does little to supplement protein. It may be used advantageously with dry milk.

Sugar

Sugar is needed as a food for the yeast. The amount used may vary with the degree of sweetness you desire. Brown sugar, honey, or molasses blend well with whole wheat flavor and are more nutritious than white sugar. They may be used interchangeably.

Shaping

Work only with lightly greased hands and bread boards. Do not add flour.

Loaves

Divide dough into portions to fit your pan. One to one and one-half pounds of dough fits a pan 9 x 5 x 2½ inches. Three-fourths to one pound of dough fits a pan 7 x 3½ x 2¼ inches. Roll the dough into balls and let rest for a few minutes (up to 15).

Pat or roll dough into a rectangle on a lightly greased board. Fold the third of the dough nearest you onto the

64

middle third of the dough and pat or roll it down securely. Then fold in the opposite one third of the dough and pat or roll it securely onto the first two thirds. Lift the mass of dough by the ends and stretch it as you slap it onto the board until it is about three times as long as your pan.

Return the elongated dough to the board. Fold an end third of the dough onto the middle third and press or roll securely. Repeat folding the other end third over the first two thirds. There should be a rectangle of dough about the length of your pan and evenly distributed from end to end. Roll the two long sides of the rectangle together pinching all seams firmly into place. Pat vigorously or roll onto the board to make sure there are no bubbles or holes left in the loaf. Grease lightly and place in the pan to rise, seam side down.

Buns or Rolls

Divide into equal portions by pinching off the dough or rolling it into a long strip and cutting with a knife or string or other means. Shape as desired into dinner rolls, wiener buns, sandwich buns, parker house rolls, crescents, cloverleaf rolls, or what have you.

Sweet Rolls

To make sweet rolls from regular bread dough, allow 1 cup brown sugar or ⅔ cup honey for each 1½ pounds (681 g.) dough. Roll or pat the dough into a rectangle on a lightly greased board. Spread with butter, then sugar, then cinnamon, dried fruits, or nuts as desired. (If brown sugar is used, sprinkle with a bit of water.) Avoid buttering the long side of the rectangle opposite you.

Roll from the long side of the rectangle nearest you, pulling the dough gently from beneath as you roll it into the tightest roll possible. Seal the roll with the unbuttered side of the rectangle. Pat and roll the long roll of dough until it is evenly distributed from end to end. Cut into the desired number of rolls with a sharp knife or thread. (If you use the latter, place the thread under the roll of dough at the places the cuts are to be made. Pull the ends up and cross them. Thread will divide even rolls filled with fruits and nuts without leaving ragged edges.) Arrange in well greased pans. Brush top side with butter. Cover with waxed paper and a damp cloth and set aside to rise.

If a tea ring is to be made, roll the dough as directed. Place it in a buttered pan or on a buttered cookie sheet in a circle, sealing the ends together. Cut almost through the roll with scissors at about ¾-inch intervals leaving the inner portion of the roll intact. Placing a spatula on one side and your fingers on the other, lift each portion up and turn it to the right so that one cut surface is on the buttered pan and the other is facing up. When all portions have been turned, brush the top surfaces with melted butter, cover, and set aside to rise.

Pizza

If a pizza crust is to be made, divide dough into amounts that will fit your pans. Roll or pat into desired thickness. Arrange in pan, pinching up the sides so the filling will not run out. Use any pizza filling desired and bake or freeze the unfilled dough for later use.

Rising

Bread dough rises best in a warm place, about 80 degrees F., protected from drafts. To keep it damp, lay a waxed paper over the dough and cover with a lightweight wet towel, or make a tent over the waxed paper by placing some kind of supports (like four quart jars) in strategic places and draping a wet towel over them. Sometimes an oven makes a good "proofing box," but be careful not to forget the dough when it is out of sight, and it must be removed from the oven long enough before the rising is completed for the oven to be preheated.

Unless flour with very strong gluten has been used or gluten or dough conditioners have been added, whole wheat dough should rise only about double in bulk. To test readiness for baking, touch the end of a loaf or roll lightly with a finger tip. If the dough holds the impression, it is ready for baking. If it springs back into place, it is not ready for baking. If the fingerprint collapses, it has already risen too much. When this happens remold the loaf or rolls and allow to rise again. It is better to remold dough two or three times than to bake a loaf that has risen beyond the strength of its gluten.

Baking

Bake at 375 degrees F. Loaves get a better "oven spring" if the oven is preheated to 425 F. with a pan of water to make the air moist, and the temperature reduced to 375 when the loaves are put in. Bake loaves 35 to 40 minutes, rolls 20 to 25 minutes. Baking is completed when crusts are solid and lightly browned, the bread sounds hollow when thumped and releases from the pan easily, and the bottom of the pans sizzle when touched with a damp finger.

Problems Sometimes Encountered

1. *Bread is coarse, dry, and crumbly.* Too much flour has been used, the dough has not been kneaded enough, or the dough has risen too high (light).

Keep the dough *soft.* It should hold its shape when put to rise but should feel soft, springy, and "alive." Bake as soon as the dough holds a fingerprint. (See instructions on flour, kneading, and rising for complete information.)

2. *Large holes appear in the bread, often just under the crust.* Air bubbles were not removed in forming the loaf or roll, the dough has risen too high and fallen away from the crust, or the crust has become too dry during rising and lost its adhesion for the rest of the loaf.

Roll and pat dough vigorously in forming loaves and rolls. If a bubble develops on rising, prick it gently with a sharp object before baking.

Bake before the volume is greater than the gluten can support. Brush the top with melted fat to hold in moisture.

67

Keep dough covered and moist while rising.

3. *Loaf is flat and has a wrinkled crust.* Not enough flour was used, or bread has risen too much and has fallen. Be sure the dough will hold its shape after kneading. Bake at proper lightness. Remold if you know it has risen too much.

4. *Crust bursts on one side of the loaf.* Air is not circulating evenly around the loaf, probably because the oven is too crowded. About one inch of space between loaves should help.

5. *Bread droops over the edge of the pan.* Dough was too soft or too light or oven was not hot enough. (See instructions for baking.)

6. *The bottom layer of loaf is heavy and the top coarse.* The dough raised too much or was not kneaded enough.

7. *The flavor is yeasty.* The temperature for rising was too high or the dough has risen too many times. A temperature of approximately 80 degrees F. (27 C.) is best. After many punchings and remoldings, yeasty flavor may develop. It is still better to remold than to bake too light a loaf, however.

8. *Other off flavors develop.* Poor ingredients were used or fluid milk was not scalded and cooled before being added. Organisms ordinarily in fluid milk must be killed before breadbaking or the long period of fermentation will provide a good culture medium for them, too, producing off flavors and odors.

9. *The bread is heavy and thick celled.* There has been too little kneading, too little rising, or both.

10. *The loaf becomes torn or mashed in cutting.* Cut with a good, serrated knife, using a sawing motion while holding the loaf lightly on its side. Cut hot bread only with a very thin "smorgasbord" knife, an electric knife, or heated knife.

EASY 100 PERCENT WHOLE WHEAT
BREAD AND ROLLS (STRAIGHT DOUGH METHOD)
(Note: Do *not* begin until you have read "Very Important Information" and "Helps for Making 100 percent Whole Wheat Bread and Rolls.")

Combine in a 4-quart bowl:
  3 eggs
  4 c. lukewarm milk (scalded and
      cooled if fluid milk is used)
  ⅓ c. honey or brown sugar
  2 Tbsp. yeast
Melt and cool:
  4 Tbsp. table fat

Sift and measure *or* weigh:
  2½ to 3 lb. whole wheat flour
      (8½ to 10½ c. granular,
      10 to 12 c. powdery)
Measure and reserve:
  1 Tbsp. salt

Allow liquid mixture to stand until yeast is softened.
Add half the flour. Beat until bubbly.
Add half the remaining flour with the salt sprinkled in. Mix. Add the table fat. Mix. Add more flour until the dough is difficult to mix with a spoon. Remove spoon and begin to knead. (See instructions on kneading in "Helps.") Continue kneading, adding flour a little at a time until you have a soft dough that will hold its shape. (Do not feel that you must use all of the flour. The amount will vary with the nature of the flour, the size of the eggs used, etc. You can add more later if it is needed.)

Select a good TV program or place interesting reading material where you can see it. Knead and read for 10 minutes by the clock. Butter bowl and dough lightly. Cover with a domed lid or damp cloth over waxed paper. Set in a warm place (80 F.) and let rise until double in bulk. Punch down. Let rise a second time until double in bulk. Divide into portions for loaves, rolls, pizza, or whatever. (See yields below for possible divisions.) Let rest a few minutes. Mold into desired shapes. (See directions for "Shaping" under "Helps.")

Place dough in buttered pans; brush lightly with melted fat; cover and let rise until it holds the imprint of a finger when touched lightly at the end of a loaf or the side of a roll.

Bake at 375 degrees F. Loaves require 35 to 40 minutes, Rolls need 20 to 25 minutes. Baking is complete when crusts are solid and lightly browned, bread sounds hollow when thumped and releases easily from the pan and the bottom of the pan sizzles when touched with a damp finger.

This recipe yields 3 loaves, 1½ pounds each (9x5x2½-inch pans) and six buns or rolls, or 4 one-pound loaves (7x3½x2¼-inch pans) and one dozen buns, or 5 dozen buns, or 5 large pizzas (1 pound dough per pizza). The loaves provide 65 Calories, 3 grams protein, 0.39 grams fiber per ounce. The buns or rolls have 90 Calories (or a little more if much fat is used in shaping them), 4.0 grams protein, 0.52 grams fiber each.

This basic dough may also be used for sweet rolls, cinnamon bread, and raisin bread.

Cinnamon Bread or Rolls

For 1½ pounds of dough (scant ⅓ of recipe for Easy 100 Percent Whole Wheat Bread and Rolls) use

2 Tbsp. soft table fat

1 c. brown sugar or ⅔ c. honey

Cinnamon to taste

If brown sugar is used, you will need a sprinkle of water.)

Cinnamon Rolls

Roll or pat the dough into a rectangle approximately 12x15 inches. Spread with soft butter or margarine. Spread sugar or honey evenly over the butter. Sprinkle with cinnamon. Sprinkle with a little water only if brown sugar is used. Roll up. (See instructions under "Shaping" among "Helps.")

Cut roll into 15 servings. Arrange in well buttered pan 9x13x2 inches. Pat tops of rolls to even them and spread their butter-sugar mixture over the tops. Cover and let rise until the dough will hold a fingerprint when touched lightly on the side.

Bake at 375 F. about 35 minutes or until lightly browned and the bottom of the pan sizzles when touched with a damp finger.

Yields 15 servings, about 175 Calories, 5.3 g. protein, 0.62 grams fiber each.

Cinnamon Bread

Roll or pat dough into a long rectangle about 8 inches wide. Proceed as for cinnamon rolls except that after the dough is rolled up and sealed, put into a greased loaf pan 9x5x2½ inches, brush lightly with butter, cover and allow to rise until it will hold the print of a finger when touched lightly on the end.

Bake at 375 F. for 45 to 50 minutes or until lightly browned and the bottom sizzles when touched with a damp finger. Yield as for cinnamon rolls if cut into 15 servings.

Tea Ring

See instructions under "Shaping" among the "Helps."

Raisin Bread

For 1½ pounds of dough (scant 1/3 of recipe)* portioned off after the dough has risen twice use

1/3 cup brown sugar or 1/4 cup honey

1/2 cup raisins

Bring raisins to a gentle boil in just enough water to cover them. Drain (reserving the water for use in cereal or syrup). Blot gently with a paper towel.

Knead the raisins and honey or sugar gently into the dough. Mold the loaf. Brush with melted butter. Cover and let rise until the dough will hold a fingerprint when lightly touched in the end.

---

* If all the recipe is to be used for raisin bread, add 1 c. brown sugar or 2/3 c. honey at the time of mixing and 1 1/2 c. raisins when the dough is punched down.

Bake at 375 degrees F. for 40 to 45 minutes or until the crust is set and lightly browned, the loaf sounds hollow when thumped, and the bottom of the pan sizzles when touched with a damp finger.

Yields 1 loaf, about 20 slices, 1½ ounce, 100 Calories, 3.6 grams protein, 0.47 grams fiber each.

Fruit Bread

Follow the same recipe as for raisin bread but use mixed candied, or dried fruit without the addition of water.

100 PERCENT WHOLE WHEAT BREAD AND ROLLS (SPONGE METHOD)

(For flour with strong gluten that can take long kneading— produces a large volume and velvety texture)

Do *not* attempt until you have read sections on "Very Important Information" and "Helps for Making 100 Percent Whole Wheat Bread and Rolls."

Measure and set aside:
   1½ pounds (about 5¼ c. granular, 6 c. powdery) hard whole wheat flour (See "Very Important Information" for *your* flour measure.)
In a 4-quart mixing bowl combine
   ¼ c. warm (not hot) water
   1 Tbsp. yeast
When yeast is dissolved add
   ¾ c. cool water
   2¼ to 3 c. flour
Make a stiff dough.

Select a good TV program or place interesting reading material where you can see it while kneading the sponge in the bowl. Knead and read or watch TV for 15 minutes. The sponge should be elastic and sticky, pull away from the bowl, and hold a ball shape. Cover with a domed lid or damp towel over waxed paper. Let stand in a warm (80 F.) place for 1 hour.

Add to the sponge:

1⅓ c. lukewarm milk (scalded and cooled if fluid milk is used)
1 egg
2 Tbsp. honey
¼ c. soft table fat
2 tsp. salt

Enough of the rest of the flour to make a soft dough that will hold its shape. You may need it all. Do not use more than is necessary. Mix and knead in the bowl for 10 to 15 minutes. Watch TV or read as you knead to avoid the temptation to stop before the time is up.

Cover and let rise in a warm place for 45 minutes or until the dough is 2 to 3 times its original volume.

Punch down, cover, and let rise again.

Divide the dough into portions, 2 for 2 loaves in 9x5x2½-inch pans, 3 for 3 loaves in 7x3½x2-inch pans, or as desired for buns, rolls, or pizza. Fashion into balls. Cover and let rest for 15 minutes. Mold into desired shapes. (See instructions on "Shaping" under "Helps.")

Place in buttered pans, brush lightly with melted fat. Cover and let rise in a warm place until about triple in bulk and light enough that it will hold the print of a finger when touched lightly in the end of the loaf or side of a roll (it may take as much as 1¼ hours).

Bake at 375 F. Loaves require 35 to 40 minutes. Rolls require 20 to 25 minutes. Baking is completed when the crust is solid and lightly browned, the bread sounds hollow when thumped and releases from the pan easily, and the bottom of the pan sizzles when touched with a damp finger.

Yield 2 loaves, 1½ pounds each, *or* 3 loaves, 1 pound each, *or* 3 dozen 1⅓-ounce rolls or buns, *or* 3 large pizzas. Loaves will provide 65 Calories, 3 grams protein, 0.39 grams fiber

73

per ounce. 1⅓-ounce buns or rolls have 90 Calories, 4.0 grams protein, 0.52 grams fiber each, or a few more Calories if large amounts of fat are used in molding the portions.

WHOLE GRAIN BREAKFASTS

Cereal Chart

Whole Grain	Water	Salt	Yield
1 c. brown rice	1½ - 2 c.	¼ tsp.	3 cups
1 c. rolled oats	2 cups	½ tsp.	2 cups
1 c. cracked wheat	3 cups	¾ tsp.	3 cups
1 c. wheat grains	3 cups	¾ tsp.	3-4 cups
1 c. cornmeal	4 cups	1 tsp.	4 cups

Directions

Rice

Measure 1 cup rice and 1½ cups cold water (2 c. if soft rice is desired). Add salt. Bring to boil. Turn heat low and steam for about 40 minutes. Toss lightly with a fork to separate grains. Do not stir! 210 Calories, 4.4 g. protein, 0.53 g. fiber per cup.

Rolled Oats*

Measure water and salt into pan. Bring to rapid boil. Add rolled oats. Return to boil. Cover. Turn heat low and simmer until thickened. Stir lightly with a fork only. (Time varies with fineness of grind.) 146 Calories, 5.3 g. protein, 0.45 g. fiber per cup.**

Cracked Wheat*

Measure salt and water into pan. Bring to rapid boil. Add wheat gradually to water, stirring with a fork. Return to a

---

*Fresh wheat germ may replace about one-third the grain to be used in preparing these cereals to add extra nutrients. Just substitute the wheat germ and proceed as usual. One third cup wheat germ provides 100 Calories, 7.5 g. protein, 0.71 g.. fiber compared with 141 Calories, 5.7 g. protein, and 0.9 g. fiber for whole wheat meal, and the mineral and B vitamin content of the germ is much higher than that of the wheat meal.
**Nutrients per cup will be fewer for all grains if more water is used in preparation.

boil. Cover. Turn heat low and simmer until thickened and starch grains are swelled. (Time varies with fineness of grind.) 146 Calories, 5.8 g. protein, 0.65 g. fiber per cup.

Whole Wheat Grains

Measure wheat, water, and salt into pan. Cover. Bring to a rapid boil. Turn off heat. Allow to stand one hour. Bring to rapid boil again. Turn off heat. Allow to stand one hour. Repeat on the third and fourth hours. After the fourth hour it should be tender with many of the shells burst, and ready for use as a cereal or in other dishes. Stir only with a fork.

Wheat grains may also be cooked in the pressure cooker, but there will be more liquid that is not absorbed, more starch in the liquid, and fewer fluffy grains.

Wheat grains may also be cooked in a thermos overnight. Fill a quart thermos with boiling water. Stopper it to allow it to heat while you prepare 1 cup wheat, 3 cups water and ¾ tsp. salt in a pan and bring it to a boil. Empty the thermos. Rinse with more boiling water. Pour boiling wheat mixture into the thermos. Put stopper in and allow to remain overnight. The wheat will be ready to serve for breakfast. A 3-cup yield = 187 Calories, 7.5 g. protein, 1.3 g. fiber per cup. A 4-cup yield = 140 Calories, 5.6 g. protein, 0.98 g. fiber per cup.

Cornmeal Mush

Bring 3 cups water and 1 tsp. salt to a boil in a deep saucepan. Combine the other cup of *cold* water with the cornmeal. Pour the cold cornmeal paste into the boiling water, stirring continuously with a fork or whisk. When thickened, turn the heat low and simmer covered about 20 minutes. Yields 4 cups, 109 Calories, 1.89 g. protein, 0.21 g. fiber per cup.

(Finely ground wheat may be prepared with this method to avoid lumping. For wheat, use a total of 3 cups water to 1 cup wheat.)

Leftover Cereals

Leftover cereals may be stored for several days in the refrigerator or frozen for later use. To reheat, bring a small amount of water, salted at a rate of ¼ tsp. per cup, to a boil. Add the leftover cereal. Break it up with a fork and stir lightly. Cover and heat, stirring occasionally with a fork, until warmed thoroughly.

Leftover cereals may also be sliced cold, fried in table fat, oil, or bacon drippings, and served with sorghum, molasses, honey, syrup, or fruit. For a more hearty dish, stir leftover meat scraps into the cereal before it is chilled. It may then be sliced and fried. This is *scrapple*. If cereal is to be fried, it must be thick. Add 100 Calories for each tablespoon of fat used, 50 to 65 Calories for each tablespoon of syrup.

Raisins or other dried fruit may be combined with cereals. For *leftover* creals, add the fruit to the hot water before the cereal is stirred in for heating. For *fresh* cereal add the fruit after the meal has been combined with the hot water for cooking. 1 oz. raisins (2 to 3 tablespoons) adds 80 Calories, 0.7 g. protein, 0.26 g. fiber to the cereal.

Wheat Nuts

(A homemade dry cereal—delicious and cheap)

Sift together:
   1¾ c. whole wheat flour *or* 1½ c. whole wheat flour and
      add ¼ c. wheat germ after sifting
   ½ tsp. salt
   ½ tsp. soda

Add and mix thoroughly:
   ¼ c. brown sugar or less

Add and mix as for muffins:
   1 c. sour milk or buttermilk

Roll very thin on a floured pastry cloth. Divide into 6 or 8 portions. Bake on a greased baking sheet at 350 F. for about 15-20 minutes or until golden brown. Cool. Place in a plastic bag and roll with a rolling pin until the desired sized pieces are obtained or grind in a coarse grinder or blender. Yields

10 ounces cereal; ¼ to ⅓ cup, depending on size of particles, 94 Calories, 3.6 g. protein, 0.46 g. fiber per ounce. Needs only milk for serving.

Granola

(One of many recipes. Create your own if you wish.)

Heat in a large baking pan until honey melts:

⅓ c. oil (Some recipes call for more than 2 times this much. Add 110 extra Calories for each tablespoon extra used.)

¼ c. honey

Add:

3 c. rolled cereal (oats, wheat, or what have you)

1 c. sunflower seeds (raw if available; if seeds are salted do not add other salt.)

2 Tbsp. brown sugar

1 tsp. salt (if no salted nuts are used)

2 Tbsp. bran

2 Tbsp. whole wheat flour

2 Tbsp. water with

1 tsp. vanilla, if desired

Mix until all particles are coated with the honey-oil mixture. Bake (stirring frequently) at 325 F. until lightly browned, about 20 minutes. Remove from oven and while still hot add:

¾ c. chopped nuts and/or coconut

1 c. wheat germ (raw germ may be included in ingredients to be baked above)

1 c. chopped dried fruits (dates, raisins, apricots, and the like)

Cool and store in a tight container. Yields 33 ounces; about 3⅓ Tbsp., 123 Calories, 3.6 g. protein, 0.51 g. fiber each. This tastes good, but watch those Calories—especially if one of the high fat recipes is used (⅔ c. oil in this recipe would raise the Calories to 140 per ounce). Commercial granolas usually have their oil from highly saturated coconut oil because it extends the shelf life of the food.

QUICK BREADS

Favorite Pancakes
Combine:
- 2 well beaten eggs
- 2 c. skim milk
- 2 Tbsp. melted table fat or oil

Sift together:
- 2 c. whole wheat flour
- 4 tsp. baking powder
- ½ tsp. salt

Add liquid to dry ingredients. Mix only until dry ingredients are moistened. Spoon onto an ungreased griddle hot enough to sizzle when a drop of water touches it. Leave until bubbly, then turn and lightly brown. Yields 12 four-inch cakes, 106 Calories, 5.1 grams protein, 0.43 grams fiber each.

Buttermilk Pancakes
In the recipe above substitute 2 cups buttermilk, sour milk, *or* sweet milk with 1 tablespoon vinegar *or* 2 tablespoons lemon juice replacing an equivalent amount of milk in each cup. Also use 1 teaspoon soda and 2 teaspoons baking powder instead of 4 teaspoons baking powder. Yield remains the same.

Everyday Waffles

In the recipe above, increase the fat to ⅓ cup. Bake in waffle iron. Yields 12 4-inch waffle squares, 135 Calories, 5.1 grams protein, 0.43 grams fiber each.

Yeast Raised Pancakes

Soften:
>2 Tbsp. yeast in
>1⅔ c. lukewarm milk (scalded and cooled if fresh fluid milk)

Add:
>1½ Tbsp. honey *or* 2 Tbsp. brown sugar

Add and mix thoroughly:
>2 cups whole wheat flour
>1 tsp. salt

Melt, cool, and set aside:
>2 Tbsp. table fat or oil

Beat until creamy and thick:
>3 eggs

Add the fat and fold in the eggs. Cover the batter and let stand in a warm place until double in bulk (20 to 30 minutes). Stir down and let rise again if it is ready before you are. Spoon onto hot griddle without stirring; leave until lightly browned on each side, turning only once. Yields 16 4-inch cakes, 90 Calories, 4.2 grams protein, 0.33 grams fiber each.

Yeast Raised Waffles

In yeast raised pancake recipe above, increase fat to ½ cup and bake in a waffle iron. Yields 16 4-inch waffle squares, 128 Calories, 4.2 grams protein, 0.33 grams fiber each.

(If there is extra dough left over, knead in enough whole wheat flour to make a soft dough and treat as bread dough. Use any way bread dough is used.)

Special Occasion Waffles

(To be prepared at night for the next morning's breakfast.)

Separate 4 eggs:
    Beat the whites until stiff but not dry. Set aside.
    Beat the yolks until thick.
Add to the yolks:
    2¼ c. milk
    2 tsp. honey *or* brown sugar
Melt and set aside to cool:
    ⅔ c. table fat *or* oil
Sift together:
    3 c. whole wheat flour
    5 tsp. baking powder
    1 tsp. salt

Combine dry ingredients with liquid mixture. Blend well. Add fat. Fold in beaten egg whites. Bake in hot waffle iron. Yields 16 large waffle squares, 172 Calories, 5.7 grams protein, 0.55 grams fiber each. Calories may be reduced to 138 by using only ⅓ cup fat. Waffles will be less crisp. Increasing the amount of sweetener will increase the crispness if desired.

Handy Pancake and Waffle Mix

Combine and sift together three times:
    10 c. whole wheat flour
    ½ c. baking powder
    4 tsp. salt
    3⅓ c. dry skim milk
Store in a tightly covered container in a cool place.

To use for cakes:
    Measure out 2½ c. mix
Combine:
    2 eggs well beaten
    1¾ c. water
    2 Tbsp. melted table fat *or* oil

Add liquid to dry ingredients. Mix only until dry ingredients are moistened. Spoon onto ungreased hot griddle, leave until bubbly. Turn and lightly brown. Yields 5 recipes, each making 12 four-inch cakes, 106 Calories, 5.1 grams protein, 0.43 grams fiber each. (For thinner cakes, add more water.)

To use for waffles:

Beat eggs in above recipe until thick and creamy. Increase fat to ⅓ cup per recipe. Bake in waffle iron. Yield per recipe is 12 4-inch squares, 135 Calories, 5.1 grams protein, 0.43 grams fiber each.

Old Fashioned Buckwheat Cakes

(To be prepared at night for the next morning's breakfast.)
Combine in a large bowl:

    2 c. milk (scalded and cooled if fluid milk is used)
    1½ tsp. yeast (half a package)
    1¾ c. dark buckwheat flour
    ½ tsp. salt

Beat thoroughly and set in a warm place to rise overnight. In the morning dissolve and add to the sponge:

    1½ Tbsp. sorghum, molasses, or brown sugar
    ¼ tsp. soda
    ⅓ c. lukewarm water

(Adjust the consistency of the dough to make the kind of cakes you like by adding more buckwheat or whole wheat flour if they are too thin, more milk if they are too thick.)
Mix well and spoon onto a lightly greased hot griddle. Yields 20 small cakes, 44 Calories, 2.1 g. protein, 0.14 g. fiber each.

If you want to serve the cakes on a fairly regular schedule, reserve a cupful of the batter for a starter. Refrigerate until the night before it is to be used. (Any leftover cakes may be returned to the leftover batter and reused as a part of the starter. They will be completely absorbed.) Combine the ingredients for a new batch as instructed above, but use the starter instead of the yeast. Reserve a starter from each batch as long as you wish to keep serving the cakes. They get better as time goes on. If off flavors do develop, start over again with fresh yeast.

French Toast

Combine:
- 3 beaten eggs
- ¾ c. milk
- ¼ tsp. salt

Have available:
- 8 slices whole wheat bread
- 1 Tbsp. oil, table fat, or pork drippings (to lightly grease the griddle)

(*Proportions are:* Equal amounts egg and milk, salted at the rate of 1 tsp. per doz. eggs. *Optional ingredients* are brown sugar, cinnamon, and nutmeg.)

Heat the griddle until a drop of water will dance on it. Brush with fat. Dip slices of bread into the milk-egg mixture one at a time. Arrange slices on griddle and fry until lightly browned. Turn and brown on the other side. Serve as pancakes or waffles. Yields 8 slices, 125 Calories, 6.9 g. protein, 0.56 g. fiber per slice if made with whole milk and bread weighing 1¼ oz. per slice; 120 Calories per slice if made with skim milk.

Suggested Accompaniments for Pancakes, Waffles, or French Toast

Instant Syrup

Combine twice as much brown sugar as water in a deep pan. Bring to a boil. Add maple flavor to taste. Syrup is ready to use. Yields about 12 tablespoons syrup, 65 Calories per tablespoonful, for each cup of sugar used.

Fruit Syrup

Save the syrup from canned fruits such as peaches, apricots, pears. Boil down to desired consistency or just heat and serve. Approximately 50 Calories per tablespoonful.

Fruit Purees

Puree in blender or food mill any soft ripe fruit such as guava, peaches, pears, apricots, or mangos. Serve with or without sweetening. May be used in addition to syrup.

Fruit Sauce

Applesauce, rhubarb sauce, cherry sauce, Scandinavian sweet soup, or others are good.

Fresh Fruits

Strawberries, Saskatoons, blueberries, raspberries, boysenberries, thimbleberries, or other berries, sliced peaches, bananas, mangos, or other fruits may be served plain, sweetened to taste if desired, with or without whipped cream or topping.

Protein Foods

Eggs, ham, bacon, sausages, cottage cheese, creamed fowl or fish, tofu, or other soybean protein foods go well with cakes, waffles and toast.

Other Syrups

Honey, sorghum, maple syrup, corn syrup, or molasses, may be served plain, thinned with water and boiled, or combined with another syrup for subtle flavors.

English Lemon Cheese

Combine in the top of a double boiler or in a heavy saucepan:

 3 large eggs beaten slightly
 grated rind and juice of 3 large lemons
 6 Tbsp. butter
 ¾ c. honey *or* 1 c. and 2 Tbsp. sugar

Optional:

 1 package unflavored gelatin dissolved in
 2 Tbsp. water

Heat gently, stirring constantly until butter melts, then for 5 minutes more. Pour into jar and refrigerate until used. Yields about 2½ cups, 36 Calories, 0.7 g. protein, 0.06 g. fiber each tablespoonful.

Facts About Doughnuts and Doughnut Making

Fat Absorption

Doughnuts can be made that either are or are *not* heavy with Calories from fat (oil). Here are some factors that affect absorption:

1. The amount of fat absorbed becomes greater with an increase in the amount of fat, sugar, or baking powder in the recipe. The proportions in the accompanying recipes give tenderness and flavor without undue fat absorption.

2. The relatively smaller the surface area, the smaller the fat absorption. Thick doughnuts with smooth surfaces absorb the least fat. Roll the dough ⅜ inch thick and cut it with a sharp, floured cutter.

3. Dough allowed to age a few minutes after cutting absorbs less fat. Don't be in a rush to cook doughnuts after they are cut. Give cake type up to 15 minutes rest. Yeast raised should double in bulk after being cut.

4. Warm dough (room temperature) absorbs less fat than chilled dough. Have all ingredients at room temperature for mixing (about 77 F.—25 C.).

5. Stiffer doughs absorb less fat. Softer doughs give greater volume and more tenderness. A choice needs to be made. If you want a light, tender doughnut, make a very soft dough, but it will absorb more fat. If you are content with a smaller, less light and less tender doughnut, use more flour and keep fat absorption to a minimum.

6. Hard wheat flours make doughnuts that absorb less fat than those made with soft wheat flour. If the latter is used, the dough should be mixed more. Hard wheat dough should be mixed just enough to combine all ingredients and be manageable, about 80 to 100 strokes. A few more strokes will

reduce fat absorption but will also reduce tenderness and volume.

7. Calories from oil absorbed may vary from fewer than 10 to more than 100 per doughnut. To find how much yours absorbs, measure your oil before and after cooking the doughnuts. For every tablespoonful used multiply by 110 to see how many Calories of oil were used for the batch. Divide by the number of doughnuts to determine how many oil Calories are in each doughnut.

8. Cooking temperatures should approximate 355 to 375 degrees F. (180 to 190 C.) to cook quickly enough to prevent excessive oil absorption.

Conserving oil:

1. Use a pan with a small diameter. A seven-inch pan requires about 20 ounces of oil and will cook 3 standard sized doughnuts at a time with room for a thermometer. Since each doughnut cooks in less than a minute, a full recipe can be cooked in 12 minutes or less in this size pan. For smaller amounts (eg. ½ recipe) a smaller pan may be used with less oil.

2. Strain leftover oil and refrigerate for later use in cooking or salads. Mix the remains from straining with dog food if you have a dog, or add to pancake or bread dough. Adjust fat in the recipe.

Sugaring:

1. Cake type doughnuts do not need added sugar for flavor. Yeast raised ones may benefit by it.

2. When cooled slightly before sugaring, each doughnut retains about 3 grams sugar when shaken in a bag of finely granulated white sugar. This represents about 12 Calories.

3. A mixture of brown sugar and cinnamon may be used for variety.

4. Save leftover sugar for breakfast cereals or making syrup.

Doughnuts (Cake Type)

Cream together:

> 2 Tbsp. table fat or oil
> 1 c. brown sugar
> ½ tsp. vanilla

Add and beat until fluffy:

> 2 eggs

Measure and set aside:

> 1¼ c. milk (skim)

Sift together:

> 4½ c. whole wheat flour
> 2 Tbsp. baking powder
> ¼ tsp. salt
> ½ tsp. cinnamon
> ½ tsp. nutmeg

Add dry ingredients alternately with the milk to the creamed mixture. Mix only enough to combine all ingredients and form a soft but manageable dough—80 to 100 strokes all together. Place dough on a lightly floured pastry cloth or board. Roll to a thickness of about ⅜ inch with a rolling pin covered with stockingnet and lightly floured. Cut with a floured cutter. Let dough rest while fat heats. Cook in deep fat (oil) at 355 to 375 F. Turn once. Drain on absorbent paper. Yields 2½ dozen doughnuts, 95 Calories *plus* fat Calories absorbed (see "Facts About Doughnuts — Fat Absorbed"), 2.7 grams protein, 0.39 grams fiber each. Add 12 Calories per doughnut if sugared.

Yeast Raised Doughnuts

Soften:

> 2 Tbsp. yeast in
> 2 c. lukewarm milk (scalded and cooled if fresh fluid milk)

Add and mix thoroughly:

> 2 eggs
> ⅓ c. honey or ½ c. brown sugar
> 2 c. whole wheat flour

1 tsp. salt

Add and mix well:

¼ c. melted and cooled table fat or oil

Add:

4 to 5 c. whole wheat flour (enough to make a soft dough)

Knead in the bowl for 10 minutes. Cover and let rise until double in bulk. Roll onto lightly floured pastry cloth or board until about ⅜ inch thick. Cut with a floured cutter. Let rise until double in bulk. Cook in deep fat (oil) at 355 to 375 F. top side down first. Drain on absorbent paper. Yields 3 dozen doughnuts about 96 Calories *plus* fat Calories absorbed (see "Facts About Doughnuts — Fat Absorption"), 3.6 grams protein, 0.43 grams fiber each. Add 12 Calories per doughnut if sugared.

Everyday Biscuits

Sift together in bowl:

1¾ c. whole wheat flour

½ tsp. salt

1 Tbsp. baking powder

Add to the flour mixture:

4 Tbsp. table fat *or* 3 Tbsp. other shortening

Use pastry blender or two knives to cut fat into dry ingredients until mixture resembles coarse crumbs.

Add all at once ¾ c. milk

Mix with a fork just until dry ingredients are moistened. Turn onto lightly floured pastry cloth or board. Dough must be *soft* but manageable. Knead 15 to 20 strokes. Roll or pat until about ½ inch thick. Cut with a floured cutter—a small can or glass will do, or cut the dough into squares, diamonds, and the like with a sharp knife. Arrange biscuits on an ungreased baking sheet. Bake at 450 F. about 12 minutes. Yields 1 dozen 2¼-inch biscuits, 93 Calories, 2.8 g. protein, 0.38 g. fiber each.

Variations on Everyday Biscuits:

1. **Pizza** - Roll or pat onto greased baking sheet or pizza pan for quick pizza crust. Top with favorite filling. Bake at 400 F. for 20 minutes. Yields one large (10x15-inch) or two smaller crusts, 12 wedges, 93 Calories, 2.8 g. protein, 0.38 g. fiber each from crust. Add Calories and proteins from filling for totals.

2. **Dumplings** - Increase milk to 1 cup. Drop by spoonfuls on top of boiling stew. Cover tightly and steam without lifting the lid for 12 to 15 minutes. Yields 12 large dumplings, 93 Calories, 2.8 g. protein, 0.38 g. fiber each plus the nutrients of the stew.

3. **Cheese biscuits** - Add ½ cup grated cheddar cheese to dry ingredients. Reduce fat to 3 Tbsp., proceed as for plain biscuits. Yields 12 biscuits, 104 Calories, 4 g. protein, 0.38 g. fiber each.

4. **Bacon biscuits** - Use bacon or ham drippings for fat. Add bits of crisp bacon. *Or* use table fat as usual and add bits of bacon flavored soya product. Yield as for plain biscuits plus bacon bits added.

5. **Luncheon biscuits** - Pat or roll dough into a rectangle about ⅜ inch thick. Spread with leftover seasoned meat or fish. Roll and cut as for cinnamon rolls. Bake on a greased baking sheet as for plain biscuits. Serve with cheese sauce, creamed peas or asparagus, mushroom sauce, gravy, or tomato sauce. Yield 6 servings for hearty eaters—12 for Calorie watchers. Nutrients vary with filling and sauce. Needs only salad or relishes and beverage to complete the meal.

6. **Buttermilk biscuits** - Substitute buttermilk or soured milk (1 Tbsp. vinegar per cup) for sweet milk. Add ½ tsp. soda to dry ingredients. Reduce the baking powder to 2 tsp. Proceed as for plain biscuits. Yield, etc., the same.

Special Occasion Biscuits

Sift together:
- 2 c. whole wheat flour
- ½ tsp. salt
- 5 tsp. baking powder
- ½ tsp. cream of tartar

Add to the flour mixture:
- ½ cup plus 1 Tbsp. table fat *or* ½ c. other shortening
- 2 tsp. honey *or* brown sugar

With pastry blender or two knives, cut honey and fat into dry ingredients until mixture resembles coarse crumbs.

Add all at once: 1 c. milk

Mix with a fork just until dry ingredients are moistened. Turn onto lightly floured board or pastry cloth. Knead about 15 strokes. Pat or roll ½ inch thick. Cut with a floured cutter—a small can or glass will do—or cut dough into a variety of shapes with a sharp knife. Arrange biscuits on ungreased baking sheet. Bake at 450 F. 10 to 12 minutes. Yields 1½ doz. 2¼-inch biscuits, 102 Calories, 2.2 g. protein, 0.29 g. fiber each.

Variations of Special Occasion Biscuits:

1. **Cinnamon Rolls** - Roll or pat dough into a rectangle about ⅜ inch thick. Spread rolled dough with table fat, honey or brown sugar, and sprinkle with cinnamon. Roll and cut as for cinnamon rolls. Bake, cut side down, in well greased muffin tins or other pans at 450 F. for 12 to 15 minutes. Yield depends on size of slice and amount of butter and sugar used. 2 Tbsp. table fat and ½ cup sugar add about 610 Calories. If cut into 12 rolls, servings will be 203 Calories, 3.4 g. protein, 0.43 g. fiber each.

Nuts and dried fruits may also be added at will. Nuts (except coconut) add about 400 Calories per ½ cup with protein content ranging from about 5 grams protein per half-cup pecan halves, 9 grams for English walnuts, 12 and 13 grams respectively for cashews and black walnuts, to 18.5 grams for peanuts. Sesame seed rates between cashews and black walnuts in protein content, and sunflower seeds rate between black walnuts and peanuts. One-half cup dried fruit adds about 200 to 250 Calories, 2 grams protein, and a varying amount of fiber.

2. *Shortcake* - Use dough as it is or add sweetening to taste. Cut and bake in desired shapes. Serve with any fresh, frozen, or canned fruit with or without whipped cream or whipped topping or just with milk. Without added sweetening yields 12 servings, 153 Calories, 3.3 g. protein, 0.43 g. fiber each *plus* fruit, sweetening, and topping or milk.

3. *Fruit Cobbler:* Double the amount of sweetening and add 1 well beaten egg to the milk. Drop in mounds *or* spread over fruit prepared in a greased baking dish, *or* line the greased dish with dough, add the fruit, and top with additional dough. Bake at 425 F. for 30 minutes or until golden brown. One full recipe provides dough for a baking dish 9x13x2 inches and yields 18 servings. One-half the recipe provides dough for an 8x8x2-inch baking dish and yields 9 servings, 110 Calories, 2.6 g. protein, 0.29 g. fiber each *plus* the fruit mixture.

Fruit preparation for cobblers is given for full recipes in 9x13x2-inch baking dishes. If more fruity cobblers are desired these amounts may be increased substantially. As given, fruit mixtures provide 60 to 70 Calories, 0.1 to 0.3 grams protein, 0.06 to 0.2 grams fiber per serving.

Peach Cobbler: Combine 4 cups sliced peaches—fresh, frozen, canned, or reconstituted dried—with 1 cup sugar or ⅔ cup mild flavored honey. (Use the syrup if peaches are canned or frozen in syrup. Add sweetener only if desired.) If you like the fruit thick, add ¼ cup whole wheat flour or 2 tablespoons quick cooking tapioca. (I prefer cobblers without thickening.) Dot with 2 tablespoons butter after the fruit is spread in the baking dish. Cover with dough and bake. (If peaches are bland in flavor or tend to darken, add 1 tablespoon lemon juice to the sweetened fruit.)

Apple Cobbler: Combine 4 cups thinly sliced and packed down tart apples with 1 cup brown sugar or ⅔ cup honey, 1 teaspoon cinnamon, and ½ teaspoon nutmeg. (Add 1 or 2 tablespoons lemon juice if apples are bland or tend to darken.) If you like thick fruit, add ¼ cup whole wheat flour. Spread in baking dish. Dot with 2 tablespoons butter. Cover with dough. Bake.

Rhubarb Cobbler: Combine 6 cups fresh rhubarb pieces (4 cups cooked rhubarb), ⅓ cup brown sugar and ⅔ cup white sugar *or* ⅓ cup brown sugar and ½ cup honey. 2 tablespoons quick cooking tapioca are optional. Spread in baking dish. Dot with 2 tablespoons butter. Cover with dough. Bake.

Cherry Cobbler: Combine 4 cups cherries, about 1 cup mild honey or 1½ cup sugar (use syrup if cherries are canned or frozen with sugar), ¼ teaspoon almond flavor, and 2 tablespoons quick cooking tapioca (if you want it thick). Let stand while preparing the dough. Spread in baking dish. Dot with butter. Cover with dough. Bake. Cherry mix provides 90 to 100 Calories per serving.

Plain Muffins

Sift together:
- 2 cups whole wheat flour
- ½ tsp. salt
- 1 Tbsp. baking powder

Combine:
- 1¼ c. milk
- 1 beaten egg
- 3 Tbsp. melted table fat *or* oil
- 1 Tbsp. honey *or* sugar

Add the liquid to the dry ingredients. Mix just enough to moisten dry ingredients (not more than 23 strokes). Fill greased muffin tins ⅔ full. Bake at 425 F. 20 to 25 minutes. Yields 1 dozen muffins, 108 Calories, 4.02 g. protein, 0.44 g. fiber each.

Boston Brown Muffins

Sift together:
    2¾ c. whole wheat flour
    1 tsp. soda
    1 tsp. baking powder
    ½ tsp. salt
Measure and set aside:
    ½ c. raisins *or* ¼ c. each raisins and nuts
Combine:
    1 egg - beaten
    1½ Tbsp. honey *or* 2 Tbsp. brown sugar
    ¼ c. sorghum or molasses
    1½ c. buttermilk or soured milk (1 Tbsp. vinegar per cup)
    2 Tbsp. melted table fat or oil

Add liquid to dry ingredients. Sprinkle raisins or raisins and nuts over all. Combine by mixing not more than 23 strokes for tender muffins. Fill well-greased muffin tins ⅔ full. Bake at 400 F. 20 to 25 minutes. Loosen from tins with a fork immediately. Yields 1½ doz. muffins, 115 Calories, 3.5 g. protein, 0.42 g. fiber each.

Refrigerated Bran Muffin Batter

Pour:
    2 c. boiling water over
    6 c. bran*
Allow bran to soak.
Cream together:
    2 c. honey *or* 2½ c. brown sugar**
    1 c. table fat
Add to the creamed mixture:
    4 eggs
Beat until fluffy.

---

*2 cups breakfast cereal bran may be used for soaking and 4 cups prepared bran flakes folded into the batter later if desired. Plain raw bran is cheaper and has fewer Calories.
**Sweetening may be increased if desired.

Sift together:
- 5 c. whole wheat flour
- 2 Tbsp. soda
- 1 Tbsp. salt

Measure and set aside:
- 5 c. buttermilk
- 2 c. raisins or chopped dates

Combine bran and creamed mixture. Add dry ingredients alternately with buttermilk. Fold in raisins or dates. Store in a tightly covered nonmetal container until needed. The batter may be kept from 1 to 2 weeks (it may darken on top).

To bake, fill greased muffin tins ⅔ full. Bake at 400 F. 20 minutes or until lightly browned. Recipe yields 1 gallon batter—6 dozen muffins, 85-90 Calories, 2.9 g. protein, 0.65 g. fiber each

Breakfast Cake

Sift together:
- 1½ c. whole wheat flour
- ¼ tsp. salt
- 2½ tsp. baking powder

Combine:
- 1 beaten egg
- 3 Tbsp. honey *or* ¼ c. sugar
- ¾ c. milk
- 3 Tbsp. melted table fat *or* oil

Add liquid to dry ingredients. Mix thoroughly. Pour into greased 8x8x2-inch baking pan. Add topping.

Topping—Mix and sprinkle on top of dough:
- ¼ c. honey *or* brown sugar
- 1 Tbsp. whole wheat flour
- 1 tsp. cinnamon
- 1 Tbsp. melted table fat
- ¼ c. chopped nuts

Bake at 350 F. for 25 to 30 minutes or until cake springs back when touched. Yields 9 pieces, 189 Calories, 4.5 g. protein, 0.43 g. fiber each *or* 12 pieces, 142 Calories, 3.4 g. protein, 0.4 g. fiber each.

Southern Corn Bread

Combine:
- 1 beaten egg*
- 1 c. sour milk or buttermilk
- 1 Tbsp. melted table fat or drippings (fat may be left out)

Sift together or stir thoroughly:
- 1½ c. cornmeal (preferably yellow)
- ½ tsp. salt
- ½ tsp. soda
- ½ tsp. baking powder

Pour the liquid into the dry ingredients. Stir until all the dry ingredients are moistened. Fill generously greased corn stick pans or muffin tins about ¾ full or pour into an 8x8x2-inch greased baking pan. Bake at 425 F. about 25 minutes or until lightly browned. Yields 1 dozen corn sticks or muffins or 12 portions crisp corn bread, 75 Calories, 2.4 g. protein, 0.09 g. fiber each when made with fat.

Conventional Corn Bread

Combine:
- 1 c. milk
- 1 beaten egg
- 3 Tbsp. melted table fat or drippings
- 2 tsp. honey (if desired)

Sift together:
- ½ c. whole wheat flour
- 3 tsp. baking powder
- ½ tsp. salt
- 1 c. cornmeal (may be stirred in)

---

*The egg may be separated and the white whipped until stiff and folded in last.

Pour liquid into dry ingredients and mix until all dry ingredients are moistened. Pour into greased 8x8x2-inch pan. Bake at 400 F. for 25 to 30 minutes or until lightly browned. Yields 12 portions, 93 Calories, 2.7 g. protein, 0.17 g. fiber each.

Egg Noodles

(Noodles are not exactly a bread but they contain the same kinds of ingredients.)

Combine:
- 1 beaten egg
- 2 Tbsp. whole milk
- ½ tsp. salt
- 1 c. whole wheat flour (more or less to form a *very stiff* dough; use all the flour you can work into the moist ingredients)

With a rolling pin dusted with flour roll *paper thin* on a floured board. Spread on dry cloths to dry for 30 minutes. Fold together and cut to desired shape and thickness, from ⅛ inch for thin noodles to 1½ inch for lasagna noodles. Spread out and allow to dry thoroughly. Store in a tight container in the refrigerator. Use wherever egg noodles are called for. Complete cooking requires 10 minutes. Yields 6 oz. noodles; 80 Calories, 3.8 g. protein, 0.43 g. fiber per oz.

CAKES

Any recipe that calls for white flour may be transformed into one using whole wheat flour. You may expect the whole wheat one to have less volume, be heavier and more moist than the one made with white flour. All the cake recipes to follow were once white flour recipes. With a little effort you can turn your favorite recipe into a whole wheat one. See the section of this book called "Very Important Information" for details. *Do not try to use these recipes without first reading the very important information given there.*

Whole Wheat Angel Food Cake

Place in large bowl:
   1⅔ c. egg whites
      (12 to 13 large)
   ½ tsp. salt
Sift together 3 times:
    1 c. whole wheat flour*
    2 Tbsp. cornstarch
    ¾ c. sugar
Allow egg whites to reach room temperature. Beat whites until foamy. Sprinkle on
   1½ tsp. cream of tartar
Beat until stiff but not dry.
Gradually beat in 1 c. sugar or ⅔ c. honey.

---
*For soft wheat flour use 1½ cups and no cornstarch.

Add:

    1 tsp. vanilla

    ½ tsp. almond flavoring

Sprinkle dry ingredients over meringue and fold in gently but quickly. Place in ungreased tube pan 10 inches in diameter, 4 inches deep. Insert spatula into dough and draw it around the pan several times to eliminate air pockets.

Bake at 375 F. for 35 to 40 minutes until lightly browned and springy to the touch. Invert the pan immediately and cool thoroughly before attempting to remove cake. Yields 16 servings, 113 Calories, 3.75 g. protein, 0.16 g. fiber each.

Nut Torte

Separate 3 eggs

To egg whites add:

    ¼ tsp. salt

Beat until fluffy but not dry.

Gradually beat in:

    6 Tbsp. sugar *or* 4 Tbsp. honey

To egg yolks add:

    6 Tbsp. sugar *or* 4 Tbsp. honey

    ½ tsp. vanilla

    ¼ tsp. almond flavoring

Beat until thick and lemon yellow.

Sift together:

    ½ c. whole wheat flour

    ½ tsp. baking powder

Add:

    1½ c. chopped nuts *or* ¾ c. chopped nuts & ¾ c. rolled oats or rolled wheat (large flakes)

Fold dry ingredients into egg yolk mixture.

Fold in egg white meringue.

Pour into greased 8x8x2-inch pan. Bake at 325 F. for 50 minutes. Remove from oven and invert on a cake rack. Cool for 30 minutes. Remove from pan.

When ready to serve, split the torte horizontally with a sharp knife. Fill and frost with date cheese topping.

Date Cheese Topping
Blend:
- 6 ounces (2 small packages) cream cheese with
- 5 Tbsp. light cream or evaporated milk and a dash of salt.

Beat until fluffy.
Add:
- ½ c. chopped dates

Mix and spread.

Decorate with maraschino cherries. Serves 12, 265 Calories, 7.5 g. protein, 0.53 g. fiber each.

Old-Fashioned Gingerbread
Cream:
- ¾ c. table fat
- ⅔ c. honey *or* 1 c. brown sugar
- ¾ c. sorghum or molasses

Add, one at a time:
- 2 eggs

Beat until fluffy.
Sift together:
- 3 c. whole wheat flour
- 1 tsp. soda
- ½ tsp. baking powder
- ¼ tsp. salt
- 1 tsp. ginger
- 1 tsp. cinnamon

Add dry ingredients alternately with
- 1 c. plus 2 Tbsp. buttermilk or soured milk (1 Tbsp. vinegar replacing 1 Tbsp. milk).

Mix until well blended.

Pour into greased and floured 9x13x2-inch pan. Bake at 350 F. 40 to 45 minutes or until cake springs back at a touch and bottom of pan sizzles when touched with a damp finger. Yields 18 servings, 218 Calories, 3.8 g. protein, 0.43 g. fiber each.

Busy Day Cake with Variations

Sift together in mixing bowl:
   1½ c. whole wheat flour
   ¼ tsp. salt
   2½ tsp. baking powder
Add:
   ⅔ c. honey *or* 1 c. sugar
Add, all at room temperature:
   ⅓ c. soft table fat
   ⅔ c. milk
   1 egg
   1 tsp. vanilla

Blend together with mixer or rotary beater, then beat at medium speed for 2 minutes. Pour into greased and floured 8x8x2-inch pan. Bake at 350 F. for 30 to 35 minutes or until cake springs back at the touch of a finger and the bottom of the pan sizzles when touched with a damp finger. Yields 12 servings, 160 Calories, 3.0 g. protein, 0.33 g. fiber. If icing is used, add nutrients noted as icing's yield.

Variations of Busy Day Cake:

1. *Spice Cake*—Omit vanilla. Sift 1 tsp. cinnamon, ¼ tsp. nutmeg and ¼ tsp. cloves with the flour.
2. *Chocolate Cake*—Add 2 squares melted, unsweetened baking chocolate and reduce table fat to ¼ cup.

Broiled Jiffy Icing for Busy Day Cake

Combine:
   3 Tbsp. table fat
   5 Tbsp. brown sugar
   2 Tbsp. cream or evaporated milk
   ½ c. shredded coconut or chopped nuts

Heat to melt table fat. Spread on cake while it is still warm. Place under the broiler or just in a hot oven until it bubbles all over the surface and browns lightly. Yields 12 servings, 80 Calories, 0.8 g. protein, 0.08 g. fiber each. If icing is used, add nutrients to those of cake.

Harvest Apple Cake

Wash, core, and chop finely:
    2 cups apples (2 medium apples)
Add and set aside:*
    ½ c. raisins
    ½ c. chopped nuts
Cream together:
    ⅔ c table fat
    1½ c. sugar *or* 1 c. honey
    ½ tsp. vanilla
Add and beat until fluffy:
    2 eggs
Sift together:
    2¼ c. whole wheat flour
    1 tsp. soda
    ½ tsp. baking powder
    ½ tsp. salt
    1 tsp. cinnamon
    ¼ tsp. nutmeg
    ¼ tsp. cloves

Add enough of the flour mixture to the apple mixture to coat fruit and nuts
Add dry ingredients not used to dredge apple mixture alternately with:
    ½ c. sour milk *or* buttermilk
Add and mix well:
    The apple-raisin-nut mixture
Pour into a greased and floured baking pan 9x13x2 inches and bake at 350 F. 40 to 45 minutes or until the cake springs

---
*You may use all raisins, all nuts, or neither.

back at a touch. Serves 18, 220 Calories, 3.4 g. protein, 0.55 g. fiber each with sugar, nuts, and raisins; 180 Calories, 2.9 g. protein, 0.45 g. fiber each with honey and no nuts or raisins. May also be served with whipped cream or whipped topping, 25 to 30 Calories per Tbsp. whipped cream, 5 to 10 Calories per Tbsp. whipped topping.

Honey Applesauce Cake

Cream:
>½ c. table fat
>⅔ c. honey *or* 1 c. sugar

Add and beat until fluffy:
>1 egg

Sift together:
>2 c. whole wheat flour *or* 1¾ c. flour and ¼ c. corn-starch
>2 tsp. baking powder
>½ tsp. salt
>½ tsp. soda
>¼ tsp. cloves
>½ tsp. cinnamon
>½ tsp. nutmeg

Add dry ingredients to creamed mixture alternately with:
>1 cup applesauce (Reduce honey or sugar if applesauce is sweetened.)

Mix well. Fold in:
>½ c. raisins or a combination of raisins and nuts

Pour batter into a well greased and floured pan, 7½x12x2 inches for a deep cake, 9x13x2 inches for a shallow cake. Bake at 350 F., 55 to 60 minutes for 7½x12x2-inch pan, 45 to 50 minutes for 9x13x2-inch pan, until cake is lightly browned and springs back at a touch. Serves 18, 150 Calories, 2.3 g. protein, 0.37 g. fiber each.

(No icing is needed, but if used, add Calories and protein from recipe following.)

Quick Caramel Icing for Applesauce Cake

Combine:
  1 c. brown sugar
  ⅛ tsp. salt
  2 Tbsp. butter
  ⅓ c. milk
Cook to soft ball stage (234 F.)
Cover and cool to lukewarm.
Add:
  1 tsp. vanilla
  1 Tbsp. cream *or* evaporated milk
Beat until spreading consistency. Spread on cool cake. Dot with nuts if desired. Serves 18, 60 Calories, 0.22 g. protein, no fiber without nuts.

Banana Loaf or Cupcakes

Cream:
  ½ c. table fat
  ⅔ c. honey *or* ⅔ c. white sugar
                ⅓ c. brown sugar

Add:
  2 eggs   ½ tsp. vanilla

Beat well.

Sift together:
  2 c. whole wheat flour
    or 1¾ c. whole wheat and ¼ c. cornstarch
  ½ tsp. salt
  1 tsp. soda   ½ tsp. baking powder

Add dry ingredients alternately with:
  1 c. banana pulp
Fold in:
  ½ c. chopped nut meats (I use ½ nuts, ½ coconut)

Bake in greased or waxed paper lined loaf pans or greased muffin tins. Loaves require 45-50 minutes at 350 F.

102

Cupcakes require 20-25 minutes. Yields 2 loaves 7x3½x2¼ inches *or* 1 loaf 9x5x2½ inches, *or* 18 cupcakes, 163 Calories, 2.95 g. protein, 0.41 g. fiber each. If each small loaf is sliced into 18 slices, each slice provides about 81 Calories, 1.5 g. protein, and 0.20 g. fiber. Large loaves provide 24 slices, 122 Calories, 2.2 g. protein, 0.31 g. fiber each.

Pumpkin Loaf

Sift into mixing bowl:
- 1⅔ c. whole wheat flour
- ½ tsp. soda
- 1 tsp. baking powder
- ½ tsp. salt
- ½ tsp. cinnamon
- ½ tsp. nutmeg

Add to dry ingredients:
- 1 c. honey
- *or* 1½ c. sugar
- ½ c. oil
- 2 eggs
- ⅓ c. water
- 1 c. thick pumpkin*

Mix until smooth. Add:
- ½ c. chopped nuts

Fold in nuts. Bake in greased or waxed paper lined loaf pans, at 350 F. for 1 hour or until cake springs back at a touch and bottom of pan sizzles when touched by a damp finger. Yields 2 small loaves—7x3½x2¼ inches—or 1 large loaf—9x5x2½ inches. If the small loaves are cut into 18 slices, each slice provides 76 Calories, 1.3 g. protein, 0.19 g. fiber. Large loaves yield 24 slices, 114 Calories, 2.0 g. protein, 0.29 g. fiber each.

---

*To prepare fresh pumpkin, cut the pumpkin into halves. Remove the seeds and adhering fiber. Place each half, cut side down, on a wet baking sheet. Bake at 375 F. until the shell is soft (about 30 minutes for a medium-sized pumpkin). Remove the soft pulp from the skin of the pumpkin. Put through a sieve or blender. Presto! Thick pumpkin with no cut fingers from peeling and no boiling down of the pulp. If this is not as thick as canned pumpkin, omit the water and use 1⅓ c. pumpkin in the above recipe.

Carrot Loaf

Beat until fluffy:
   3 eggs
Add and mix thoroughly:
   ½ c. oil
   ⅔ c. honey *or* 1 c. sugar
   1 tsp. vanilla
Sift together:
   1½ c. whole wheat flour
   ⅛ tsp. salt
   1 tsp. baking powder
   ½ tsp. soda
   1 tsp. cinnamon
Add dry ingredients, then:
   1 c. grated raw carrots*
   1 c. chopped nuts

Mix thoroughly. Bake in greased or waxed paper lined loaf pans, 350 F. for 1 hour or until loaf springs back at a touch and the bottom of the pan sizzles at the touch of a damp finger. Yields 2 small loaves—7x3½x2¼-inch pans—or 1 large loaf—9x5x2½-inch pan. If the small loaves are cut into 18 slices, each slice provides 78 Calories, 1.4 g. protein, 0.19 g. fiber. Large loaves yield 24 slices, 117 Calories, 2.1 g. protein, 0.29 g. fiber each.

Zucchini Loaf

Beat until fluffy:
   3 eggs
   1 c. oil *or* table fat
   1 c. sugar *or* ⅔ c. honey
   2 tsp. vanilla

     Add and mix
        2 c. grated zucchini squash**

---

*½ pound carrots as purchased or harvested makes about 1 cup grated raw carrot.
**One pound zucchini makes about 2 cups grated.

Sift together:
    3 c. whole wheat flour
    1 tsp. soda
    1½ tsp. baking powder
    ½ tsp. salt
    1 tsp. cinnamon

Add and mix:
    The dry ingredients
Optional—Fold in:
    ½ c. chopped nuts

Bake in greased or waxed paper lined loaf pans, 350 F. for 1 hour or until loaf springs back at a touch and the bottom of the pan sizzles when touched with a damp finger. Yields 3 loaves, 7x3½x2¼-inch pans, *or* 1 large loaf, 9x5x2½-inch pan, and 9 cupcakes. (Cupcakes require 20 to 25 minutes for baking.)

If the small loaves are cut into 18 slices, each slice provide 80 Calories, 1.43 g. protein, 0.22 g. fiber with nuts. Cupcakes provide 160 Calories, 2.86 g. protein, 0.43 g. fiber each. Large loaves provide 24 slices, 120 Calories, 2.1 g. protein, 0.33 g. fiber each.

Devil's Food Cake

Cream together:
    ½ c. table fat
    1½ c. sugar
    1 tsp. vanilla
    ¼ tsp. maple flavoring
        (optional)

Add and beat until fluffy:
    3 eggs

Sift together at least twice:
    2 c. whole wheat flour
    ⅓ to ½ c. cocoa *or* carob
    1½ tsp. soda
    ½ tsp. baking powder
    ½ tsp. salt

Add dry ingredients alternately with:
  ½ c. sour milk or buttermilk*

Mix thoroughly and add:
  ½ c. boiling water   Mix thoroughly.

Bake in a buttered and floured pan, 9x13x2 inches, at 350 F. for 35 to 40 minutes or until the cake springs back at a touch and a toothpick tester comes out clean. Yields 18 servings, 173 Calories, 3.4 g. protein, 0.39 g. fiber each made with cocoa; 174 Calories, 3.15 g. protein, 0.53 g. fiber with carob. Top with whipped cream or whipped topping *or* vanilla or caramel fudge.

Vanilla or Caramel Fudge

Combine and cook until a small portion dropped into cold water will form a soft ball:
  1 c. sugar
  ½ c. light cream
Remove from heat. Add but do not stir:
  1 tsp. vanilla
  1 Tbsp. butter
Cover and cool until the top can be touched comfortably. Beat until it is thick and loses its shiny appearance. Spread on cake quickly.
For caramel fudge, allow sugar-cream mixture to brown slightly, but do not burn. Proceed as for vanilla fudge. Chopped nuts may be added or whole nutmeats may be used to decorate the top. Yields 18 servings. 77 Calories, 0.39 g. protein each, without nuts. Added to Devil's Food Cake, each serving totals 250 Calories, 3.5 to 3.8 g. protein.

---

*Add 1 Tbsp. vinegar to the sour milk for a rich dark color. Leave out the extra vinegar for a red colored cake. With the vinegar, more B vitamins are retained.

Oatmeal Cake

Combine:
- 1½ c. boiling water
- 1 c. quick oats (uncooked)
- ½ c. table fat

Let stand 20 minutes. (You may use 1½ c. leftover cooked oats or whole wheat cereal instead of uncooked oats and water.)

Add 2 eggs. Beat well.

Add 1 c. brown sugar
  1 c. white sugar *or* ⅔ c. honey

Beat well.

Sift together:
- 1½ c. whole wheat flour
- 1 tsp. soda
- 1 tsp. cinnamon
- ½ tsp. nutmeg
- ½ tsp. salt

Add dry ingredients. Beat well.

Pour batter into greased and floured 9x13x2-inch pan. Bake at 350 F. about 45 minutes or until it springs back at the touch. Cool slightly. Add topping.

Topping

Combine:
- 6 Tbsp. table fat
- ½ c. brown sugar
- 1 c. coconut (or less)
- 1 c. chopped nuts (or less)
- ¼ c. cream *or* evaporated milk
- ½ tsp. vanilla

Heat until fat is melted.

Spread topping on hot cake. Replace in oven or broil until lightly browned and bubbly. Yields 24 servings, 240 Cal., 3.3 g. protein, 0.50 g. fiber each.

Date Nut Loaf

Combine:
- 1 c. boiling water
- 1 c. chopped dates
- ½ c. chopped nuts

Let date mixture stand.

Sift together:
- 1¾ c. whole wheat flour
- 1 tsp. soda
- ½ tsp. baking powder
- ½ tsp. salt

Cream together:
- 1 Tbsp. table fat
- ½ c. honey *or*
- ¾ c. sugar

Add:
- 1 tsp. vanilla
- 1 egg. Beat well.

Add dry ingredients alternately with date mixture. Last of all *add ⅔ cup water*. Mix well. Bake in greased or waxed paper lined loaf pans at 350 F. for 50-60 minutes or until it springs back at the touch. Yields 2 loaves 7x3½x2¼ or one loaf 9x5x2½ inches. If small loaves are cut into 18 slices, each slice provides 65 Calories, 1.3 g. protein, 0.27 g. fiber. Large loaf yields 24 slices, 98 Calories, 1.95 g. protein, 0.41 g. fiber each.

Old-Fashioned Shortcake

Cream:
- 2 Tbsp. table fat
- ⅔ c. honey *or*
- 1 c. sugar

Add:
- 1 egg, and beat until fluffy

Sift together:
- 1¾ c. whole wheat flour
- ¼ tsp. salt
- 2 tsp. baking powder

Add dry ingredients alternately with:
- ¾ c. milk

Mix thoroughly. Pour into greased and floured or waxed paper lined round cake pan or pans. One pan gives a thick cake, two pans give two thin layers to be filled and topped with fruit. Bake at 350 F. for about 25 minutes or until the cake springs back at a touch and the pan sizzles when touched with a damp finger. Yields 12 servings, 140 Calories, 3.3 g. protein, 0.38 g. fiber each. (Add fruit and topping or milk.)

Pineapple Upside-Down Cake With Variations

Melt in a 9x13x2-inch pan:
    3 Tbsp. table fat

Add:
    ¾ c. brown sugar
    ¼ c. pineapple juice

Spread evenly over bottom of pan. Arrange in the syrup:
    12 slices pineapple
    12 maraschino halves (upside down in the center of each pineapple ring)

Cream:
    ½ c. table fat
    ⅔ c. honey *or*
        1 c. sugar

Add and beat until fluffy:
    3 large egg whites

Sift together:
    2 c. *plus* 2 Tbsp. whole wheat flour
    2 tsp. baking powder
    ¼ tsp. salt

Add dry ingredients alternately with:
    ¾ c. milk

Mix well and spread over the pineapple slices. Bake at 375 F. about 50 minutes or until lightly browned and the cake springs back at a touch. Serve, bottom side up, with each pineapple ring and attached cake one serving. Yields 12 servings, 30 Calories, 4.2 g. protein, 0.57 g. fiber each. (You may use pineapple chunks patterned with cherries and serve smaller portions.)

Variations:

Cherry Upside-Down Cake: Substitute 3 cups drained pie cherries and ¼ cup cherry juice for pineapple and juice and add ¾ tsp. cinnamon to the sugar.

Cherry or Pineapple or Rhubarb Puffs: Grease 12 custard cups. Divide fruit and sugar mixture between them. Add batter to fill cups about ⅔ full. Cover each cup with aluminum foil or waxed paper held in place by string.

Steam for 20-25 minutes or until the cake springs back at a touch. Serve fruit side up with or without whipped topping or milk.

Fruit Cobbler (Cake Type)

(Rhubarb, cherry, peach, apple, apricot, Saskatoon, or other berries)

In a greased baking dish 7½x12x2 inches or pan that will hold 2 quarts spread:*

    4 cups fruit (sliced or chunked if fruit is large; smaller amounts if fruit is cooked)

Cream:

    3 Tbsp. table fat
    ¾ c. sugar *or* ½ c. honey
    1 tsp. vanilla

Sift together:

    1 c. whole wheat flour
    ¼ tsp. salt
    2 tsp. baking powder

---

* Small fruits may be placed on top of batter instead of in dish.

Add dry ingredients alternately with:
    ½ c. milk   Beat batter until smooth.
Spread batter over the fruit. Sprinkle over top of batter:*
    ½ c. sugar mixed with
    1 Tbsp. cornstarch
Pour over all:
    1 c. boiling fruit juice, fruit juice and water, *or* just water.

Bake at 350 F. 50-60 minutes or until lightly browned and the cake springs back at a touch. Yields 10 servings, 157 (rhubarb), 175 (average) Calories, 2.1-2.7 g. protein, 0.32-077 g. fiber each.

Carrot Pudding

Cream:
    ½ c. table fat
    1 c. brown sugar
Add and beat until fluffy:
    1 egg

Add:
    1 c. grated raw carrots
    1 Tbsp. sorghum or molasses
Sift together:
    2 c. whole wheat flour
    1 tsp. soda
    1 tsp. cinnamon
    ½ tsp. nutmeg
Add dry ingredients and mix until just moistened.
Add:
    1 c. raisins or mixed fruit
Fold in fruits. Fill greased molds (empty cans, deep pans, etc.) ⅔ full. Cover with aluminum foil, waxed paper, or baking plastic. Steam for 3 hours or until the pudding (cake) springs

---

* Brown sugar and cinnamon are especially nice with some fruits.

back at a touch. Serve hot with pudding sauce. (May be cooled, even frozen, and reheated for serving.) Yields 18 servings, 170 Calories, 2.4 g. protein, 0.41 g. fiber each.

Pudding Sauce

Combine:
- 2 Tbsp. whole wheat flour
- 1 c. brown sugar
- 1 Tbsp. butter
- ½ c. corn syrup
- 1 c. boiling water

Boil until slightly thickened.

Add:
- 4 Tbsp. lemon juice
- 2 Tbsp. grated lemon rind
- Salt to taste if desired

Serve warm on steamed puddings.
Yields 1¾ c. sauce, 51 Calories, 0.2 g. protein, 0.08 g. fiber per Tbsp.

COOKIES

Cowboy Cookies

Cream together:
- 1 c. table fat
- 1 c. white sugar
- 1 c. brown sugar

Add:
- 2 eggs
- 1 tsp. vanilla

Beat until fluffy.

Sift together:
- 2 c. whole wheat flour
- ½ tsp. soda
- ½ tsp. salt
- ½ tsp. baking powder

Add dry ingredients.

Mix well.

Add 2 c. rolled oats (old-fashioned preferred)
Mix.

Add:
- ½ c. chocolate chips or raisins
- ½ c. chopped nuts

Drop by teaspoonfuls on ungreased cookie sheet. Bake at 350 F. for about 12 minutes. Yields 60 cookies, 90 Calories, 1.3 g. protein, 0.15 g. fiber each.

Old-Fashioned Oatmeal Cookies

Cream together:
- ¾ c. table fat
- ½ c. white sugar
- 1 c. brown sugar
- 1 tsp. vanilla

Add:
- 2 eggs. Beat well.

Sift together:
- 1½ c. whole wheat flour
- 1 tsp. soda
- ½ tsp. salt
- 2 tsp. cinnamon
- ½ tsp. nutmeg
- Pinch of cloves

Combine all ingredients. Mix well.

Add:
- 3 c. old-fashioned rolled oats (uncooked)
- 1½ Tbsp. wheat germ (if desired)

Mix. Then add:
- ½ c. nuts and ½ c. raisins. Mix.

Drop by teaspoonfuls on ungreased cookie sheet. Bake at 350 F. for 8-10 minutes. Yields 60 cookies, 75 Calories, 1.4 g. protein, 0.14 g. fiber each. (You may chill dough, roll it to ¼ inch thick on a board sprinkled with powdered sugar, and cut with a cookie cutter. Bake as above.)

Applesauce-Nut Cookies

Cream together:
- ½ c. table fat
- ⅓ c. brown sugar
- ½ c. white sugar
- 1 tsp. vanilla

Add and beat well:
- 1 egg

Sift together:
- 2 c. whole wheat flour
- ¼ tsp. cinnamon
- ¼ tsp. salt
- ¼ tsp. soda
- 1 tsp. baking powder

Add dry ingredients alternately with
  ½ c. cold applesauce

Mix well and add:
  ½ c. raisins
  ½ c. nuts chopped

Drop by teaspoonfuls onto ungreased cookie sheet. Bake at 400 F. about 10 minutes. Yields 45 cookies, 65 Calories, 1.05 g. protein, 0.32 g. fiber each.

Oatmeal Date Bars
(Canadian Matrimonial Cake)

Combine in saucepan:
  1 c. chopped dates
  ½ c. sugar *or* ⅓ c. honey
  ¾ c. water
  ½ c. chopped nuts

Boil until thick.

Mix together with pastry
blender, knives, or fingers:
  1 c. brown sugar
  1 c. table fat
  2 c. whole wheat flour
  ½ tsp. salt

Add:
  2½ c. oatmeal (old-fashioned preferred)

Add:
  1 tsp. soda dissolved in
  ¼ c. hot water

Mix with your hands. Pat ½ of the dough into 9x13x2-inch, more or less, baking pan. Spread with the date mixture. Cover with the rest of the dough mixture that has been patted to size on a waxed paper. Bake at 350 F. for 20 to 25 minutes depending on the temperature of the date mixture used. Cool in the pan. Cut into serving pieces while still warm. Yields 60 bars, 96 Calories, 1.15 g. protein, 0.22 g. fiber each.

German Love Cookies

Beat 4 eggs until frothy.
Add 1 pound brown sugar.
Beat until thick.

Sift together:
    2 c. whole wheat flour
    1 tsp. salt

Add dry ingredients. Mix well.
Add ¾ c. chopped nuts.

Spread evenly in greased pan, approximately 9x13x2 inches. Bake at 350 F. 30 minutes or until golden brown. Cool in pan. Cut while warm. Yields 60 bars, 55 Calories, 1.1 g. protein, 0.11 g. fiber each.

Fudge Brownies

Cream:
    ⅔ c. table fat
    1 c. brown sugar
    1 c. white sugar
    ½ tsp. vanilla
    ⅛ tsp. maple or almond flavor

Add:
    4 eggs. Beat until fluffy.

Sift together:
    1½ c. whole wheat flour
    1 tsp. salt
    ⅓ c. cocoa or carob.

Add dry ingredients. Mix well.

Add:

½ c. chopped nuts

Spread batter in well greased baking pans—2 pans 8x8x2 inches or an equivalent larger pan. Bake at 325 F. for 30 minutes or until top looses its shiny look and the edges begin to pull away from the sides of the pan. Do not overcook. The idea is to have fudge brownies. Cool in the pans. Cut while warm. Yields 40 bars, 98 Calories, 1.4 g. protein, 0.19 g. fiber each.

(To make cake-type brownies, sift 1½ tsp. baking powder with dry ingredients and bake at 350 F. 30 to 35 minutes or until cake springs back at a touch and the bottom of the pan sizzles at the touch of a damp finger.)

Coco Mints

Cream:

Add:

¾ c. table fat

1 egg. Beat until fluffy.

1 c. sugar

Sift together:

2 c. plus 2 Tbsp. whole wheat flour
1 tsp. baking powder
½ tsp. soda
⅓ c. cocoa or carob

Add dry ingredients alternately with:

½ c. milk
½ tsp. vanilla

Mix well. Drop by teaspoonfuls onto ungreased baking sheet and bake at 325 F. 10-12 minutes. Yields 5 dozen 2-inch fudgy cookies, 50 Calories, 0.8 g. protein, 1.1 g. fiber each. Use plain or with mint filling. For thicker, less moist cookies use 2½ c. whole wheat flour. Yields 4 dozen cookies, 65 Calories, 1.1 g. protein, 1.6 g. fiber each. Serve plain or with mint frosting.

Mint Filling or Frosting for Coco Mints

Cream:
    2 Tbsp. table fat
    1½ c. sifted powdered sugar
Add:
    2 Tbsp. milk
    4 or 5 drops mint flavor

Beat until spreading consistency. If used to make 30 coco mint fudgy cookie sandwiches, each sandwich provides 130 Calories, 1.6 g. protein, 2.2 g. fiber. If used to frost 30 cookies, add 30 Calories per cookie.

Dough may also be formed into rolls, wrapped in wax paper or plastic, and frozen to be used later. Slice thinly and bake as above, allowing a little extra time for frozen dough. Makes good ice-cream sandwiches.

Gingersnaps

Cream together:
    ½ c. table fat
    ½ c. sugar
    ½ c. sorghum *or* molasses

Sift together
    2½ c. whole wheat flour
    1½ tsp. ginger
    1½ tsp. cinnamon
    ½ tsp. cloves
    ½ tsp. soda
    ½ tsp. salt

Add dry ingredients alternately with ¼ c. water. Mix well. Dough must be soft but manageable. Form 1-inch balls. Place on ungreased cookie sheet. Sprinkle with granulated sugar if desired. Bake at 375 F. about 15 minutes. Yields 4 dozen cookies, 54 Calories, 0.81 g. protein, 0.14 g. fiber each.

Peanut Butter Cookies

Cream together:
    ⅔ c table fat
    ¾ c. peanut butter
    ⅔ c. white sugar
    ⅔ c. brown sugar
Add 2 eggs. Beat well.

Sift together:
    2½ c. whole wheat flour
    1 tsp. soda
    ½ tsp. baking powder
    ½ tsp. salt

Add dry ingredients to creamed mixture. Mix well. Roll into balls about 1 inch in diameter. Flatten with a fork dipped in cold water, creating your own pattern on the surface, or use a meat tenderizer.

(You may, if you desire, shape the dough into rolls, 1 to 2 inches in diameter, wrap in wax paper, and chill in the refrigerator or freeze. Cut in thin slices with a sharp knife when ready to bake.)

Bake on ungreased baking sheets at 375 F. for 10 to 12 minutes. Yields 5 dozen cookies, 71 Calories, 0.9 g. protein, 0.11 g. fiber each.

Dainty Tea Cookies (pressed)

Cream together:
    1 c. butter
    ⅔ c. sugar
    1 tsp. almond flavor
Add and beat until fluffy:
    1 egg

Sift together:
    2⅓ c. whole wheat flour
    ⅛ tsp. salt

Add dry ingredients to creamed mixture. Mix. Put through cookie press onto a *cold*, ungreased baking sheet. Decorate with colored sugars, nonpariel, chocolate candies, etc. Bake at 450 F. about 5 minutes. Watch it closely. Yields 6 dozen cookies, 43 Calories, 0.6 g. protein 0.02 g. fiber each.

Carrot Cookies

Cook enough carrots to make 1 cup mashed. Set aside to cool (or use leftover carrots).
Cream:

    1 c. table fat
    ½ c. honey *or* ¾ c. sugar

Add and beat until fluffy:

    1 egg.

Add:

    1 c. mashed carrots
    1 tsp. grated orange rind
    ¼ tsp. salt
    ½ tsp. vanilla

Sift:

    2 c. whole wheat flour
    1 tsp. baking powder

Add: Dry ingredients. Drop by spoonfuls on ungreased cookie sheet.

Bake at 375 F. 12-15 minutes.

(May be frosted with butter-powdered sugar frosting made with orange juice and grated orange rind.) Yields 5 dozen cookies, 50 Calories, 0.65 g. protein, 0.12 g. fiber each without frosting.

Party Date Balls

Combine in a saucepan:

    1 c. chopped dates
    ¼ c. honey *or* ⅓ c. sugar
    ½ c. table fat
    1 beaten egg
    ½ tsp. orange flavoring
    ⅓ c. coconut

Cook until dates are well blended. Remove from heat.
Add:

4 c. high protein cereal

Mold into balls the size of a walnut and roll in:

1 c. finely chopped coconut. Chill thoroughly.
Yields 36 balls, 77 Calories, 1 g. protein, 0.28 g. fiber
each.

Quick Peanut Butter Bars

Combine in a large (4 qt.) saucepan:

⅓ c. honey *or* ½ c. sugar

¾ c peanut butter

½ c. corn syrup

Heat until peanut butter melts. Remove from heat and stir in:
6 c. high protein cereal.

Press into greased pan 9x9x2 inches.

Cool. Cut into bars and serve. Yields 18 bars, 135 Calories,
4.9 g. protein, 0.24 g. fiber each.

Bars may be topped with:

1-6 oz. bag semi-sweet chocolate chips melted and
drizzled over the top. The chocolate will add 58 Calories and
0.48 g. protein per serving and increase the cost.

Oatmeal Nut Crisps

Melt in 10-inch skillet and brown slightly:

½ c. table fat

Add:

1½ c. uncooked rolled oats

⅓ c. chopped walnuts

Stir often until lightly toasted.

Cool.

Beat until thick and lemon colored:

1 egg

Add gradually and beat until very thick:

½ c. honey *or* ¾ c. sugar

Fold in oat and nut mixture. Drop by level tablespoonfuls on a greased cookie sheet about 2 inches apart. Bake at 300 F. for 15-20 minutes until lightly browned around the edges. Remove from pans immediately. Store in tightly covered container. Yields 3 dozen crisp, large cookies, 51 Calories, 0.6 g. protein, 0.05 g. fiber each.

Coconut Kisses

Separate 6 eggs.
Beat the whites until they stand in peaks.
Add:
    1 tsp. vanilla
    ½ tsp. lemon *or* almond flavor

Sift together and set aside:
    1 c. whole wheat flour
    ¼ tsp. salt

Slowly beat into the egg white mixture:
    1⅓ c. honey *or* 2 c. sugar

Beat until peaks are stiff and shiny.
Fold flour mixture into meringue.

Add:
    2 c. shredded coconut
Blend with rubber spatula.

Drop by spoonfuls on an ungreased cookie sheet. Bake at 325 F. for 10 minutes or until delicately browned. Loosen from cookie sheet and serve as they are *or* loosen from sheet but leave there to keep warm. Gently fold sugary crust into the soft center to form each cookie into a loose ball if desired.

Yields 5 dozen cookies, 50 Calories, 0.8 g. protein, 0.18 g. fiber each.

PASTRIES

Whole Wheat Piecrust

Combine and blend to the size of peas with pastry blender or knives:
- 2 c. sifted whole wheat flour
- 1 c. table fat (2 to 4 Tbsp. less if lard or other shortening is used)
- ¼ tsp. salt

Form a paste of:
- ½ c. whole wheat flour
- 6 Tbsp. cold milk (necessary for rich color)

Immediately pour paste over blended mixture. Mix with a fork until all is moist.

Form into balls, one ball for each crust. Yields crusts for:

Number	Size	Item	Servings	Calories	Protein	Fiber
1	9-10-inch	2-crust pie	8	320	5.2	0.82
2	9-10-inch	1-crust pies	16	160	2.6	0.41
2	8-inch	lattice crust pies	16	160	2.6	0.41
3	8-inch	1-crust pies rolled thin	24	107	1.8	0.27
8	4½-inch	potpies	8	320	5.2	0.82
30	2½-inch	tarts, moderate crusts	30	86	1.4	0.22

Roll out on floured *pastry cloth* (heavy cotton fabric) with a rolling pin covered with a stockingnet to the desired size and shape. (*Do not* try to handle whole wheat pastry dough with a bare rolling pin on a floured pastry board.) Line pastry pans or plates.

For two-crust pies:

Fill the bottom crust. Draw designs on top crust or otherwise puncture it to permit the escape of steam. (This may be done after the crust is fitted into place. If the pie is to be frozen, leave top crust whole until time to bake.)

Fit crust to top of filled pie. Trim crusts until about ½ inch larger than pan. Press edges together until sealed. This is usually done by fluting to make a pretty crust edge. If a very juicy filling is used, trim the lower crust to ½ inch bigger than the pan. Leave the top crust 1 inch larger than the pan. Fold the top crust over the bottom crust and flute for a juice-tight seal. Brush top with a mixture of milk and honey or brush with milk and dust with granulated sugar for a nice glaze.

Bake at 450 F. for 10 minutes. Reduce heat and complete baking according to the directions for the kind of pie in the making. Most pies are finished at 350 or 375 F. Cool on a rack for crisp bottom crusts.

For one-crust pies:

Fit crust to pie pan or plate. Trim evenly about 1 inch larger than the pan. Flute the edges above the edge of the pan. Fill and bake at 450 F. for 10 minutes. reduce heat and complete baking according to the kind of pie in the making. Cool on a rack for crisp bottom crusts.

For crusts to be baked without filling:

Prepare crust as for one-crust pie. Prick crust generously to allow air and steam to escape without causing the crust to bubble or shrink. Bake at 450 F. for 10 to 15 minutes, just until golden brown. Do not allow thin spots or they may burn.

Note: Whole wheat crusts are especially good with stronger flavored pies but may be used with any filling you choose.

For main dish pies:

Handle most as any two-crust pie, except do not glaze with sugar or honey. Bake until crust is lightly browned and filling is bubbly. Use recipes for fish, poultry, or other meat fillings. Quiche Lorraine is handled as a one-crust pie. Serve immediately after baking or reheat.

Saskatoon Butter Tarts

Cream together:
    1 c. brown sugar
    3 Tbsp. butter
Add and beat until fluffy:
    1 egg
Add and mix:
    ½ c. milk

Fold in:
    ½ c. coconut (shredded)
    ½ c. walnuts (chopped)
    Pinch of salt
    ¼ c. raisins

Line tart tins with pastry. Fill half full with butter mixture. Bake at 400 F. 15 to 20 minutes until filling and crust are lightly browned. Fills 21 2½-inch tarts, 101 Calories, 1.1 g. protein, 0.17 g. fiber each *plus* crust for a total of 187 Calories, 2.5 g. protein, 0.39 g. fiber each tart.

Cream Puffs or Eclairs

Melt:

¼ c. table fat in

½ c. boiling water

Add all at once and stir vigorously:

½ c. plus 1 Tbsp. whole wheat flour

⅛ tsp. salt

Cook, stirring continuously, until mixture forms a ball that does not separate.

Remove from heat. Cool slightly. Add, one at a time, 2 eggs; beat vigorously until batter is smooth after each addition.

Drop by spoonfuls 2 inches apart on a greased baking sheet. Bake at 450 F. 15 minutes. Then reduce heat to 325 F. and continue baking for 25 minutes more. Remove to rack and cool.

When puffs are cool, split one side of each. Fill with cold milk pudding (any flavor) blended with whipped cream or topping, heavenly hash, chicken or fish salad. Serve elegantly. Yields 12 small puffs, 60 Calories, 1.5 g. protein, 0.12 g. fiber each *or* 6 large puffs, 120 Calories, 3.0 g. protein, 0.24 g. fiber each.

Graham Cracker Crust

In a 9-inch pie pan melt:

⅓ c. table fat

Reduce to fine crumbs with blender or rolling pin:

12 graham crackers (1½ c. crumbs)

Add the graham cracker crumbs to the melted fat. Mix thoroughly and press evenly over the bottom and sides of the pan. Chill. May be used for unbaked or for baked pies like the cottage cheese cake. Yields 8 servings, 150 Calories, 1.5 g. protein, 0.23 g. fiber each when made with homemade crackers from the following recipe.

When commercial graham crackers are used, recipes usually call for the addition of ¼ to ⅓ cup sugar, which brings the

Calorie count about equal to that above. Protein and fiber, however, are reduced by about half if commercial crackers are used.

Graham Crackers

Cream together:
   ½ c. table fat
   ⅔ c. brown sugar
Sift together:
   2¾ c. whole wheat flour
   ½ tsp. baking powder
   ¼ tsp. cinnamon
Add dry ingredients to creamed mixture alternately with:
   ½ c. skim milk
Mix well, and let dough rest a few minutes. Roll to ⅛ inch thickness on a well floured pastry cloth. Cut into 2½-inch squares with a sharp knife. Place squares on a greased cookie sheet and prick generously with a fork. Bake at 350 F. about 15 minutes or until golden brown. Be careful not to allow them to get dark brown or burn. Yields 1½ pounds, 4 dozen delightful squares—if you can get them baked. (The dough is so good that my family eats as much as I will allow before the squares get to the oven.) 50 Calories, 1 g. protein, 0.15 g. fiber each. Calories may be reduced by using less sugar. Excellent for making graham cracker crusts.

Cottage Cheese Cake (Pie)

Prepare a graham cracker crust in a deep 9-inch pie pan, reserving some of the crumbs for topping. Put crust into refrigerator to chill while preparing filling.
Blend smooth in a blender or by pressing through a sieve:
   1 c. creamed cottage cheese
Add and mix well:
   ⅓ c. light cream *or* evaporated milk
   ⅛ tsp. salt

127

4 tsp. whole wheat flour
1 Tbsp. lemon juice
1 tsp. grated lemon rind *or* ¼ tsp. nutmeg

Beat with a rotary beater until very light:

2 eggs

Gradually beat in:

3 Tbsp. honey *or* 5 Tbsp. sugar *or less*

Spread the cottage cheese mixture over the egg mixture and fold gently until the whole is well blended. Pour into the chilled crust. Sprinkle crumbs on top. Bake at 325 F. for one hour. Turn off heat. Leave in the oven another hour. (If your oven retains heat very well, reduce baking time to 45 minutes.) Chill before serving. Yields 8 servings, 96 Calories, 5.6 g. protein, 0.03 g. fiber each for filling alone. With crust, Calories total 246, protein—7.1 g., fiber—0.26 g. per serving. Excellent topped with fruit or fruit pie filling, or with half this recipe used to top half a cherry pie filling in a crumb crust. Fill crumb crust half full with cherry pie filling. Add half this recipe of cheese filling and bake as above. 8 servings provide 260 Calories, 4.7 g. protein, 7.2 g. fiber each.

Favorite Pumpkin Pie
(Or Custard)

Combine:

¾ c. brown sugar *or*	¼ tsp. ginger or less
½ c. honey*	¾ tsp. cinnamon
1 Tbsp. whole wheat flour	½ tsp. nutmeg
½ tsp. salt	pinch of cloves

---

*If honey is used, add it to the pumpkin instead of to the dry ingredients.

Combine:
   1¼ c. thick pumpkin*
    1 Tbsp. sorghum or molasses
    1 Tbsp. melted fat
Combine:
    2 beaten eggs
    1 tsp. vanilla
   1¼ c. whole milk *or* diluted
           canned evaporated milk

Add dry ingredients to pumpkin mixture. Blend well. Add liquid ingredients. Blend. *For Pie:* Pour gently into pastry-lined 9-inch pie plate. Bake at 400 F. for 10 minutes. Reduce heat to 350 F. and bake until custard is set—about 40 minutes more. Yields 8 servings, 316 Calories, 7.0 g. protein, 0.9 g. fiber each.

For Custard: Pour into a quart baking dish. Bake at 350 F. about 45 minutes until custard is set. Yields 6 servings, 208 Calories, 5.9 g. protein, 0.65 g. fiber each.

Pecan Pie

Combine:
    3 beaten eggs
    ½ c. sugar *or* ⅓ c. honey
    1 c. corn syrup (light, dark, or
           a combination)
    ⅛ tsp. salt
    1 tsp. vanilla
    ¼ c. melted table fat

Place 1 c. pecan kernels** in the bottom of whole wheat pastry lined pan. Gently pour in the filling. Bake at 400 F. for 10 minutes. Reduce heat to 350 F. and continue baking for about 50 minutes, until custard is set. Yields 8 servings, 486

---

*See Pumpkin Loaf recipe for instructions for preparing fresh pumpkin.
**You may substitute for the pecans:
   ⅔ c. rolled oats *or* rolled wheat
   ⅔ c. coconut

Calories, 6.1 g. protein, 0.72 g. fiber each. This pie tastes good, but watch *those* Calories!

Fresh Fruit Pies
(For peaches, apples, cherries, berries, or combinations
of fruits—general instructions)

Prepare fruit—wash, slice, cut into pieces, peel, etc.) For each 9-inch pie combine:

3-4 c. fruit
⅔ to 1 c. honey *or*
     1 to 1½ c. sugar
⅛ tsp. salt
2 to 4 Tbsp. flour *or* 1 to 2 Tbsp. cornstarch
     or quick-cooking tapioca

Line 9-inch pie pan with whole wheat pastry. Fill with fruit mixture. Dot with 1 Tbsp. butter or margarine. (Adjust sweetening and thickening to sweetness and juiciness of fruit. If fruit is bland, add 1 to 2 Tbsp. lemon juice. If fruit is dry, add ¼ c. water.)

Adjust top crust and follow directions for 2-crust pies under whole wheat pastry recipe. Yields 8 servings, approximately 450 Calories, 3.3 g. protein, 0.76 g. fiber each.

Bake at 450° for ten minutes, reduce heat to 375°, bake 40 to 50 minutes or until fruit is soft and filling bubbly.

Canned or Cooked Fruit Pies
Combine:

2 to 2½ c. drained fruit, sliced if needed
¾ c. juice
¼ to ¾ c. sugar (according to sweetness of fruit)
¼ tsp. salt
2 to 4 Tbsp. whole wheat flour *or*
     half that much cornstarch or tapioca

Proceed as for fresh fruit pies. Yield is about the same.

Apple Pie

Peel and slice thin:

6 to 8 tart apples—enough to make 4 cupfuls.

Arrange in 9-inch pie pan lined with whole wheat pastry.

Combine and sprinkle over the apples:

½ c. honey *or* ¾ c. sugar (white or brown)

⅛ tsp. salt

½ tsp. cinnamon

¼ tsp. nutmeg

2 Tbsp. flour

If the apples are bland, add

1 to 2 Tbsp. lemon juice

Dot with

1 to 2 Tbsp. table fat

Adjust top crust and proceed as for 2-crust pies under whole wheat pastry. Apple pies require about 1 hour total baking time. Yield is about the same for other fresh fruit pies.

Bake at 450° for ten minutes, reduce heat to 375°, bake 40 to 50 minutes more or until fruit is soft and filling bubbly.

Mince Pie
(Mock Mincemeat)

Combine and cook until apples are soft:

2 c. chopped unpeeled apples

½ c. raisins (whole)

¼ c. water

½ c. light molasses or sorghum

Add and simmer 2 minutes:

2 Tbsp. table fat

1½ c. raisins ground or chopped fine

½ c. chopped English walnuts

½ tsp. cinnamon

¼ tsp. salt

¼ tsp. nutmeg

⅛ tsp. cloves

Grated rind of:

2 lemons

1 orange

2 Tbsp. orange juice
Optional:
   3 Tbsp. chopped citron
   ¼ tsp. allspice

Allow to stand at least an hour before using (a day is better). Fill 2 8-inch pastry-lined pans with the mix. Use strips of pastry to make a lattice crust. (Use half as much pastry as would be used for a bottom crust.) Secure the ends of the strips by fluting them with the lower crust. Brush top pastry with milk and sprinkle with granulated sugar or brush with a honey-milk mixture. Bake at 450 F. for 20 minutes. Reduce heat to 375 F. and bake 25 to 30 minutes longer until top crust is lightly browned and filling is bubbly. Yields 16 servings, 298 Calories, 3.5 g. protein, 1.20 g. fiber each.

Tarts—1 Tbsp. filling per 2½-inch tart provides 132 Calories, 1.7 g. protein, 0.28 g. fiber each, with pastry.

Real Mincemeat

(Mother made it from the cooked heads of freshly butchered hogs. This recipe is from her file. Not tested for this book.)

Simmer until tender, cool, and grind:
   2½ pounds lean meat (cooked weight)
Add:
   5 pounds chopped, unpeeled apples
   1 pound raisins
   ½ pound currants
   1 pint vinegar
   1 quart water
   1 c. sorghum
   1 c. sugar
   2 Tbsp. butter
   2 tsp. cinnamon
   ½ tsp. cloves
   Salt and pepper to taste

Simmer together 2 hours. (Liquid should be absorbed). Can,

freeze, or use immediately in pies or tarts. Yields filling for 8 pies, 8 servings per pie, 437 Calories, 10.9 g. protein, 0.97 g. fiber each serving.

Rhubarb Custard Pie

Cut into 1-inch pieces and wilt:
    5 c. (1¼ lb.) rhubarb
      (Frozen rhubarb will wilt on thawing. Fresh rhubarb may be heated gently, *or* it may be covered with boiling water for 1 minute, then the water drained away and reserved for fruit beverage and use in the pie.)

Separate 3 eggs. Set the whites aside.
Combine:
    1 c. sugar *or* ⅔ c. honey
    ¼ c. whole wheat flour
    2 Tbsp. rhubarb juice
    2 Tbsp. melted table fat
    3 egg yolks (beaten)
    ¼ tsp. nutmeg if desired

Line a 9-inch pie pan with whole wheat pastry. Fill with wilted rhubarb. Pour egg yolk mixture over rhubarb. Bake at 425 F. for 15 minutes. Reduce heat to 350 F. and bake 35 minutes more or until custard is set. Cool.

Prepare meringue: To the three egg whites add
    ⅛ tsp. salt. Beat until frothy.
Add:
    ¼ tsp. cream of tartar and beat
      until foam begins to stiffen.
Add gradually while beating constantly,
    ¼ c. honey or 6 Tbsp. sugar

Beat until meringue stands in stiff, lustrous peaks. Spread on cooled pie, being certain to seal to edges of crust. Return to the oven and bake at 350 F. until lightly browned—about 15 minutes. ⅛ of a 9-inch pie provides 196 Calories, 3.1 g. protein, 0.56 g. fiber *plus* crust. Total Calories 356, 5.7 g. protein, 0.97 g. fiber per serving.

Plain Rhubarb Pie

Combine:

  3 c. cut rhubarb
  ⅔ c. honey *or* 1 c. sugar
  3 Tbsp. whole wheat flour
  ¼ tsp. nutmeg if desired
  ⅛ tsp. salt

Line 9-inch pie pan with whole wheat pasty. Fill with rhubarb mixture. Dot with butter. Top with second crust in strips arranged in lattice fashion or entire with designs cut to permit steam to escape. Seal top and bottom crusts together. Glaze if desired. Bake at 450 F. for 10 minutes. Reduce heat to 375 F. and bake 25 to 35 minutes more until crust is lightly browned and filling is bubbly. ⅛ of a 9-inch pie provides 115 Calories, 0.7 g. protein, 0.35 g. fiber *plus* crust. Total—435 Calories, 5.9 g. protein, 1.17 g. fiber per serving if all the crust is used; 355 Calories, 4.6 g. protein, 0.96 g. fiber for lattice crust. (Two crust pies are especially poor choices for those who need to restrict their Calories.)

Custard Pie
(With carrot pie variation)

Combine:

  3 well-beaten eggs
  ¼ c. honey *or* ⅓ c. sugar
  ½ tsp. vanilla
  ¼ tsp. salt
  ¼ tsp. nutmeg
  2 c. milk (warm)

Pour gently into a 9-inch pastry-lined pan. Bake at 450 F. for 10 minutes, then 325 for about 25 minutes or until custard is set. Do not overbake. Overbaking or excessive amounts of sugar will cause it to be watery. Yields 8 servings, 233 Calories, 7.1 g. protein, 0.41 g. fiber each.

Carrot Pie (We called it mock coconut during the Depression.)
Peel, grate, and pile into the pastry before the custard mix:
 1 c. (loosely filled) carrot (about ¼ lb. as purchased)
Optional:
 1 Tbsp. cornstarch (added to the sugar if sugar is used or made into a paste with cold milk if honey is used)
 Dash of cinnamon and a dash of cloves
Proceed as for custard pie. Yields 8 servings, 239 Calories, 7.3 g. protein, 0.56 g. fiber each.

Dutch Apple Pie

Cover 2 ounces dried apple slices or rings with water and soak two hours or until no longer leathery.

Combine and mix:
 1 c. light whipping cream (may be sour)
 1 c. sugar (or less)
 2 Tbsp. flour
 Dash of salt
Pour gently into pastry-lined 9-inch pan. (It bubbles up. Be sure the sides are fluted high.) Blot the apple slices or rings on a paper towel, arrange over top, place into the filling and dust with nutmeg.*
Bake at 425° F. for ten minutes, reduce heat to 350° and continue baking until filling is set and slightly browned and apples are tender, about 50 minutes.

---
*You may use fresh apple slices or rings *or* even add 2 cupfuls of chopped apples to the mix. If fresh apples are used, add 1 large beaten egg and ½ tsp. vanilla. Yields 8 servings, 385 Calories, 3.7 g. protein, 0.84 g. fiber with dried apples; 379 Calories, 4.5 g. protein, 0.75 g. fiber with fresh apples and egg.

FRUIT DESSERTS

Applesauce with Variations
Remove cores and blemishes from 3 to 4 (1 pound) tart apples.* Slice (makes 1 quart slices). Place in heavy saucepan. Add ¼ c. water. Cover and cook, stirring occasionally, until apples are soft and clear. Add sweetening to taste (1 to 2 Tbsp. honey or sugar). Serve hot or cold. Yields 1½ c. sauce, 3 servings, 102 Calories, 0.3 g. protein, 1.5 g. fiber each when sweetened with 1 Tbsp. honey.

Smooth Applesauce—blend sauce in blender. (You may pass cooked apples through a sieve or food mill before adding the sweetening. This removes skins and reduces nutrients and fiber some. It may benefit appearance and flavor.)

Spiced Applesauce—Sweeten with brown sugar. Add cinnamon, nutmeg, and maybe mace to taste.

Blushing Applesauce—Reduce or eliminate sweetening and cook 1 Tbsp. red cinnamon candies with the sauce.

Park Avenue Applesauce—Drop a scoop of vanilla ice cream into a dish of applesauce. Dust with cinnamon. Serve.

Fried Apples—Heat 1 Tbsp. table fat in a heavy skillet. Add sliced apples and water, cook and sweeten as above. Serve

---
*Add 1 Tbsp. lemon juice if apples are bland.

with sausage, bacon, ham, cottage cheese, eggs or other breakfast or dinner entrees. The fat adds 35 Calories to each of 3 servings.

Baked Apples with Variations

Wash medium sized apples (3 to a pound). Core by making a hole from stem to blossom end of the apples with a peeler or small knife. Place apples in a deep baking dish or dishes. In the hole in the center of each apple place

1 tsp. honey
¼ tsp. butter or margarine
1 tsp. whole wheat flour (if desired)
Dash of cinnamon

Pour 2 Tbsp. water per apple around the apples. Bake covered at 375 F. about 45 minutes or until the apples are tender, or bake uncovered and baste frequently. Serve plain, with cream, milk, whipped topping, or stirred custard. Plain, each apple provides about 110 Calories, 0.4 g. protein, 1.55 g. fiber.

Variations:

1. Fill the cavity of apples prepared for baking with one of the following:

A mixture of brown sugar, flour, and cinnamon.

Jelly or jam.

Chopped dried fruits and nuts. Drizzle honey on top after baking.

Candied ginger. Drizzle honey on top after baking.
Bake according to directions for plain baked apples.

2. Prepare apples as for baking. Leave whole or cut crosswise into rings ¾ inch thick. Simmer in syrup made by combining:

2 c. water
½ c. sugar
¼ c. cinnamon candies

When tender, lift gently from syrup. Drain and serve (these go particularly well with fish or pork). Use syrup for pancakes, waffles, or French toast.

Apple (or Rhubarb) Crumble

Grease a pan 8x8x2 inches and arrange in it:

3 medium sized (1 lb.) tart apples sliced *or*
4 c. (1 lb.) diced rhubarb

Sprinkle with:
¼ c. water
1 Tbsp. lemon juice*
½ c. sugar
½ tsp. cinnamon

Mix together:
¾ c. whole wheat flour
½ tsp. baking powder
⅛ tsp. salt
⅔ c. rolled oats

Cream together:
⅓ c. brown sugar
¼ c. table fat

Combine and spread over fruit:
The creamed mixture and
The flour mixture

Bake at 375 F. for about 40 minutes or until the fruit bubbles up through the crumbled topping and the topping is lightly browned.

---

*Orange juice may be substituted for the water and lemon juice, and the amount may be increased for dry apples.

Stewed Rhubarb

Cut into 1-inch pieces:

   4 cups (1 lb.) rhubarb

Add:

   ¼ c. honey *or* ⅓ c. sugar (*or* add an equivalent amount
      of low Calorie sweetener after the rhubarb is cooked).

Simmer gently until rhubarb is soft. Yields 4 ½-cup servings,
18 Calories per serving with low Calorie sweetener, 82 with
honey, 91 with sugar, 0.7 g. protein and 0.79 g. fiber per
serving.

Fruit Betty

Prepare:

   2½ c. stewed rhubarb *or*

          6 medium apples, sliced

Combine:

   2 c. buttered whole wheat toast crumbs

   ½ c. brown sugar

   1 tsp. cinnamon

Optional:

   1 Tbsp. lemon juice

   1 tsp. grated lemon or orange rind

Butter a 2-quart casserole or baking pan. Arrange alternate
layers of bread and fruit beginning with ⅓ of the crumbs,
adding ½ of the fruit, another third of crumbs, the rest of the
fruit and finally, the rest of the bread.

Pour over all:

   ½ c. hot water (maybe less for rhubarb)

Bake at 375 F. about 40 minutes or until fruit is bubbly and
tender. Serve with milk or lemon sauce (see Apple Crisp with
Lemon Sauce recipe). Yields 9 servings, 151 Calories, 1.5 g.
protein, 1.21 g. fiber each with apples, 144 Calories with pre-
sweetened rhubarb (sweetened with sugar) or 102 with
rhubarb unsweetened except for sugar in the pudding. (a
pinch of salt helps reduce the amount of sweetening needed
by fruits.)

Cheese Apple Crisp

Grease a 9x13x2-inch baking dish and slice into it:

   6 medium sized tart apples (2 pounds)

Add:

   ¼ c. water
   2 tsp. lemon juice

Combine:

   1½ c. sugar
   1 tsp. cinnamon
   1 c. whole wheat flour
   ¼ tsp. salt

Add:

   ½ c. table fat to the sugar-flour mixture. Cut it in with a
       pastry blender, knives, or your fingers.

Add:

   1½ c. (⅜ pound) grated cheddar cheese. Toss lightly.

Cover apples with the sugar-flour-cheese mixture. Bake at 350 F. until apples are tender and crust is crispy (about 30-35 minutes). Serve with lemon sauce. Garnish with whipped cream if desired. Crisp alone yields 18 servings, 195 Calories, 3.29 g. protein, 0.65 g. fiber each.

Lemon Sauce

Combine:

   ½ c. sugar *or* ⅓ c. honey
   1 Tbsp. cornstarch
       Pinch of salt

Add:

   1 c. boiling water. Boil until thick and clear. Continue
       cooking over low heat or boiling water until starchy
       flavor is gone (about 20 minutes).

Add:

   2 Tbsp. butter
   2 Tbsp. lemon juice
   1 Tbsp. grated lemon rind
       Dash of nutmeg

Sauce alone yields 18 servings, 33 to 36 Calories, 0.01 g. protein, and 0.01 fiber. Total Yield, 18 servings, 229 Calories, 3.3 g. protein, 0.66 g. fiber per serving without whipped cream. 1 Tbsp. whipped cream adds 25 Calories.

Cranberry Sauce

Rinse and pick stems from
    4 c. (1 lb.) cranberries
Boil together until sugar dissolves:
    2 c. sugar
    2 c. water

Add cranberries to syrup. Boil until all are popped (5 to 10 minutes). Skim off white froth. Pour into molds or dish for serving. Cool and serve. Yields 4 cups sauce, 27 Calories, trace of protein, and 0.1 g. fiber per tablespoonful.

Scandinavian Sweet Soup

Combine:
    2 c. (about 1 lb.) raisins
    2 c. (about ¾ lb.) prunes or a
       combination of dried fruits
    8 c. cold water
    2 three-inch sticks cinnamon bark

Let stand several hours or overnight. Add 1 large or 2 smaller lemons sliced very thin, skin and all. Bring to a boil. Boil gently for 10 minutes. Add ⅔ c. honey. Return to boiling. Add ½ c. quick cooking tapioca. Boil 2 minutes. Serve hot or cold. Yields 11 cups, 22 servings, 138 Calories, 0.9 g. protein, 0.46 g. fiber each. (May be kept in the refrigerator for more than a week or frozen for later use. Good to have on hand for emergencies.)

Fruit Compote

Combine varying amounts of available fruits and melons, fresh, frozen or canned. Accent with color whenever possible by including red apples, watermelon, cherries, and the like. Use sweet fruits, such as bananas, to sweeten the compote, and juices, such as pineapple, to keep fruits from darkening. Include some crisp fruit when possible. Cut most fruit into small pieces, but leave some large or natural (such as orange sections, whole grapes, etc.) and arrange attractively. Nutrients and fiber depend on fruits used. Unsweetened fresh or frozen fruit can be expected to average less than 50 Calories per ½ cup serving and provide from 0.5 to 1. g. protein and about the same fiber. Fruits canned in heavy syrup, will easily double the Calories.

Ambrosia
(Fruit Compote with coconut)

Prepare for each serving:
- ½ medium orange sectioned
- ⅓ of a medium banana sliced
- 2 Tbsp. orange juice
- ¼ c. pineapple chunks (fresh or canned)
- 2 Tbsp. flaked coconut

Arrange the fruit and coconut in layers in large serving bowls or individual bowls. Pour juice over all. Chill and serve. Other fruits may be used. Strawberries make a beautiful ambrosia. Yields 167 Calories, 1.8 g. protein, 1.66 g. fiber each serving as described. Coconut alone provides 68 Calories, 0.45 g. protein.

Bride's Salad
(For a crowd)

Combine, cook until thick, and cool:
- 2 eggs, well beaten
- ⅓ c. honey or ½ c. sugar
- 1 Tbsp. flour
- ¼ c. orange juice
- ¼ c. lemon juice
- ½ c. pineapple juice

Combine and set aside:
    2 c. drained pineapple chunks
    1 lb. tokay grapes
    1 lb. marshmallows (tiny or cut up)
    ½ c. chopped walnuts
Whip until stiff
    2 c. whipping cream
Fold whipped cream into cooled sauce. Fold fruit mixture into cream sauce mixture. Refrigerate for several hours before serving. Yields 30 servings, 150 Calories, 1.7 g. protein, 0.2 g. fiber each.

Prune (or Apricot) Whip

Cook gently until soft, drain* and pit:
    12 oz. dried prunes (48 medium)
        in water to cover
Blend or mash pulp. There should be 1½ cups of it.
Add to pulp 1½ Tbsp. lemon juice
Separate 3 eggs
To the whites add a pinch of salt.
Whip until foam begins to stiffen.
Gradually add (beating until stiff, shiny peaks form)
    ¼ c. honey *or* ⅓ c. sugar
Fold the fruit mixture into the meringue. Pile lightly into a greased 6-cup baking dish or into 6 greased individual baking dishes. Bake at 325 F. 15 to 20 minutes for individual dishes, 25 to 30 minutes for the larger dish, or until lightly browned. Yields 6 servings, 180 Calories, 3.2 g. protein, 0.90 g. fiber each when made with honey, 194 Calories made with sugar.

---

*Use any water not absorbed for cereals, beverages, or syrups.

Cranberry Ice

Combine:
   2 cups cranberries
   1¼ c. water
Combine to soften:
   ¼ c. cold water
   1 tsp. plain gelatin
Boil cranberries until they pop. Sieve.
Add ⅔ c. honey *or* 1 c. sugar
Boil until sweetening is dissolved.
Add:
   Juice of 1 lemon   Softened gelatin
Stir until gelatin is dissolved. Cool. Freeze, stirring frequently, beating with a rotary beater occasionally until frozen.
Yields 8 servings, 102 Calories, 0.7 g. protein, 0.8 g. fiber per serving.

Lemon Chiffon Ring with Fresh Fruit

Separate 6 eggs
To egg yolks add pinch of salt
Combine to soften:
   ½ c. cold water
   4 tsp. plain gelatin
Beat until light yellow and fluffy.
Combine:
   ½ c. honey *or* ⅔ c. sugar
   ⅔ c. lemon juice
      (4 large lemons)
Add sweetened lemon juice mixture to beaten egg yolks, stirring constantly. Cook mixture until it coats a spoon. Remove from heat. Add softened gelatin. Stir until gelatin is dissolved.
Wash beaters thoroughly.*
Beat egg whites until they begin to stiffen.

---

*A bit of egg yolk, or any fat, left on the beaters will prevent the whites from whipping up properly.

Gradually add (beating until stiff, lustrous peaks are formed) ¼ c. honey or ⅓ c. sugar
Pour hot custard-gelatin mix into meringue in a steady stream, whipping gently but constantly until combined. Pour into large ring mold. Chill to set. Unmold. Fill center with fresh fruit and garnish with sprigs of mint, fresh fruit, and whipped cream if desired.
Yields 16 servings, 95 Calories, 2.8 g. protein per serving without fresh fruit or garnish.

Pineapple Chiffon

Separate 8 eggs
Add to the yolks and cook until thick and glossy:
  2 c. juice-packed crushed pineapple
  ⅔ c. honey *or* 1 c. sugar
  1 Tbsp. lemon juice (optional)
  1 tsp. grated lemon rind (optional)

Prepare 2 c. (6-7 oz.) graham cracker crumbs
Butter a 9x13x2-inch baking dish*
Sprinkle ¾ of the crumbs over the butter
        (Reserve ¼ c. for topping)
Soften:
  1 Tbsp. (pkg.) unflavored gelatin** in
  2 Tbsp. pineapple juice (drained from fruit)
Add the softened gelatin and stir until dissolved.
Add pinch of salt to the whites.
Beat until foam begins to stiffen. Gradually add (beating until stiff, lustrous peaks are formed) ⅔ c. honey *or* 1 c. sugar.
Pour the hot custard-gelatin mix into the meringue in a steady stream, whipping gently but constantly. Pour over crumbs in buttered dish. Top with remaining crumbs. Chill until gelatin is set. Garnish with whipped cream or topping

---

*For half the recipe, use a pan 8x8x2 inches. Serves 9.
**3 oz. (1 small package) lemon gelatin dessert powder may be substituted for the gelatin and lemon. It will add about 290 Calories in sugar, 16 Calories per serving unless sugar in the recipe is reduced by ⅓ cup.

and a cherry if desired. Yields 18 servings, 173 Calories, 4.0
g. protein, 0.2 g. fiber when made with honey, 182 Calories
made with sugar (without garnish).

Easy Fruit Gelatin Dessert

(Orange, pineapple, grape, apple, strawberry, any available
fruit*)
Soften:
    1 Tbsp. (pkg.) unflavored gelatin in
    2 Tbsp. fruit juice (cold)
Add and stir until gelatin is dissolved:
    1 c. minus 2 Tbsp. fruit juice (boiling)
Add and mix thoroughly:
    1 c. fruit juice (cold)
Place in molds or a quart bowl or pan. Chill until set. Yields
4 servings. Nutrients vary with the fruit chosen and will
equal ½ cup of the juice plus about 6 Calories, 1.5 g. protein
for the gelatin. E.g. pineapple-gelatin has 73 Calories, 2.0
protein, 0.12 g. fiber per serving.

Fruited Fruit Gelatin Dessert

Follow instructions for Easy Fruit Gelatin Dessert until it is
all combined. Allow it to cool until it begins to gel. Then add
solid fruits of your choice such as fruit cocktail, sliced
bananas, cooked or canned pineapple chunks,** strawberries,
or a combination of fruits. Fill molds or place in a quart bowl
or pan to set. Each additional cup of fruit may increase the
number of servings by 2 and may change the Calories per
serving very little. E.g. pineapple gelatin with 1 cup
pineapple chunks and 4 small or 2 very large bananas yields
9 servings, 78 Calories, 1.4 g. protein, 0.20 g. fiber each.

---

*Raw pineapple has an enzyme that prevents gelatin from gelling.

**Fruit flavored gelatin dessert powder may be substituted for gelatin and fruit with about the same Calories
and protein but little other nutritive value. If fruit juice is used instead of water with dessert powder, Calories
total about 73 *more* per serving than the juice and gelatin alone. Use only cooked pineapple juice.

Quick Fruited Gelatin Dessert
(With dessert powder)

Place in a 2-quart heat-proof bowl or 9x13x2-inch baking dish:
6 oz. (1 c.) gelatin dessert powder

Add, and stir until gelatin is dissolved:
2 c. boiling water

Drain juice from a 19 or 20 oz. can juice-packed pineapple, crushed or chunks.

Add to pineapple juice:
Crushed ice to make 2 cups liquid

Add the crushed ice and juice to the dissolved gelatin and mix thoroughly.

Add and mix thoroughly:
The drained pineapple
4 to 6 bananas, sliced

Chill to set. Serve plain or with whipped cream or topping. Yields 18 servings, 70 Calories, 1.3 g. protein, 0.24 g. fiber without topping.

Heavenly Hash

Prepare 6 oz. gelatin dessert powder with pineapple juice and cold water as for quick fruited gelatin dessert. We prefer strawberry and raspberry mixed, but choose your own flavor. When the liquid is thickened but not set, whip with a mixer or rotary beater until light and fluffy. Refrigerate while you whip 2 c. whipping cream until it stands in peaks but does not separate, *or* prepare 4 cups topping.

Add to whipped cream and mix carefully:
2 Tbsp. honey or sugar
1 tsp. vanilla

Fold whipped cream into whipped gelatin. Then fold in
- The drained pineapple
- 6 to 8 sliced bananas

Chill to set and serve. Yields 25 servings, 108 Calories, 1.5 g. protein, 0.36 g. fiber each. You may use unflavored gelatin and juices instead of prepared powder and water, but do not use raw pineapple juice (gelatin will not set with it).

MILK DESSERTS

Low Calorie Whipped Topping

Dissolve:
    ½ tsp. unflavored gelatin in
    3 Tbsp. boiling water
Cool to room temperature. Pour into 6-cup bowl (small bowl with mixer holds 6 cups)

Add:
    ½ c. *cold* water
    ½ c. instant dry milk (skim)
Beat at high speed until peaks form when the beater is lifted.

Gradually beat in:
    2 Tbsp. honey *or* 3 Tbsp. sugar
    ½ tsp. vanilla
Beat until stiff. Keeps fluffy several hours in the refrigerator.

Yields 4 cups topping, 4 Calories, 0.2 g. protein, per Tbsp. when made with honey. Volume may be less if sugar is used, and there may be up to 9 Calories per tablespoon.

Baked Custard

Combine:
- 3 slightly beaten eggs*
- 3 Tbsp. honey *or* ¼ c. sugar
- ¼ tsp. salt

Slowly add:
- 2 c. scalded milk
- ½ tsp. vanilla

Pour into a 1-quart baking dish or 6 custard cups. Sprinkle nutmeg over top. Bake in a pan of hot water at 375 F. until set and a knife inserted into the middle comes out clean (about 30-40 minutes). Yields 6 servings, 100 Calories, 6 Grams Protein per serving if honey and skim milk are used. 126 Calories per serving if honey and whole milk are used.

Easy Bread or Rice or Whole Wheat Pudding**

Place 2 c. cooked rice or whole grain wheat or bread (4 oz.) cubes in a baking dish 8x8x2 inches (6 c.). Scatter ¼ c. raisins over the cereal or bread. Pour custard mix above over all. Sprinkle cinnamon or nutmeg or both over pudding. Bake as for custard. Yields 9 servings, about 122 Calories, 5.8 g. protein, 0.09 g. fiber each with whole milk, 105 Calories with skim milk.

*Egg yolks may be used instead of whole eggs. 2 egg yolks have approximately the same thickening power as 1 egg.

**A variety of breads, biscuits, muffins, cake crumbs, toast, French toast, pancakes, waffles, and the like may be used for a variety of flavors. Serve plain or with a fruit sauce, milk, or cream.

Vanilla Pudding with Variations
(May also be used for pie filling)

Combine in a heavy saucepan and heat:
- 1½ c. milk
- 3 Tbsp. honey *or* ½ c. sugar**

Combine:
- 6 Tbsp. finely ground whole wheat flour *or*
    - 3 Tbsp. cornstarch
- ⅛ tsp. salt
- ½ c. cold milk

Combine and set aside:
- 1 well beaten egg*
- 2 Tbsp. cold milk
- 1 tsp. vanilla

Slowly add flour mixture to the hot milk, stirring constantly, preferably with a French whip or whisk. Allow pudding to boil 3 minutes. Add the beaten egg mixture, slowly, stirring constantly. Remove from heat. Pour into dessert dishes and serve, warm or cold. Yields 5 half-cup servings, 155 Calories, 5.9 g. protein, 0.54 g. fiber each when made with whole wheat flour and whole milk, 127 Calories made with skim milk. With cornstarch there is practically no fiber and protein is reduced to 5.1 g. per serving.

Meringue

Combine and whip until foam begins to stiffen:
- 2 egg whites
- pinch of salt

Gradually add and continue beating until stiff, lustrous peaks are formed:
- 3 Tbsp. honey *or* ¼ c. sugar

---

*2 egg yolks may be used instead of 1 egg, or 2 eggs may be separated, the yolks used in the pudding and the whites made into a meringue (see following recipe) for a topping or to be beaten into the hot pudding to fluff it. (Pour the hot pudding into the meringue in a steady stream while beating constantly but gently.)

**If sugar is used, mix it with the flour or cornstarch.

Pile onto cooled puddings or pie.* Bake at 375 F. for 12 to 15 minutes or until lightly browned. 5 servings provide 47 Calories, 1.7 g. protein each.

Chocolate Pudding—Use vanilla pudding above except:
Sift with the flour:
   3 Tbsp. cocoa or carob
Add to the hot milk:
   ¼ c. milk
   ½ Tbsp. honey
Yields 5 servings. 176 Calories, 6.5 g. protein, 0.27 g. fiber each made with whole milk and cocoa and without meringue, 181 Calories, 6.35 g. protein, 0.35 g. fiber made with carob.

Butterscotch Pudding

In the basic vanilla pudding recipe, substitute:
   ¼ c. brown sugar for honey or white sugar
Add:
   1 Tbsp. butter
Five servings provide 189 Calories, 5.9 g. protein, 0.54 g. fiber each, made with whole milk, served without meringue.

Raisin Pudding

To the basic vanilla pudding add:
   1 c. raisins
   Lemon juice to taste
Serves 6 to 8. Six servings provide 208 Calories, 5.7 g. protein, 0.7 g. fiber each; eight servings provide 156 Calories, 4.2 g. protein, 0.52 g. fiber each when made with whole milk and served without meringue.

---

*Most pies need meringues made from 3 egg whites. Follow above procedure using 1½ Tbsp. honey or 2 Tbsp. sugar per egg white. Seal meringue to crusts. Pudding recipe with 3 egg yolks fills one 8-inch baked crust, yields 8 servings, 261 Calories, 7.6 g. protein, 0.61 g. fiber each, made with flour and whole milk.

Stirred Custard

Combine:
- 2 beaten eggs
- ⅛ tsp. salt
- ½ tsp. vanilla

Heat in a heavy saucepan or double boiler:
- 2 c. milk
- 3 Tbsp. honey *or* ¼ c. sugar

Slowly add ¼ c. of the hot milk to the eggs, then slowly pour the egg mixture into the hot milk stirring continuously, preferably with a French whip or whisk. Cook over low heat until the mixture begins to thicken and will coat a spoon. Remove from heat and chill rapidly by setting the pan (be sure it is not breakable) in a pan of cold water or by pouring the custard into a shallow dish. (Do not overcook or the custard will curdle. If curdling occurs, combine chilled custard with whipped topping and serve anyway.)

Serve alone or with cake or fruit (over, under, or beside). Garnish with a sprinkle of nutmeg if desired. Made with whole milk, one recipe makes 6 small servings, 113 Calories, 5.0 g. protein, no fiber each, or 4 servings, 170 Calories, 7.5 g. protein each. With skim milk, 6 servings have 86 Calories each and 4 servings have 130.

Homemade Ice Cream
(For a 1½-gallon freezer)

Separate 5 eggs
Combine and cook until thick, stirring constantly:
- 5 egg yolks, beaten
- 2 c. milk
- ⅔ c. honey *or* 1 c. sugar
- 4 Tbsp. cornstarch (mixed with the sugar or with some cold milk)

Whip until stiff but not dry:
- 5 egg whites
- ½ tsp. salt

Remove from heat and pour custard slowly into beaten egg

whites, continuing to beat until thoroughly mixed. Cool.
Add:

    2 c. sugar *or* 1⅓ c. honey
  14 c. whole milk, approximately*
    2   c. whipping cream
    2 Tbsp. vanilla**

Note: Portions of this mix may be frozen in the freezing compartment of a refrigerator. Whip the cream. Fold in the cooled custard. Add other ingredients. Place in bowl or flat pans in the freezing compartment. Remove frequently as it freezes and whip vigorously, preferably with an electric mixer. Adding 1 Tbsp. softened gelatin to the hot custard will help keep it smooth.

The full mix yields 24 one-cup servings (few people eat less), 286 Calories, 7.8 g. protein, negligible fiber each when made with light cream and sugar, 246 Calories made with honey and light cream. Add 10 Calories per serving if heavy cream is used.

For a richer ice cream, use more cream and less milk or substitute 1 large can evaporated milk for 2 cups of the milk. Substituting 2 cups evaporated milk adds 14 Calories and 0.6 g. protein per serving. Substituting 2 cups heavy cream adds 57 Calories and reduces the protein by 0.3 g. per serving.

For a low-fat dessert, use 3 cups noninstant or 4 cups instant dry skim milk instead of cream in the basic recipe. Each serving provides 266 Calories, 11.8 g. protein made with sugar, 226 Calories made with honey.

Lemon Fluff

Dissolve and cool until nearly gelled:

    4 oz. (⅔c.) lemon gelatin mix
  1¾ c. boiling water

Whip gelatin until fluffy and add:

    1 c. sugar
   ¼ c. lemon juice

---

*Leave a little more than an inch headspace for expansion as the cream whips and the mix freezes.
**Other flavorings may be used such as maple, peppermint, lemon, or chocolate. For the latter add 2 oz. chocolate or ⅓ c. cocoa or carob to the custard mix. Fresh fruit may be substituted for some of the milk.

Place in freezer until ice crystals form:

1 large (15 oz.) can evaporated milk

Remove from freezer and whip until light and fluffy
Fold whipped milk into the whipped gelatin mixture.
Prepare for use:

2¼ c. graham cracker crumbs

Spread 2 c. graham cracker crumbs in the bottom of a baking
dish 9x13x2 inches. Pile whipped gelatin-milk mix lightly on
top. Sprinkle the remaining ¼ c. cracker crumbs on top.
Garnish with cherries. Chill until set. Cut and serve. Yields
18 servings, 144 Calories, 3.3 g. protein, 0.12 g. fiber each or
15 servings, 172 Calories, 4.0 g. protein, 0.14 g. fiber each.

Haupia
(A coconut "milk" Hawaiian treat)

Select an uncracked coconut that has lots of liquid in it and
weighs about 1½ pounds. Puncture the "eyes" of the coconut
and drain the fluid, reserving it. Crack the nut with a ham-
mer or heavy tool. Cut the "meat" in small sections and pry
it out. Peel off the dark fiber. Grate the "meat" finely.
Combine and allow to stand 20 minutes, stirring frequently:

3-4 c. grated coconut (loosely filled cups—about 1 pound)

2 c. boiling water (enough to cover the coconut)

Drape a cheesecloth or loosely woven cotton cloth over a
bowl. Pour the coconut mix into it and strain out the "milk,"
twisting the cloth and massaging the "meat" to get every
drop of moisture possible.* There should be 2 cups "milk." If
there is not, add some of the fluid drained from the coconut *if*
it is sweet and tasty. If it is not, add enough cow's milk to
make the 2 cups.
To the 2 cups of "milk" add:

3 Tbsp. sugar mixed with

2½ Tbsp. cornstarch

⅛ tsp. salt

---

*Place the "meat" in a large shallow pan in a 350 F. oven and toast it, stirring frequently, until it is lightly
browned—about 1 hour. Cool in the oven, still stirring frequently, to be sure it is dry. Store in a tightly closed
container and use as you would use nuts.

Use any extra fluid from the coconut as a beverage or in beverages.

Cook, stirring continuously until thick. Turn heat low and continue cooking several minutes until the starchy flavor is gone. Pour into an 8x8x2-inch pan or a pie pan. Cool. Cut and serve. Yields 9 small servings, 90 Calories, 0.8 g. protein each.

MAIN DISHES

MAIN DISHES FOR SUMMER MEALS

Chopstick Tuna

Combine:
- 1 can (10 oz.) cream of mushroom soup
- ¼ can water
- 1 can (6½-7 oz.) chunk tuna
- 1 c. celery sliced thin
- ¼ c. chopped onion
- ½ c. chopped toasted cashews

Add and toss lightly:
- 1 c. chow mein noodles

Pour into baking dish that holds 6 to 8 cups. Sprinkle on top.
- 1 c. chow mein noodles

Bake at 375 F. 15 to 30 minutes or until bubbly. (You may speed baking time by heating ingredients except noodles on top of the stove.) Garnish with parsley. Yields 6 servings, 292 Calories, 14 g. protein, 0.34 g. fiber each *or* 4 large servings, 440 Calories, 21 g. protein, 0.51 g. fiber each when made with tuna in oil. Water packed tuna makes small servings provide 242 Calories and large servings 365. For a low Calorie dish, use water packed tuna and eliminate the cashews. Small servings now provide 175 Calories, 10 g.

protein, 0.25 g. fiber and large servings provide 265 Calories, 15 g. protein and 0.33 g. fiber each.

Tuna Noodle Casserole

Combine:
 2 cans (6½-7 oz. each) chunk tuna
 1 can (10 oz.) cream of mushroom soup
 1 c. milk
 1 c. (¼ lb.) grated cheddar cheese
Combine in a skillet:
 ¼ c. melted table fat
 2 c. (4 oz.) diced whole wheat bread crumbs
Toast bread lightly and set aside
In a large saucepan bring to a boil:
 4 c. water
 1 tsp. salt
Gradually add.
 8 oz. egg noodles
Reduce heat, cover, and continue to boil 5 to 7 minutes until noodles are tender. Combine tuna and noodle mixtures. Pour into a 3-quart baking dish. Top with toasted crumbs. Bake at 375 F. 15 to 25 minutes or until bubbly. Yields 8 servings, 432 Calories, 21.8 g. protein, 0.41 g. fiber each if tuna in oil and whole milk are used *or* 360 Calories, 23.2 g. protein, 0.41 g. fiber if water packed tuna and skim milk are used.

Tuna, Salmon, Mackerel, Chicken, or Turkey Pie

In skillet melt:
 ¼ c. table fat or chicken fat
Add and lightly brown:
 1 c. sliced mushrooms* 2 Tbsp. chopped green pepper
 3 Tbsp. minced onion
Add and blend:
 3 Tbsp. flour
Cook until thickened.

---

*Cream of mushroom soup may be substituted for mushrooms, fat, milk and flour (1 - 19 oz. can).

Beat: 1 egg yolk
Stir some of hot mixture into egg yolk and return yolk and all to hot mixture.
Add: 2½ c. (1 lb.) chunk tuna, mackerel or salmon, diced cooked chicken, or turkey
    2 Tbsp. finely chopped pimiento
Line deep pie dish, casserole, or individual pie plates with whole wheat pastry. Fill with hot mixture. Adjust slashed top crust. Bake at 450 F. for 10 minutes. Reduce heat to 375 F. and continue baking until top crust is lightly browned.

Crust may be baked separately and simply filled with hot mixture for quick serving.

Yields filling for 8 pies, 165 Calories, 19.5 g. protein, 0.38 g. fiber each if water packed fish is used. Poultry adds 38 Calories per pie and reduces the protein by about 3.8 grams per pie. Oil packed fish add about 90 Calories per pie. 1 recipe pastry makes 8 pies. 320 Calories, 5.2 g. protein, 0.82 g. fiber each *plus* filling.

Creamed Salmon, Tuna, or Shrimp
(Also chicken or turkey for winter meals)

Melt: 4 Tbsp. table fat
Add: 4 Tbsp. flour   ½ tsp. salt
Cook until lightly browned.
Add: 2 c. milk
Boil until thickened
Add: 1 pound (about 2½ c.) chunk tuna, salmon, shrimp or cubed poultry.

Yields 6 servings, 197 Calories, 24.4 g. protein, 0.11 g. fiber per serving with water packed tuna. Varies with other ingredients up to 261 Calories and down to 19.6 g. protein for poultry.

Serve on hot biscuits, toast, waffles, *or* mashed potatoes. May be combined with a green vegetable such as peas for serving.

Quiche Lorraine with Variations

Line one 9-inch pie plate with whole wheat pastry.* Flute the edges high.

Scatter evenly over bottom of pastry:
> 2 Tbsp. soy-bacon bits
> 2 Tbsp. minced onion (if desired)

Combine:
> 5 well beaten eggs
> 1¾ c. whole milk *or* light cream
> ½ tsp. salt
> ¼ tsp. pepper (if desired)
> ¼ tsp. nutmeg
> 1 c. grated cheese (combine cheddar and parmesan or other flavors to taste, about ¼ lb. cheese)

Pour custard mix gently into pastry shell. Bake at 450 F. for 10 minutes. Reduce heat to 350 F. and continue baking until custard is set (30 to 40 minutes). A knife inserted in the middle will come out clean when it is done. Serve immediately. Yields 6 servings, 415 Calories, 16.8 g. protein, 0.56 g. fiber each, including the pastry, when made with whole milk, 100 Calories more and 0.6 g. protein less if made with cream.

Tomato and Cheese Quiche Lorraine—Filling only. Follow instructions above.

Cover the bottom pastry with:
> 3 medium tomatoes, peeled and sliced in ¼-inch slices

Over the tomato slices arrange:
> 4 slices processed cheddar cheese cut on the diagonal

Combine:
> 4 well beaten eggs
> 2 c. whole milk *or* light cream
> 1 Tbsp. minced onion fried golden brown in 1 Tbsp. table fat

---

*Pastry accounts for 213 Calories, 3.5 g. protein, 0.55 g. fiber in each serving of Quiche Lorraine.

1 Tbsp. flour
½ tsp. salt
⅛ tsp. dry mustard
Dash of cayenne

Pour custard mixture gently over the tomatoes and cheese. Bake as above. Yields 6 servings, 438 Calories, 16.5 g. protein, 1.08 g. fiber each, including pastry, when made with milk; 553 Calories, 15.8 g. protein when made with cream.

Cottage Cheese-Potato Quiche Lorraine—Filling only. Follow instructions above.

Blend in blender *or* sieve:

2 c. (16 oz.) cottage cheese (creamed)

Add:

2 beaten eggs
½ c. sour cream (cultured)
2½ c. lightly packed riced or mashed potatoes
1 tsp. salt
¼ tsp. pepper (if desired)

Spoon into pastry-lined pan. Brush top with whole milk. Dot with butter *or* sprinkle bacon chips over the top.

Bake as above. Yields 6 servings, 414 Calories, 17.9 g. protein, 0.85 g. fiber each, including pastry.

Mackerel Patties

Combine:

1 pound can mackerel (you may remove oil floating on top if desired, but otherwise do not drain)
2 or 3 eggs
2 slices whole wheat bread or equivalent crumbs (2 oz.)

Grease griddle or skillet with oil or bacon drippings.

Drop by spoonfuls onto hot griddle or skillet.

Cook until lightly browned on both sides.

Serve with brown rice, parsley potatoes, potatoes and kale *or* corn (on or off the cob), and a tossed salad for a quick, inexpensive, and delicious meal.

Yields 6 servings, 208 Calories, 18.6 g. protein, 0.2 g. fiber per serving when made with 3 eggs.

Mackerel Loaf

Combine:

    1 pound can mackerel
    ¾ c. whole wheat bread crumbs
    ¾ c. milk
    2 eggs
    ½ tsp. salt
    1 Tbsp. melted table fat
    1 tsp. minced onion
    ¼ c. pickle relish

Mix well. Pack into greased loaf pan or individual casseroles. Bake at 350 F. about 30 minutes or until loaf becomes firm and lightly browned.

Serve plain *or* with white sauce to which minced onion has been added and garnish with hard-cooked egg slices and sliced stuffed olives.

Yields 6 servings, 222 Calories, 18.7 g. protein, 0.24 g. fiber each without white sauce or garnish.

See regular recipe books for recipes for salmon loaves, salmon patties, croquettes, etc.

Fried Fish

Clean fish, removing heads, viscera (innards), and scales or skin, according to the fish being prepared. Fillet large fish (remove strips of flesh from bones) or cut them into steaks (make vertical cuts through the fish approximately 1 inch thick). Or simply defrost or unpackage ready prepared fish. Rinse if needed. Blot excess moisture, but do not dry. Complete the process in one of the following ways:

    1. *Butter fried* (for very fresh fish). Place fish directly into hot butter in a skillet and fry until lightly browned on the under side and moisture begins to appear on the top side.

Turn and fry until lightly browned and the flesh flakes easily. Add salt to taste. Drain and serve.

2. *Meal Dipped* (for a tasty, low-Calorie coating, to help seal in juices).

Combine in a plastic or paper bag:

¼ c. cornmeal, finely ground

¼ c. flour

1 tsp. salt

¼ tsp. paprika

Dash of pepper if desired

Drop the fish, one piece at a time, into the meal and shake until coated. Fry one of two ways:

(1) *Drop into deep fat* heated to 375 F. and fry until the fish rises to the top and is lightly browned—3 to 5 minutes.

(2) *Fry in a skillet* with ¼-inch moderately hot (sizzle but not smoke) fat. Follow directions for butter fried. Total frying time 5 to 8 minutes. *Do not overcook*. Drain on absorbent paper.

Serve with lemon wedge or tartar sauce. Each pound of prepared flesh yields 3 servings, varying with the kind of fish from 192 Calories, 26 g. protein for cod to 230 Calories for fresh water catfish and halibut with the halibut providing an extra 3.7 g. protein. (Four servings give adequate protein for a meal but make small servings.)

3. *Egg dipped* (for a more crusty fish and less fish odor in the house).

Combine:

1 beaten egg

1 Tbsp. water or milk

Dip the fish first in the egg mixture, then into the meal mixture or finely ground bread or cracker crumbs. Fry in deep fat or in a skillet as directed above. Expect Calories to rise about 20 per serving and protein to increase 1 to 2 grams.

Broiled or Barbecued Fish
(In oven broiler, hibachi, or barbecue pit)

Prepare fish as for frying but do not dip. Treat with butter or barbecue sauce.

1. *Butter broiled:* Brush fish with melted butter. Dust with paprika and onion powder or fish seasoning if desired. Place on a greased rack 2 inches or more from the heat source - 2 inches for thinner fillets, more for thicker fillets, whole fish, or steaks. Turn with a spatula when golden brown if the piece needs turning. (Thin fillets often cook completely without turning. If the flesh flakes easily, serve.) Baste generously while broiling. Salt when cooking is complete. Total broiling time, 5 to 10 minutes.

2. *Barbecued:* Marinate fish in barbecue sauce. Follow directions for butter broiled for cooking, basting with sauce instead of butter.

3. *Barbecued fish, Hawaiian style*—Marinate in teriyaki sauce before cooking. See Teriyaki Steak recipe among the meats for sauce.

Yield varies with the kind of fish and the amount of fat used in cooking. At 3 servings per pound, halibut, trout, and fresh water catfish have 150-155 Calories plus 35 Calories for each teaspoon of fat used in cooking, with 31.2 g. protein per serving for the halibut, 26 g. for the catfish, and 29 for the trout. Cod, ocean perch, pike, or Jacks range from 118 to 143 Calories with 26 to 29 g. protein per serving, plus the fat used in cooking. (All values are based on prepared flesh, not whole fish.)

Baked Fish, Stuffed

Select a whole fish, cleaned and dressed but not skinned, filleted, or steaked. Rub the inside and outside with salt. Stuff with any desired dressing (see bread and celery dressing recipe to follow for one suggestion). Skewer or sew the sides together. Brush with melted butter, margarine, or oil. Place on a greased rack in a shallow baking pan or on an ovenware platter, skewered or sewn side down. Bake, uncovered, at 375 to 400 F., 10 to 15 minutes per pound. Baste occasionally. Fish flakes easily and pulls away from skin and bones when done. *Do not overcook.* Garnish with lemon slices, tomato wedges, and parsley. Yields 3 servings per pound, nutrients similar to butter broiled fish *plus* nutrients of dressing.

Whole Wheat Bread and Celery Dressing
(For stuffing fish, chicken, turkey, pork chops,
or serving alone)

For 6 cups dressing—enough to serve 12 half-cup servings and to stuff 2 good-sized fish or chickens or one turkey weighing ten to fifteen pounds.

Toast, butter, and cube whole wheat bread or split, butter, and cube whole wheat biscuits to make:

6 c. buttered bread crumbs (about 12 oz.)

Add and toss lightly but thoroughly:

1 c. (or less) chopped onion
2 c. diagonally sliced celery, stalk and leaves
1 tsp. salt
1½ tsp. fish seasoning, poultry seasoning *or* sage, marjoram, and thyme to taste.

Add:

Any meats to be added (see instructions for poultry)
Broth to moisten bread mixture (about 1 cup)

For Baked Fish—Prepare broth by dissolving 2 chicken flavored boullion cubes in 1 cup hot water or use 1 cup chicken broth or clam broth. Use fish seasoning if desired, and proceed as directed in recipe for stuffed baked fish. Each of 12 servings provides 110 Calories, 3.5 g. protein, 0.62 g. fiber with yeast bread.

For Poultry—Remove giblets and neck from the bird. Cover with water in a saucepan. Bring to a boil. Reduce heat and simmer until neck meat is tender. Cool. Remove meat from bones and chop into bite-sized pieces. (Heart and gizzard may also be sliced and used in the dressing or may be served separately with the liver to those who enjoy them.) Add chopped meat to the dressing along with 1 c. broth developed in their cooking.

To use, sprinkle body and neck cavities of the bird with salt. Fill with dressing. Secure with skewers or string and bake according to directions found on the package with the bird or in a standard cookbook. Remove dressing from the fowl to a serving dish or serve directly from the bird. Yields 12 half-cup servings, 150 Calories, 7.7 g. protein, 0.62 g. fiber each made with yeast bread and meat from a large turkey neck; 187 Calories, 6.8 g. protein with biscuits instead of yeast bread.

Dressing baked alone—(to be served with canned or stewed poultry, fish, or pork creamed or in gravy). Use broth if available or make broth using boullion cubes. Add 2 beaten eggs to the mixed dressing. Place in a buttered baking dish and bake at 375 F. 30 to 45 minutes or until eggs set and top lightly browned. Time varies with shape of baking dish. Nutrients vary with broth used but approximate 123 Calories, 4.5 g. protein when made with yeast bread.

Baked Fish Fillets

Cut fillets into serving sized pieces.
Sprinkle every surface of each piece with:
> salt
> onion powder
> paprika
> celery salt

Dot each piece with butter if desired. Arrange in buttered baking dish. Bake at 400 F. for 20 minutes or until fish flakes easily. Garnish with parsley. Serve immediately. 1 pound ocean perch* yields 4 servings, 125 Calories, 21.6 g. protein each.

---

*Halibut has more Calories, cod has fewer. Both have less protein.

Saucy Fish Fillets

Melt: 2 Tbsp. table fat
Add and toss lightly:
    ¼ c. chopped onion
    1½ c. whole wheat bread cubes
Spread half of this mixture in the bottom of a baking dish approximately 8x8x2 inches. Arrange 1 pound fish fillets cut into serving pieces on the crumbs.

Prepare sauce by combining:
    2 Tbsp. melted table fat
    2 Tbsp. flour
    ½ tsp. dry mustard
    ¼ tsp. salt
    ¼ tsp. pepper (if desired)
Cook until smooth and bubbly.
Add:
    1½ c. milk
    1 cube chicken boullion
Stir over low heat until thickened. Spread over fish. Top with the rest of the crumb mixture. Bake at 350 F. for 35 minutes or until fish flakes easily. 1 pound ocean perch yields 4 servings, 320 Calories, 27.1 g. protein, 0.45 g. fiber each *or* 5 servings, 256 Calories, 22.5 g. protein, 0.36 g. fiber each, made with whole milk, 290 and 232 Calories respectively made with skim milk.

Fish Baked in Tomato Sauce

Combine in baking dish approximately 8x8x2 inches:
    2 c. tomato juice
    1 tsp. onion flakes
    Dash of garlic powder
    1½ c. chopped celery
    ½ tsp. parsley flakes
    ½ tsp. butter flavored salt
Heat. When hot add:
    1 pound fish fillets cut into serving pieces.

Bake at 350 F. for about 30 minutes or until fish flakes easily. Baste with sauce occasionally. 1 pound ocean perch yields 4 servings, 133 Calories, 22.7 g. protein, 0.50 g. fiber each.

Macaroni, Cheese, and Egg Casserole

Hard cook: 6 eggs. Peel and slice them.
Prepare 1 quart (4 cups) medium white sauce:
  Melt: ½ c. table fat
  Add: ½ c. flour
      1 tsp. salt
  Cook until bubbly, but not browned.
  Add: 1 quart (4 cups) milk
  Cook, stirring constantly, until thickened.
  Remove from heat.
  Add: ½ pound grated sharp cheese. (Other cheeses will do
      but are not so tasty.)
In separate container, bring to boil
      1 quart (4 cups) water
Add:
      1 tsp. salt
      8 oz. enriched macaroni
Stir lightly with a fork. Cover tightly. Turn heat low and simmer until tender (about 7 minutes).

Grease a 3-quart baking dish. Spread macaroni over bottom of dish. Add sliced eggs. Pour cheese sauce over all.
Melt 2 Tbsp. table fat. Add 1 c. whole wheat bread crumbs or cubes. Mix well. Sprinkle over top of casserole. Brown in oven at 350 F. about 30 minutes.

Yields 10 servings, 384 Calories, 17.1 g. protein, 0.27 g. fiber per serving when made with skim milk, 415 Calories made with whole milk.

Whole Wheat Goulash

In skillet melt
>2 Tbsp. table fat or drippings

Add and heat through, but do not brown:
>1 small onion chopped
>1 c. sliced celery
>1 small green pepper chopped
>½ c. chopped parsley
>½ pound sliced mushrooms *or* 1 10-oz. can, drained
>1 tsp. salt

Add
>1 14-oz. can Spanish tomato sauce
>4 cups precooked whole wheat

Cover and simmer about 15 minutes. Yields 6 servings, 200 Calories, 7.6 g. protein, 1.96 g. fiber per serving. Serve with grated Parmesan cheese, wedges of cheddar cheese, cottage cheese salad, or a cheese, egg, or milk dessert to supply additional protein.

Lasagna

Place 4 ounces beef-flavored textured soya protein in small bowl. Add ⅔ c. water. Let stand 15 minutes while preparing other ingredients.

Shred and set aside:
>½ lb. mozzarella cheese

Heat in skillet:
>1 Tbsp. oil

Add to brown
>1 clove minced garlic
>1 medium onion minced

Add
>Reconstituted soya protein
>1 14-oz. can pizza sauce *or* Spanish tomato sauce
>1 tsp. salt

Allow to simmer while you cook noodles as follows:
Boil together:

> 6 c. water
> 1 tsp. salt

Add slowly so water continues to boil:

> 8 oz. lasagna noodles

Cover and keep boiling 15 minutes.
Drain 2 c. water from noodles and add to sauce.* Put a bit of the sauce into a 9x13x2-inch baking dish. Arrange half of the noodles over the sauce to cover the bottom of the dish.
Spread over the noodles:

> 1 pound cottage cheese
> ½ of shredded mozzarella

Pour half of the sauce over the cheese.
Arrange the rest of the noodles on top of the sauce.
Top with the rest of the sauce.
Sprinkle the rest of the mozzarella cheese evenly over the top of it all.

Bake at 350 F. for 30 minutes or until it is bubbly and the cheese slightly browned. Remove from oven and allow to sit for about 15 minutes before cutting into squares for serving. Yields 8 servings, 325 Calories, 25 g. protein, 0.6 g. fiber per serving. (For winter meals, eliminate oil, reduce cottage cheese to ½ pound, and substitute 1 pound lean hamburger for the textured protein. Calories, protein, and fiber remain about the same.)

Sweet-Sour Ham

Combine and let stand 15 minutes:

> 2 3½-oz. (100 gram) packages ham flavored textured soya protein**
> 1⅓ c. water

---

*You may prefer to use 2 cups tomatoes instead of water in the sauce.
**1 pound chopped ham may be substituted.

Combine and cook until thickened:

2 Tbsp. cornstarch
3 Tbsp. brown sugar
1 Tbsp. soy sauce
⅓ c. vinegar
¾ c. water
1 14-oz. can pineapple chunks

Heat in skillet:

2 Tbsp. table fat or oil

Add reconstituted ham flavored protein. Brown lightly.
Add and heat, but do not brown:

1 medium onion, thinly sliced
1 c. celery sliced thin on the diagonal
½ large green pepper cut into thin strips

Add sauce. Heat gently. Serve on fluffy brown rice.

Yields 6 servings, 185 Calories, 18 g. protein, 0.56 g. fiber per serving when textured protein is used. Lean ham will add about 35 Calories per serving and reduce the protein slightly.

Basic Methods for Cooking Dried Beans, Peas, and Lentils

(Great Northern, Navy, Pinto, Kidney, Dry Limas, Soybeans, and Others)

For 2 cups beans, select a 3- to 4-quart kettle. Carefully sort the beans, removing the stones, pieces of dirt, damaged beans. Wash quickly but thoroughly through several waters. A strainer or a sieve is helpful for draining the beans between washings. Place the clean beans in the kettle and add:

4 to 6 cups water. (Lentils, dried peas, and some beans need less water than pinto or soybeans. Start with the smaller amount and add water as needed.)

Optional:

2 Tbsp. table fat, oil, ham or bacon drippings* *or* cook

---

*Fat helps prevent foaming during cooking and adds flavor. It also adds 100 Calories or more per tablespoonful. Soybeans have 11 times as much fat as other beans and need little if any extra fat for seasoning.

with a piece of ham bone, ham skin, or slices of ham fat or bacon (2 oz. or less).*

Near the end of the cooking period add:

Salt to taste. With ham or bacon, there may be no need for additional salt. For plain beans that need salt, start with ½ teaspoonful. Lean ham or ham flavored soya protein may be added for protein and flavor.

Method I (For plump, whole beans and low energy cost)— Bring beans to a boil. Turn off heat. Allow to stand one hour. Return to boiling. Turn off heat. Let stand one hour. Repeat on the third hour and again on the fourth. By the fourth hour they are ready to serve. (Lentils and peas will take less time).

Method II—Boil beans for 2 minutes. Turn off heat. Allow to soak one hour. Bring to a boil again. Turn heat low and simmer until tender (½ hour for lentils and peas, 1 to 2 hours for other beans), *or* place in a slow cooker and cook until tender.

Method III—Combine only water and beans and soak 5 to 6 hours. Add fat if desired. Bring to a boil in the soaking water. Turn heat low and simmer until tender (time as for Method II).

Yields vary with the type of bean and seasonings added. For most, the total yield is from 5 to 6 cups beans and liquid. With a 6-cup yield and 2 Tbsp. fat per recipe, each cupful averages about 230 Calories, 13 g. protein, 2.4 g. fiber for pintos and kidney beans to 250 Calories, 15 g. protein, 2.8 g. fiber for common white beans and lentils. 5 cups with seasoning average 276 Calories, 15.6 g. protein, 2.88 g. fiber per cup of pintos or kidney beans; 300 Calories, 18 g. protein, 3.36 g. fiber for white beans and lentils. Without extra fat, a 5-cup yield of soybeans provides about 305 Calories, 25.8 g. protein, 4.3 g. fiber per cup.

Serving—All beans, peas, etc., may be served plain. Small amounts of animal protein such as ham, eggs, beef, cheese, milk, or fish or whole wheat breads served with beans enhance the protein quality and increase the protein available.

---

*When I buy a ham, I remove the fat, skin, and bone and divide them into packets to be frozen for later use as seasonings.

These vegetable proteins also may be used in many ways. Some examples are tacos, tostados, chili, baked beans, bean soup, split pea soup, and casseroles, (some of which follow). For more information on the use of soybeans and soya products, order USDA Home and Garden Bulletin No. 208, *Soybeans in Family Meals*, from the Superintendent of Documents, U.S. Government Printing Office, Washington, D.C., 20402, or pick it or other literature up at your local Extension Service office or department of public health.

Tacos
(Pinto Beans Preferred)

Prepare or purchase 16 tortillas (corn masa), 1 oz. each.

Pour oil 1 inch deep in a pan large enough to accommodate a single tortilla. Hold each tortilla with tongs and pass it through the oil, turning once, quickly for soft ones, longer for crisp ones. Blot on absorbent paper. (*Or* heat tortillas in a bun warmer or oven without oil.) Have each person fill his/her own.

Serve for filling, in separate containers:

- 3 cups cooked beans, mashed if desired
- 8 chopped, hard-cooked eggs *or* 1 pound lean hamburger browned and seasoned with 1 tsp. salt and a dash of garlic powder
- ½ medium head lettuce shredded and seasoned with a dash each of onion and garlic powder.
- 2 medium tomatoes chunked and tossed with the lettuce
- 1 large onion chopped finely

Sprinkle on sparingly:

Salsa Picante (hot sauce) made by grinding together in a Mexican moler or blender:

- 1 Tbsp. cumin (camino) seed
- 2 plump cloves of garlic
- 1 or 2 chili peppers (fresh or dried) depending on size of pepper and degree of hotness desired.

2 medium, peeled tomatoes (fresh or canned)
Salt to taste

Each tortilla provides approximately 58 Calories, 1.1 g. protein, 0.2 g. fiber without oil. Divided into 16 portions, the filling and hot sauce provide 100 Calories, 6.5 g. protein, 0.52 g. fiber per taco with eggs; 111 Calories, 9.4 g. protein, 0.52 g. fiber with beef. Allow 2 to 4 tacos per person. Leftover beans, beef, and Salsa Picante make good chili.

Tostados

Use the same ingredients as in tacos except substitute grated cheese for the eggs or beef or use less of the eggs and beef and top with grated cheese, and mash the beans.

Method—Fry the tortilla until crisp. Leave flat. Blot. Spread with mashed beans. Sprinkle with hot sauce. Arrange shredded lettuce and tomato mixture. Sprinkle on onion, if desired, and top with cheese. Calories and protein are about as for tacos with beef if ½ pound of cheese is used.

Chili

Combine:

4 c. cooked, seasoned beans—pintos preferred
4 oz. beef flavored textured soya protein *or* ½ pound lean hamburger browned with 1 tsp. salt and a dash of garlic powder.
2½ c. peeled, fresh or canned tomatoes
1 medium onion chopped
Chopped fresh celery leaves and parsley *or* celery salt and parsley flakes to taste.
Salsa Picante (hot sauce) to taste. (You may use chili powder but the flavor will not equal that of the sauce.)
Simmer until flavors are well blended.

Yields 8 servings, 185 Calories, 15 g. protein, 5.15 g. fiber per serving when textured protein is used. With hamburger there are about 10 more Calories and 1 gram less protein per serving.

Bean Soup

Combine:
- 2 cups cooked beans with liquid, seasoned with table fat, drippings, or ham
- 2 Tbsp. chopped onion (more or less, as desired)
- Chopped celery leaves as available and desired
- 2 cups additional liquid. May be bean stock (liquid from cooking beans), water seasoned with ½ tsp. salt and 1 tsp. table fat, liquid drained from other vegetables, noodles, etc.

Simmer until flavors are well blended, 10 to 15 minutes at least. Yields 4 servings, about 134 Calories, 6.6 g. protein, 1.25 g. fiber each.

Baked Beans
(Preferably Navy or Great Northern Beans)

Cook 2 cups beans as directed in "Basic Method for Cooking Beans, etc."

Combine seasoned beans and liquid in a 2-quart baking dish or bean pot(s) with:

4 Tbsp. sorghum *or*	
2 Tbsp. brown sugar	¼ c. catsup *or*
2 Tbsp. molasses	1 Tbsp. vinegar
½ tsp. dry mustard *or*	½ c. tomato puree
2 tsp. prepared mustard	Dash of pepper if desired

Cover the top of the beans with onion sliced thin. Dot with butter or uncooked bacon pieces. Bake at 350 F. until beans are well seasoned and browned, onions are cooked, and liquid is of desired consistency. Baking time may be from 1 to 3 hours or more, according to your wishes. If for more than 1 hour you may need to start the beans covered or add more liquid as they bake. Yields 8 servings, 277 Calories, 12.4 g. protein, 2.25 g. fiber each.

Quick and Easy Baked Beans may be made using 6 cups pork and beans instead of home-cooked beans. Reduce other ingredients by half. Baking time about 1 hour. Yields 8 servings, 280 Calories, 12.7 g. protein, 2.82 g. fiber each if a total of 2 Tbsp. fat are used in seasoning. Add 13 Calories per serving for each additional Tbsp. fat.

Bean Rarebit
(Preferably Pinto or Kidney Beans)

Grate and set aside
  ½ pound cheddar cheese*
Melt in a skillet
  1 Tbsp. table fat
Add and sauté until crisp tender:
  2 Tbsp. minced onion
  2 Tbsp. chopped sweet pepper
Add and heat through:
  2 c. beans (cooked)
  2 Tbsp. catsup
Optional:
  ½ tsp. Worchestershire sauce
  Pinch of salt

Turn off heat. Add the grated cheese and stir until melted. Do not overcook or it will get stringy. Serve on crisp whole wheat toast. Delicious! Serves 4 to 6. Four servings with cheddar cheese provide 361 Calories, 21 g. protein, 1.39 g. fiber without toast. With processed cheese, reduce Calories by 16 and protein by 1 gram per serving. If 6 are served, each receives 240 Calories, 14 g. protein, 0.93 g. fiber with cheddar.

---

*Processed cheese may be used, but the flavor is not as good. It does not get stringy, however.

Pizza

Crust:
1. Use a portion of whole wheat bread dough (see recipe for 100 percent whole wheat bread).
2. Use biscuit dough. 1 recipe everyday biscuit dough makes 1 large or 2 small crusts.
3. Create a simple pizza dough following these instructions for 2 large pizzas.

Combine:
   1½ c. lukewarm milk (scalded and cooled if fluid milk is used)
   1 Tbsp. yeast
   1 tsp. brown sugar or honey

Sift and measure:
   4 c. (1 lb.) whole wheat flour

Add: half of the flour to the liquid and beat thoroughly.
Add:
   1 tsp. salt
   2 tsp. melted table fat or oil

Continue to add flour to make a *soft* dough that will hold its shape. You may or may not need it all. *Knead* in the bowl about 5 minutes. Grease dough and bowl lightly. *Cover* and allow to rise until double in bulk. Punch down. If there is time, let rise again.

Divide into two portions. Pat or roll thin to fit 2 large well-greased cookie sheets or pizza pans. Flute edges to prevent bubbling over. *Spread* the dough with one 14-17 oz. can pizza sauce or Spanish tomato sauce.

Use your favorite fillings. Here are some suggestions:
1. *Tuna Pizza*
Combine:
   2 cans (6½ to 7 oz. each) tuna
   1 medium onion chopped
   Dash of garlic powder

Spread the mixture over the sauce-covered dough. Sprinkle generously with oregano.

Cover with ½ pound grated mozzarella cheese

Bake at 400 F. 20 minutes or until filling is bubbly and crust is lightly browned. Loosen from pan immediately after removing from oven. Cut into wedges. Garnish with parsley. Serve with a tossed salad and beverage. Allow 2 to 3 wedges per person (some will want more).

Yields 24 wedges, 135 Calories, 10.1 g. protein, 0.55 g. fiber each when made with water-packed tuna. Add 25 Calories per wedge and subtract 0.6 g. protein if oil-packed tuna is used.

2. *Hamburger Pizza* (for winter meals)

Substitute 1 pound lean hamburger and 1 tsp. salt for the tuna.

Heat but do not brown the meat with the onion and garlic. Proceed as for tuna pizza. Yield is about the same as for oil-packed tuna.

3. *Hamburger-Sausage Pizza*—Arrange slices of sausage so each serving will contain one or two. Calories and protein vary with kind of sausage and amount used.

4. *Mushroom and Cheese*

Sprinkle garlic salt and oregano over the sauce-covered dough.

Chop and sprinkle over all:

    1 small onion
    1 small can pimiento
    1 green pepper
    1 pound mushrooms (raw)*

Grate and sprinkle over the vegetables:

    1 c. parmesan cheese (5 oz.)
    1 c. cheddar cheese (4 oz.)
    1 lb. Mozzarella**

Proceed as for Tuna Pizza. Yields 24 wedges, 212 Calories, 9.6 g. protein, 0.68 g. fiber each.

---

*Two fourteen-ounce cans mushrooms may be used. Drain, slice, and scatter on sauce.

**Mozzarella cheese may be reduced to ½ pound. Reduce Calories to 177 and protein to 6.9 g. per wedge. Allow 2 to 3 wedges per serving. Needs only a salad and a beverage for a meal.

EGGS
"Butter" Poached Eggs
(Good for one or as many as the skillet will hold)

Choose a skillet with a tight fitting lid. Heat table fat in skillet—just enough to flavor the eggs. One teaspoonful may be enough for a whole skillet.

Break each egg first into a dish, then pour into the hot fat. Sprinkle with salt and pepper, if desired.

Add 1 Tbsp. water or less per egg—enough to produce steam for cooking.

Cover the skillet with lid. Steam until the eggs are of the desired consistency. Separate and serve. Each large egg provides about 80 Calories, 6 g. protein, plus the fat. Fat is about 35 Calories per teaspoonful.

Hard-Cooked Eggs
(Boiled eggs get tough when they get hard. Slow cooked they remain tender.)

Cooking:
Place eggs in water about the temperature they are. Allow to *heat* slowly. Too fast heating of cold eggs will cause them to burst. If one should crack and begin to leak, pour salt at the site of the leak; this will help coagulate the protein and seal the leak. Bring to a *boil. Turn heat low* and simmer 20 minutes to half an hour. *Remove* from heat. *Drain.*

Cooling:
Plunge eggs immediately into *cold* water. Change water as needed to *cool rapidly.* The iron and sulfur of the egg combine to form a green coloring at lukewarm temperatures. Rapid cooling can usually prevent this. If it forms, it does not harm the egg except in appearance.

Peeling:
Crack open the big end of the egg. Break through the inner membrane. Crush the shell and plunge into cold water again. The cold water *usually* helps loosen the membrane. If the eggs are very fresh, however, it may not help enough. If it

doesn't peel easily, use a spoon to slice under the membrane and lift off the shell.

Serving:

1. For lunches, eat out of hand (with the addition of salt if desired).
2. Chop and use in sandwich filling (see recipe) or in tacos (see recipe).
3. Use in casserole (see macaroni, cheese, and egg casserole), cream sauces, or as garnishes for creamed dishes, salads, etc.
4. Serve in salads, alone as wedges on lettuce with tomato wedges, or chopped as in tuna, ham, chicken, salmon, turkey, potato, and other salads and in sandwiches.
5. Fix deviled eggs (recipe follows).

Deviled Eggs

Hard-cook 6 eggs, peel, and slice lengthwise.
Remove the yolks and mash them smooth with

2 Tbsp. mayonnaise type salad dressing *or* combined salad dressing and sweet pickle vinegar
1 tsp. prepared mustard
¼ tsp. salt

Sprinkle whites lightly with salt and refill with egg yolk mixture. Garnish with paprika and parsley. (They are beautiful when the yolk mixture is dispensed by a pastry tube.)
Serve alone, with tomato wedges, beet pickles, or other brightly colored vegetables in salads or as a separate dish, or serve as garnish for casseroles, salads, and creamed dishes. Excellent picnic fare! Yields 12 halves, 51 Calories, 3 g. protein each.

Creamed Egg

Combine and heat until bubbly but not browned:

    4 Tbsp. melted fat*

    4 Tbsp. flour

Cut into wedges and set aside:

    6 hard cooked eggs

Add, stirring rapidly, preferably with a French whip:

    2 c. milk

    ½ tsp. salt

Cook, stirring continuously until thickened. Turn heat low.
Add, and heat thoroughly:

    6 hard cooked eggs previously cut in wedges

    Salt to taste if needed

Optional:

    a dash of onion salt

    1 Tbsp. chopped pimiento (or more)

    2 Tbsp. parsley (chopped)

Serve on whole wheat toast, in prebaked whole wheat pastry shells, on mashed potatoes, over steamed asparagus spears, salmon or mackerel loaves, or on biscuits. Yields 4 main dish servings (6 to 8 servings on fish loaves), 284 Calories, 14.5 g. protein, 0.16 g. fiber each when made with full fat and skim milk, 324 Calories made with whole milk. Fiber increases with pimiento and parsley.

Omelet with Variations

For each serving

Combine:

    2 well beaten eggs

    2 Tbsp. milk

    ⅙ tsp. salt

In a heavy skillet, heat:

    1 tsp. table fat or drippings

---

*2 Tbsp. fat may be used to reduce Calories by 200, but more care must be exercised to keep the sauce smooth.

Prepare and set aside:

½ oz. chopped or grated cheese

½ Tbsp. bacon-flavored soya

Pour the egg mixture into the skillet when fat is hot but not browned. Cook, lifting the edges of the omelet frequently to allow the fluid portion to run underneath. When omelet is almost set, remove from heat. Scatter cheese and "bacon" on one half. Gently fold other half onto the bacon and cheese. Transfer to a hot platter or serving plate. Serve immediately, garnished with parsley. Each serving provides 290 Calories, 22.1 g. protein, no fiber except for the parsley.

Variations:

1. Serve plain without cheese or "bacon," 215 Calories, 17.1 g. protein each.
2. Use ½ tsp. chopped onion and 1 Tbsp. chopped sweet pepper instead of "bacon" and cheese, 220 Calories, 17.4 g. protein, 0.24 g. fiber each.
3. *Fluffy Omelet*—Separate the eggs. Beat the whites until stiff but not dry. Beat the yolks until thick before adding the milk and salt.

   Preheat the oven to 375 F. Use a skillet that may be placed in the oven. Pour eggs into hot fat in the skillet and cook until bottom is lightly browned. Place in oven and continue cooking until top springs back at a touch (about 15 minutes). Fold and serve as above.
4. Use very crisp bacon or ham alone or in combination with onion, sweet pepper, and the like. Crisp bacon adds 45 Calories, 2.5 g. protein per slice (7.5 g.). Ham adds about the same for each ½ oz.

Scrambled Eggs

Use the same proportions as for omelets. When the egg mixture is poured into the hot fat, stir continuously until eggs are almost set. Remove from heat while partially liquid because they will continue to cook from contained heat. All the variations suggested for omelets, except fluffy omelet, may be used with scrambled eggs by combining the ingredients with the eggs.

Egg Foo Yung

Chop fine or cut into thin strips:

  1 large onion (½ lb.)
  ½ pound carrots
  ½ pound celery (use leaves, slice diagonally)
  ½ pound any dark green vegetable (broccoli, kale, parsley)

Other vegetables such as cauliflower, green beans, rutabaga, jicama, and radishes may be used also. Frozen vegetables or leftovers are acceptable. Total volume without compressing vegetables should not exceed 3 quarts (12 cups), 1 cup per egg.

Add:

  12 eggs
  2 tsp. salt

Stir with a fork until eggs are frothy and everything is well mixed. Brush hot griddle with a small amount of oil, table fat or bacon drippings. Drop mixture by spoonfuls to make servings approximately 4 inches in diameter. Brown on one side. Turn with a spatula. Cook until lightly browned and egg is set. Serve with fluffy brown rice and soy sauce.

Yields about 18 patties, about 75 Calories, 5 grams protein, 0.6 g. fiber each. Allow 2 to 3 patties per serving or more. Leftovers are excellent for lunches or snacking.

Green Rice

Combine and mix thoroughly:

  3 c. cooked brown rice
  2 c. chopped parsley
  1 small onion chopped (green onion is nice)
  ½ large sweet pepper (green or red)
  3 eggs slightly beaten
  1½ c. milk
  1 tsp. salt or to taste

183

Pour into a greased baking dish or casserole that will hold 6 cups. Place dish in a pan of warm water. Bake at 350 F. for 30 to 45 minutes or until set. (To speed cooking, warm the rice and milk before mixing.)

Yields 6 servings, 200 Calories, 8.4 g. protein, 0.8 g. fiber each made with whole milk, 180 Calories made with skim milk.

Serve with creamed tuna, shrimp, salmon, chicken, turkey, ham, or any of these a la king, or add 1 cup (¼ lb.) grated sharp cheese to the recipe. One-fourth pound cheddar cheese adds 75 Calories, 4.7 g. protein per serving.

Fried Rice

Heat in skillet:
>   1 Tbsp. table fat *or* bacon drippings

Add, mix, and heat thoroughly:
>   3 c. cooked brown rice
>   2 Tbsp. soya bacon chips *or* crumbled crisp bacon from 2 medium slices

Add, stirring constantly:
>   3 slightly beaten eggs
>   1 c. (or more) mixed vegetables* (cooked or fresh, chopped)
>   1 Tbsp. soya sauce *or* salt to taste
>   3 or 4 chopped green onions

Yields 4 servings, 283 Calories, 10.5 g. protein, 0.98 g. fiber each made with soya bacon and table fat, 285 Calories and 10 g. protein with real bacon and bacon fat. Six small servings provide 188 Calories, 7.0 g. protein, 0.65 g. fiber each. If you add more fat, add 100 Calories per Tbsp. for table fat, 110 Calories for bacon fat.

---

*Nutrients were calculated for this recipe using equal amounts of parsley, green peas, green beans, and corn. Any available vegetable may be used. Some will enjoy additional round onions. Be sure to include a dark green vegetable such as parsley, kale, or broccoli. Carrots and celery are nice.

SANDWICH SPREADS

Tuna Sandwich Spread

Combine:
1 can (6½-7 oz.) chunk tuna
2 Tbsp. pickle relish (optional)
3 Tbsp. salad dressing
Dash of garlic powder
Onion powder *or* onion chopped fine to taste

Yields filling for 6 sandwiches, 127 Calories, 7.5 grams protein per sandwich if oil-packed tuna is used *or* 78 Calories, 8.7 g. protein, negligible fiber if water-packed tuna is used. Add nutrients for bread and spread.*

Pimiento Cheese Spread

Grate:
1 lb. mild or medium cheddar cheese
Add:
1 small can pimientos
1 tsp. grated onion
3 Tbsp. salad dressing
dash Worchestershire Sauce

Mix well. Serve as cheese ball rolled in nuts or on crackers, croutons, fruit wedges, celery sticks or other vegetables, or make into sandwiches.

Yields filling for 1 dozen sandwiches, 170 Calories, 9.7 g. protein, 0.1 g. fiber each, filling only.

Egg Salad Sandwich Spread

Cover 1 dozen eggs with cold water. Bring slowly to a boil. Turn heat down and simmer for 20 minutes.
Cool quickly. Peel. Chop finely.

---

*Note: Each ounce slice whole wheat bread adds about 65 Calories, 3 g. protein, 0.45 g. fiber. Butter adds 35 Calories per teaspoon. With the sandwich, 8 ounces of skim or buttermilk adds 85 Calories and another 9 grams protein. 8 ounces of 2% milk (with milk solids added) adds 145 Calories and 10 grams protein. 8 ounces whole milk adds 160 Calories and a bit less protein. 8 ounces soft drink adds 104 Calories and no protein.

Add:

1 tsp. salt
1 Tbsp. onion chopped fine
1 tsp. prepared mustard
2 Tbsp. pickle relish
3 Tbsp. salad dressing

Mix thoroughly. Add pickle juice to spreading consistency if needed.

Yields filling for 8 sandwiches, 150 Calories, 9 grams protein each, or 12 sandwiches, 100 Calories, 6 grams protein, negligible fiber each. Add nutrients for bread and spread.

MAIN DISHES FOR WINTER

Eggplant Parmesan

Peel and cut into ½-inch slices:

2 pounds (1 large or 2 small) eggplants

Dip the slices into a mixture of:

1 beaten egg
3 Tbsp. water

Prepare:

4 oz. fine cracker crumbs

Measure out and set aside:

¼ c. oil
½ c. grated Parmesan cheese

Roll dipped slices in cracker crumbs and brown in hot oil, using 1 to 2 tablespoonfuls oil per skillet full, depending on size of the skillet. Arrange half of the slices to cover the bottom of a 9x13x2-inch baking dish. Set the rest aside.

Combine and brown in a skillet or form into balls and brown:

1 medium potato, scrubbed and grated
1 pound lean hamburger
1 tsp. salt
2 cloves garlic, minced, or a dash of garlic powder

Remove browned meat mixture or balls to the baking dish and spread evenly over the eggplant. Pour off excess fat, if any. Leave just enough to grease the skillet. Add and cook until clear

1 medium onion (½ lb.) chopped

Add and simmer 5 minutes:

2½ c. whole tomatoes, fresh peeled or canned

2 tsp. brown sugar

Pour half the sauce over the meat mixture in the baking dish. Sprinkle half the Parmesan cheese over the sauce and meat. Arrange the remaining eggplant over the top of the contents of the baking dish.

Spread the remaining sauce over the top layer of eggplant. Sprinkle remaining Parmesan cheese over top of all. Bake uncovered at 375 F. for 1 hour. Yields 8 servings, 342 Calories, 21.1 g. protein, 1.5 g. fiber each.

(For summer meals, substitute 7 oz. beef-flavored textured soya protein, reconstituted, for the hamburger and brown in 2 tablespoons oil or table fat. Calories are slightly reduced and protein increased about 1.3 g. per serving.)

Pot Roast of Beef

Select a rump or chuck rib, shoulder, or round bone roast, allowing 1 pound for each 3 or 4 *small* (2 or 3 average) servings of lean anticipated. (See chart for amounts to be expected.)

Rub all surfaces with salt (½ teaspoon per pound of roast), with pepper and onion powder to taste.*

Heat a heavy pot or dutch oven until a drop of water will dance on it.

Brown all surfaces of the meat, beginning with the fat side to render out enough fat to prevent the lean from sticking to the pot. When meat is browned, slip a rack or trivet, if one is available, under it. Add ½ cup water.

Cover with a tight fitting lid and turn heat to simmer *or* place in a 300 F. oven or slow cooker to cook until tender. Add

---

*The meat may be dredged in flour (¼ c. for a 4 to 6-pound roast) seasoned with the salt, pepper, and onion powder if desired. If flour is used, trim some of the fat from the roast and render out 3 or 4 tablespoons fat before browning process is begun.

more water if needed as it cooks. Allow 30 minutes or more cooking time per pound of roast (still more if slow cooker is used).

If vegetables are to be cooked with the pot roast, arrange them around and over the roast early in the cooking period. Salt lightly. Allow 1 medium scrubbed potato, 3 or 4 small carrots or sections of large ones, 2 small onions or quarters of large ones per person to be served. Rearrange vegetables occasionally to allow each to come into contact with the meat juices during cooking.

(If a slow cooker is being used, follow instructions for vegetable placement.)

To serve, arrange meat and vegetables on a hot platter. Serve juices in a gravy boat.

YIELD OF SEPARABLE LEAN EXPECTED FROM ONE POUND RAW MEAT

CUT	WITH BONE		BONELESS	
	Choice grade	Good grade	Choice grade	Good grade
	Oz.	Oz.	Oz.	Oz.
Chuck rib roast	6.2	6.6	7.4	7.8
Arm or round bone	8.1	8.4	9.1	9.4
Rump	7.4	7.4	8.8	8.9

Each 2.2 oz. lean meat provides about 130 Calories, 18 g. protein. Add 35 Calories for each adherring teaspoon fat. Fat may be reduced by skimming excess from juices or chilling and lifting hard fat away.

Beef Curry
(A good way to use less expensive cuts)

Dice and brown in a heavy pot or skillet
    1 lb. lean beef (less tender cuts)

Remove beef and brown slightly in the drippings:
    1 lb. chopped onion (1 large to 5 small)
    ½ lb. (3 medium) or more carrots, chopped
    ⅓ lb. (1 medium) or more apple, chopped

Add and cook for one minute:

  1 Tbsp. curry powder

Add, stirring constantly until well distributed and slightly browned:

  ¼ c. flour

Slowly add, stirring constantly until thickened:

  2 c. beef stock (made by cooking bones or scrap meat or by dissolving 2 boullion cubes in water)

Add:

  ⅓ c. raisins

  1 tsp. sugar, jam, or chutney

Return beef to sauce and simmer 2 hours or until tender. (A slow cooker may be used and the curry allowed to cook for several hours.)

Serve with fluffy brown rice, a salad, and perhaps a green vegetable. Curry alone yields 6 servings, 240 Calories, 17.7 g. protein, 1.2 g. fiber each.

Meat Loaf

Combine and mix thoroughly:

  1 lb. ground meat*

  1 tsp. salt

  sage, pepper to taste

  1 c. whole wheat bread crumbs (soft)

  1 c. tomato (fresh peeled, canned, or sauce)

  1 small onion, chopped fine

  1 large egg

Pack firmly into a loaf pan 7x3½x2¼, rounding the top like a loaf of bread. Bake at 350 F. for about 45 minutes. Yields 5 servings, 233 Calories, 22.4 g. protein, 0.64 g. fiber each made with all lean beef; 313 Calories, 19.8 g. protein made with regular hamburger. Reduce Calories by 20 per serving for each tablespoon fat drained away. If all beef-flavored

---

*May be all beef, ¾ beef and ¼ pork, ½ beef and ½ beef-flavored textured soy protein, or all beef-flavored textured protein. If all beef-flavored textured protein, use Spanish-style tomato sauce.

textured soy protein is used, reduce Calories of lean beef loaf by 50 and add 2 g. protein per serving.

Teriyaki Steak
(An Oriental treat)

Prepare the sauce. For each pound, prepare ½ cup or less. Combine:

    1-inch piece of fresh ginger root mashed
    1 plump garlic clove mashed
    ½ c. soy sauce
    1 to 2 Tbsp. brown sugar according to taste

Slice round steak across the grain to ¼ inch thick. (Have the butcher do it for you and ask him also to run it through his tenderizer twice.) Trim off fat and tough fibers. (Simmer them for soup stock, which has nothing to do with this recipe.) Pound the lean with a meat mallet until it is very thin but still holds together well. Cut into pieces easily handled with a tong at the grill. Dip each piece into the sauce. Pile into a dish. Allow to marinate for at least 1 hour, turning occasionally so all will marinate evenly. Barbecue on a charcoal grill or in the oven. Brown lightly. Do not overcook. The pieces should be juicy but cooked. Serve with brown rice, a green vegetable, and a tossed salad plus dessert and beverage for a festive meal.

One pound serves 4, 187 Calories, 26.2 g. protein, no fiber each.

Beef Stroganoff
(For a crowd)

Brown, drain fat, and set aside:

    2 pounds lean hamburger

Slice across the grain into ¼-inch-thick finger length strips

    2 pounds sirloin tips or round steak

In a paper or plastic bag combine:

¼ c. flour	1 tsp. salt
dash of pepper	¼ tsp. paprika

Toss the steak strips a few at a time into the flour mix until all are floured.
Brown the floured strips in:
    ¼ c. butter (or more if needed)
Remove the meat. Replace in skillet with:
    2 large white onions sliced thin
    1½ pound mushrooms sliced

Saute onions and mushrooms 3 to 5 minutes. Return browned hamburger and browned steak to the skillet with the onions and mushrooms. Add:
    1 bunch chopped green onions
    5 ten-oz. cans cream of mushroom soup
  1½ c. water
    Dash of garlic powder
    2 tsp. salt
    pepper to taste

Cover and simmer until meat is tender—1 to 1½ hours. Just before serving add 12 oz. sour cream

Serve over wide noodles prepared according to instructions on package. To serve 20 use 1 lb., 4 oz. noodles. Yields 20 servings, 389 Calories, 25 g. protein, 0.77 g. fiber each with noodles; 110 Calories, 3.6 g. protein, 0.2 g. fiber less without.

Liver and Onions
(For beef or calves liver)*

Slice 1 pound liver about ⅜ inch thick
Rinse liver to remove excess blood
Blot excess moisture
Combine in a bag:
    ¼ c. flour
    ½ tsp. salt
     Dash of paprika
Drop slices into seasoned flour
Shake until coated

---

*Pork liver is more nutritious and usually much cheaper than beef or calves liver, but it is also stronger flavored and requires thorough cooking. It usually gets tough when prepared this way.

Heat in a skillet

¼ c. fat (oil, bacon drippings)

Arrange coated slices of liver in the hot fat (sizzling but not burning). Fry until moisture appears on the top of the slices and the under side is golden brown. Turn, salt lightly, and brown the other side. *Do not overcook.* Overcooked liver is tough.

Remove the fried liver to a hot platter and place in a warm oven. Drain all the fat possible from the skillet, leaving the browned crumbs of flour and liver.

Slice thin and place in the skillet:

2 large onions (about 1½ pounds)

¼ c. water

½ tsp. salt

Cover tightly and steam, stirring frequently, until onions are clear and lightly browned. Add more water if necessary. All the water should be evaporated when the onions are done. Pile cooked onions on the liver slices and serve. Crisp bacon makes a tasty addition. Liver alone makes 5 servings, 208 Calories, 24 g. protein each. With onions 5 servings provide 260 Calories, 26 g. protein, 0.82 g. fiber each. Each medium slice crisp bacon adds about 45 Calories, 1.8 g. protein.

Liver in Sour Sauce
(For pork liver especially)

Slice, coat, and fry liver as for liver and onions except that slices should be cut into 2-inch or so lengths. When liver is all fried, drain off excess fat, leaving about 3 Tbsp. visible fat. To the liver and fat add:

2 c. chopped onions

¼ c. flour (use any leftover seasoned flour for part of this)

Brown the flour and cook the onions, stirring constantly. Add:

2½ c. milk

Cook, stirring constantly until the sauce is thick. Add

2 Tbsp. vinegar, or vinegar to taste

Serve over crisp toast or mashed potatoes. Serves 5, 294 Calories, 25 g. protein, 0.4 g. fiber each.

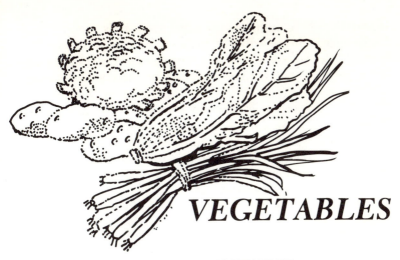

VEGETABLES

SAUCES FOR VEGETABLES

Sauces for Vegetables

Basic White Sauces

Proportions for	fat	flour	milk	salt	yield	use
Thin white sauce	1 Tbsp.	1 Tbsp.	1 cup	¼ tsp.	1 cup	cream soups
Medium white sauce	2 Tbsp.	2 Tbsp.	1 cup	¼ tsp.	1 cup	creamed vegetables, cheese sauce, scalloped dishes
Thick white sauce	3-4 Tbsp.	3-4 Tbsp.	1 cup	¼ tsp.	1 cup	croquettes

¼ cup thin white sauce provides 51 Calories, 2.5 g. protein, 0.04 g. fiber, ¼ c. medium white sauce provides 82 Calories, 2.7 g. protein, 0.08 g. fiber, ¼ c. thick white sauce provides 113-144 Calories, 3-3.2 g. protein, 0.13-17 g. fiber.

Cheese Sauce

To 2 cups medium white sauce add 1 cup (4 oz.) grated cheese and stir until cheese is melted. Do not overcook, especially if a natural cheddar cheese is being used (overcooked cheese will get stringy). Processed cheeses are less apt to overcook. Each ¼ c. serving provides 94 Calories, 4.2 g. protein, 0.06 g. fiber when made with cheddar cheese.

Mushroom sauce

Saute 1 cup mushrooms in 4 Tbsp. table fat.
Add 4 Tbsp. flour and stir until bubbly.
Add 2 cups milk, stirring constantly until sauce is thickened.
Add a dash of Worcestershire sauce if desired.
Yields about 2½ cups sauce.
Each ¼ cup sauce provides about 84 Calories, 3 g. protein, 0.14 g. fiber.

Lemon-Butter Sauce

(Good on greens and broccoli for those who can afford the Calories)

Melt 4 Tbsp. table fat. Add 1½ Tbsp. lemon juice. Yields ⅓ cup sauce. Each tablespoon provides 75 Calories and negligible protein and fiber.

Green Vegetables
(General Instructions)

1. Prepare vegetable—wash, peel, shell, or whatever needs to be done.
2. Heat a small amount of water to boiling.
3. Drop vegetable in and *tend carefully* with lid *off* until
   (1) Chlorophyll is redistributed and the vegetable is bright green.
   (2) Volatile acids have escaped. If the acids return to the water, they will cause the vegetable to lose its bright color.
4. When the vegetable is bright green all over, cover and cook further if needed.
5. Serve all the cooking liquid with the vegetable or in beverage, soup, or sauce.

Kale, Spinach, Turnip, Mustard, Wild Greens, and Others
(For highest vitamin E content, pick in the morning
and refrigerate until ready for use)

1. Wash through several waters. If there is danger of worms being present, salt the wash water. Worms will be detached from leaves more readily. Lift leaves from water. Do not pour water off leaves.
2. Remove coarse middle ribs as from kale if desired. Ribs are not very nutritious but may be used if they are tender.
3. Chop with a sharp knife immediately before cooking if leaves are too large for rapid cooking or easy serving. If leaves are small, leave whole.*
4. Place in container for cooking with only the moisture that clings to the leaves from washing. Leave the lid off.
5. Salt lightly—½ to 1 tsp. salt per pound.
6. Toss lightly with a fork as leaves heat. Tend carefully until every leaf is bright green.
7. Turn heat low and continue to cook if desired. Do not allow cooking to continue long enough to change the color of the leaves.

Each 3½ oz. serving provides about 25 to 55 Calories, 3 g. to 6 g. protein, 0.6 to 1.1 g. fiber. Spinach and turnip greens have fewer Calories and less protein, Kale has the higher values. If fat is used for seasoning, add 35 Calories per teaspoonful. Vinegar added for flavor adds only a trace of Calories or protein, lemon juice about 4 Calories per tablespoon and a trace of protein.

Broccoli

1. Select dark green heads. Wash thoroughly, using salted water if there is any probability of worms being present.
2. Cut off heavy stems at the point where head stems branch off.
3. Strip away leaves, chop into serving sizes.

---

*For extra flavor, add chopped onion to taste.

4. Peel the heavy stems by stripping off the tough outer skin. Cut the tender inner portion into strips or chunks that will cook quickly, serve them raw as relishes or in salads, or slice them thin and use them in egg foo yung.
5. Separate the head stems, peeling any tough skin from the bottoms of the stems.
6. Split large stems up to the heads to assure even, quick cooking.
7. Arrange broccoli in cooking pot, stem and leaves in the bottom, the rest standing heads up, stem ends down.
8. Salt lightly, ½ to 1 tsp. salt per pound.
9. Pour in a small amount of hot water (½ to 1 cup is usually enough).
10. Heat quickly, tending carefully with fork or tong, making sure every head gets steamed until it is bright green, but do not leave the heads in the water.
11. When the broccoli is all bright green, turn the heat off, cover the pot, and allow it to continue cooking in its own heat, but be sure it does not overcook. (If it loses its color, it is overcooked.)

Each 3½ oz. serving provides about 26 Calories, 3.1 g. protein, 1.5 g. fiber. If fat is added for seasoning, add 35 Calories per teaspoonful. Broccoli may be combined with cauliflower and baby carrots, each cooked separately, for a beautiful and delicious dish. Broccoli alone or in combination with other vegetables is excellent served with cheese sauce. (See sauces for vegetables.) Each ¼ c. serving of cheese sauce provides 94 Calories, 4.2 g. protein, 0.06 g. fiber.

Seven-Minute Cabbage
1. Wash cabbage. Discard only those leaves which are very coarse or severely damaged, and the core with the bitter portion attached. The dark green outer leaves are more nutritious than the inner white ones.
2. Cut into wedges that will separate into pieces large enough for attractive serving, small enough to be easily handled.

3. Bring a small amount of water to a boil—½ cup is enough for most pans.
4. Drop cabbage wedges into hot water.
5. Salt lightly—½ to 1 tsp. per pound of cabbage.
6. Heat, tending carefully with a fork or tong, until every piece of cabbage is green. (Even the white leaves will take on a green cast.)
7. Serve immediately or cover and allow to cook a few minutes. Do not permit the beautiful green to fade.

Each 3½ oz. serving provides about 14 Calories, 1.4 g. protein, 0.6 g. fiber. If fat is added for seasoning, toss it lightly with the cooked cabbage and add 35 Calories per teaspoonful.

Brussels Sprouts

1. Wash sprouts. Discard very coarse or damaged leaves.
2. Heat a small amount of water to boiling—½ to 1 cup, depending on the amount to be cooked and the size of the pan.
3. Drop the sprouts into the boiling water.
4. Salt lightly—½ to 1 tsp. salt per pound.
5. Tend the sprouts with a fork or tong until every sprout is dark green. Cover and steam until the sprouts are cooked through. Test with a fork. Do not let the bright color fade.

Each 3½ oz. serving provides 36 Calories, 4.2 g. protein, 1.6 g. fiber. If fat is used for seasoning, toss lightly with cooked sprouts and add 35 Calories per tsp.

Asparagus, with Variations

1. Remove portions of the stalk that will not snap easily. Scrub gently with a brush, being certain no earth remains behind a scale.
2. Snap into 1- to 1½-inch pieces *or* snap the lower, less tender parts into pieces and leave the top in about 4-inch spears.
3. Heat ½ to 1 cup water to boiling. Add the less tender

parts first, then the spears. Salt lightly, ½ to 1 tsp. per pound. Tend carefully until all the asparagus is bright green. Turn off heat. Cover and let cook in its own heat a very few minutes before serving.

Each 3½ oz. serving provides 20 Calories, 2.2 g. protein, 0.7 g. fiber. Add 35 Calories for each teaspoon table fat if it is used for seasoning.

"Creamed" Asparagus—Cook asparagus as above in 1 cup of water or more.

For each cup liquid, combine and mix thoroughly:

2 Tbsp. flour

2 Tbsp. soft table fat or 4 Tbsp. heavy cream

When the asparagus is bright green, stir in the flour-fat combination and continue stirring gently with a fork until the sauce is thickened. Season with salt and pepper, if desired. Serve on crisp whole wheat toast.

Each ¼ c. sauce adds 62 Calories, 0.5 g. protein, 0.08 g. fiber. (This is a good way to stretch a little asparagus to serve a lot of flavor.)

Asparagus with Cheese Sauce—Arrange cooked spears of asparagus on a platter or on plates. Pour cheese sauce across the middle of the spears (see "Sauces for Vegetables" for cheese sauce recipe). Each serving of cheese sauce adds 94 Calories, 4.2 g. protein, 0.06 g. fiber.

Cauliflower
(Whole Head)

1. Cut cauliflower head out of green leafy base but retain the base. Wash both head and base, using salt water if worms may be present.
2. Use the whole base or just a few of the leaves in the cooking pot to form a support for the head to keep it out of the water while it steams.
3. Turn the head upside down and split the core into 6 or 8 sections, but do not divide the head. Splitting the core allows for quicker and more even cooking.

4. Bring 1 cup water to a boil. Arrange the leaves or the base of the cauliflower in the bottom of the pan with the head on top. Salt lightly. Allow to steam with the lid off until the leaves are bright green and the flowerets of the head begin to take on a green cast. Cover and continue to steam until the head is tender, removing the lid occasionally to allow any volatile acids that may accumulate to escape. Do not let it lose its green cast. If it turns pink or brown, it has overcooked. Add more boiling water if necessary, but plan to use all you add.
5. Remove the head to a platter or serving bowl. Arrange the green leaves around the head if desired. Otherwise, use them in soup or stew. Serve plain, or seasoned with table fat and garnished with a sprinkling of paprika, *or* drizzle cheese sauce over the head, sprinkle with paprika, and serve.

Plain, each 3½ oz. portion provides 22 Calories, 2.3 g. protein, 1 g. fiber. Add 35 Calories for each teaspoon table fat used *or* 94 Calories, 4.2 g. protein, 0.06 g. fiber for each ¼ c. cheese sauce.

Cauliflower
(Flowerets)

1. Prepare as for whole head, except divide the head into flowerets. Use enough leaves to add color or plan to use them in egg foo yung, as a separate dish, or in soup or stew.
2. Heat a small amount of water to boiling. Add the flowerets. Salt lightly. Tend carefully until all have a green cast. Cover and allow to steam a few minutes until tender. Do not overcook. Serve plain, buttered, or with cheese sauce. Yields are as for whole head.

Snap Green Beans

(Follow the same procedure for wax beans, but they provide less than half the vitamin A value.)

1. Wash the beans. If they have a fibrous string that must be removed, snap the stem end off and pull the string away with it. If there is no string, use a chopping board and a sharp knife. Line up a handful of beans by their stem ends. Cut off those ends and discard. Cut the rest of the beans into 1- to 1½-inch lengths (do not remove the blossom end unless it is necessary to remove the string), *or* leave whole if they are young and tender, *or* cut lengthwise for French style.

2. Bring a small amount of water to a boil. Add the beans. Salt lightly. Tend carefully until all the beans are bright green (or have a greenish cast in the case of wax beans).

3. Turn heat low and allow to simmer until just crisp-tender. Do not overcook. The beans should keep their bright color.

A 3½ oz. serving will provide about 25 Calories, 1.6 g. protein, 1 g. fiber. Add 35 Calories for each teaspoon table fat, bacon, ham drippings, or other fat used as seasoning.

Green Lima Beans

Shell limas. Rinse. Cook as other green beans (except these will take a little longer, and you may want to have smaller servings). A 3½ oz. serving of green limas provides 111 Calories, 7.6 g. protein, 1.8 g. fiber, and vitamin A value comparable with wax beans. Add 35 Calories per teaspoonful if fat is added for seasoning.

Green Soybeans

Place unshelled beans in boiling water for 4 minutes (they may be in a loosely woven cloth bag, a strainer, or still on the stem). Dip into cold water so they can be handled. Press each pod to expel the bean. (Do not try to shell otherwise unless you want trouble.)

Cook as other green beans, but do not add fat. They are already rich in it. Crumble crisp bacon or soy bacon to add flavor (but these also add Calories). 1 slice crisp bacon adds 45 Calories, 2.5 g. protein; 1 Tbsp. soy bacon adds 40 Calories, 3 g. protein. 3½ ounces of the beans served plain provide 118 Calories, 9.8 g. protein, 1.4 g. fiber.

Garden Peas with Variations
(Also called green or English or sweet peas)

1. Shell peas and rinse.
2. Bring a small amount of water to a boil (½ to 1 cup, depending on size of pan and amount of peas to be cooked).
3. Add peas, salt lightly—½ to 1 tsp. salt per pound; heat quickly, tending carefully with a fork until all the peas are bright green. Cover, turn heat to simmer until peas are tender but still keep their color.

A 3½ oz. serving (about ⅔ cup) provides 71 Calories, 5.4 g. protein, and 2 g. fiber without added fat for seasoning. Add 35 Calories for each teaspoon fat if fat is used.

Creamed Peas—Cook peas as above, except with a cup or more water.

For each cup of liquid, combine and mix thoroughly:

2 Tbsp. flour

2 Tbsp. soft table fat or 4 Tbsp. heavy cream

When peas are tender, stir in fat-flour mixture and continue stirring gently until sauce is thickened. Season with salt and pepper, if desired, to taste. Each ¼ c. serving sauce adds 62 Calories, 0.5 g. protein. 0.08 g. fiber.

Creamed Peas and New Potatoes—Scrub new potatoes. Cut into pieces about 1 inch in diameter or use small potatoes. Cook covered in lightly salted water. When the potatoes are beginning to be tender, add the peas. Leave the lid off until all the peas are bright green. Cover and cook until the potatoes and the peas are tender. Prepare sauce as for Creamed Peas. Nutritive values will vary with the proportion of peas and potatoes. If there are about equal weights of each, a 3½ oz. serving (drained weight) plus ¼ c. sauce (about a ⅔ c. serving) will provide 130 Calories, 4.1 g. protein, 1.33 g. fiber. A chopped green onion added with the peas is delicious.

Sugar or Chinese Sweet Peas
(Peas with edible pods)

Wash pods. Remove coarse stems. Cook as green beans. Nutritive information not available. (See also recipes for Oriental or Wok cookery.)

ROOT VEGETABLES AND TUBERS

Beets with Variations

Method I:

Scrub beets. Leave about 3 inches of stem and all of root intact. Cover with boiling water. Cover and cook until tender. Cool and slip skins off. Slice or dice. Salt lightly. Reheat and serve with or without butter.

Method II:

Peel beets. Slice or chop as desired. Salt lightly. Cook in a small amount of water until tender. Add a few drops of vinegar or lemon juice if beets begin to lose their color. Serve with or without butter.

A 3½ oz. serving, plain, provides 32 Calories, 1.1 g. protein, 0.8 g. fiber. Add 35 Calories per teaspoon fat used.

Harvard Beets—Combine and cook until thickened:

    ¼ c. vinegar
    ¾ c. beet stock (liquid from beets)
    Salt to taste
    1 Tbsp. cornstarch
    2 Tbsp. sugar or 1⅓ Tbsp. honey

Add 1 Tbsp. table fat (or more) if desired.

Add cooked beets (about 1 pound as purchased) and heat through. Yields 4 servings, 58 Calories, negligible protein or fiber plus the beets for a total of 90 Calories, 0.3 g. protein, 0.2 g. fiber each with 1 Tbsp. fat.

Beet Pickles—The easy way is to save the vinegar solution from sweet pickles, heat it to boiling, and drop small whole or sliced beets in. Allow to stand several hours before using. If sweet pickle vinegar is not available combine:

 ½ c. water from cooking the beets
 ½ c. vinegar
 1 Tbsp. brown sugar
 ¼ tsp. salt
 1 tsp. pickling spices

Heat to boiling and drop 2 cups small whole or sliced beets in. Allow to stand several hours before using. ¼ c. serving provides 40 Calories, 0.9 g. protein, 0.68 g. fiber.

Leftover beet pickle juice may be diluted with beet stock and thickened with cornstarch to form the sauce for Harvard beets. Use equal amounts of beet stock and pickle juice with 1 Tbsp. cornstarch per cup.

Carrots with Variations

1. Scrub carrots, remove stems and blemishes, and peel thinly if desired. Carrot skins do not contribute large quantities of minerals as potato skins do and so may be discarded if doing so increases the desirability of the food.
2. Cut into lengthwise pieces, crosswise slices, or leave whole as desired.
3. Heat a small amount of water to boiling and add carrots. Salt lightly—½ to 1 tsp. salt per pound. Cover tightly and bring to a boil. Turn heat low and simmer until carrots are crisp tender. Serve with or without butter or other fat. 3½ oz. provide 42 Calories, 1.1 g. protein, 1 g. fiber without fat. Add 35 Calories for each teaspoon fat used.

Peas and Carrots—Combine cooked sliced carrots with cooked peas with or without butter or other fat. A good way to use leftovers.

Parsley or Mint Carrots—Add finely chopped parsley or mint to carrots before serving. Adds color and flavor without adding many Calories.

Serve with Lemon-Butter Sauce (see Sauces for Vegetables).

Glazed Carrots (good, but watch those Calories)
Combine and bring to a boil:

⅓ c. brown sugar
3 Tbsp. table fat
¼ c. carrot stock (water drained from cooking carrots)

Pour over 8 medium cooked carrots (1 pound as purchased) cut into strips lengthwise, or 1 pound smaller carrots left whole, in a skillet or baking dish. If in a skillet, heat, turning frequently until carrots are glazed. If in a baking dish, bake at 375 F. for about 20 minutes, basting frequently with the syrup. Yields 4 servings, 185 Calories, 1.1 g. protein, 1 g. fiber each; or 6 servings, 124 Calories, 0.7 g. protein, 0.67 g. fiber each.

Parsnips

Prepare and cook as carrots, with the same variations. A 3½ oz. serving without fat provides 66 Calories, 1.5 g. protein and 2 g. fiber. Add 35 Calories for each teaspoon fat.

Sweet Potatoes with Variations

Baked Sweet Potatoes—Scrub potatoes. Remove blemishes. Brush with table fat. Arrange on tray or rack. Bake in a hot (400 F.) oven until potatoes soften. Time will vary with the size of the potatoes; small potatoes take about 30 minutes, large ones up to 1 hour. A 3½ oz. serving without seasoning fat provides about 140 Calories, 2.1 g. protein, 0.9 g. fiber (1 pound as purchased serves 4—3½ oz. servings).

Boiled Sweet Potatoes—Scrub potatoes. Remove blemishes. Cook in a small amount of boiling water in a pot with a tight fitting lid until tender. Watch that it does not boil dry. Serve whole, cut into pieces, or mashed and seasoned with a small amount of salt and table fat. They may be mashed, seasoned, placed in a greased baking dish, topped with marshmallows, and baked until the marshmallows are lightly browned. Alone the potatoes provide 114 Calories, 1.7 g. protein, 0.7 g. fiber per 3½ oz. serving. Each teaspoon fat adds 35 Calories, each regular marshmallow adds 23 Calories and 0.1 g. protein.

Candied Sweet Potatoes (tastes good, but watch those Calories)
    Boil or bake sweet potatoes as directed above. Cut into serving sizes. Arrange in a skillet or baking dish.
Combine and bring to a boil:
    ⅓ c. brown sugar
    3 Tbsp. table fat
    ¼ c. sweet potato stock (water from cooking potatoes) or fresh water
If in a skillet, add the syrup and cook, turning frequently until potatoes are glazed and heated through. If in a baking dish, place in a 375 F. oven and bake, basting frequently, until potatoes are glazed and heated through—20 to 30 minutes. Yields 4 servings, 258 Calories, 1.7 g. protein, 0.7 g. fiber each *or* 6 servings, 172 Calories, 1.1 g. protein, 0.47 g. fiber each.

Potatoes with Variations

Scrub potatoes thoroughly (a nylon pot scrubber will remove dirt and the coarsest fiber without disturbing the minerals and other nutrients). Remove blemishes, green spots, remains of sprouts, and any dark streaks inside the potatoes. Green spots and sprouts have a high concentration of solanine (poison) and dark streaks may be dangerous for pregnant mothers. Properly prepared, potatoes are an excellent food.

Boiled potatoes—Cut the clean potatoes into pieces that will cook quickly. Select a pot with a tight fitting lid. Bring a small amount of water to boil. Add the potatoes. Salt lightly. Cover tightly and return to boiling. Turn heat to simmer and continue cooking until potatoes are tender. Serve with or without added fat. A 3½ oz. serving (1 small to medium potato) provides about 75 Calories, 2.1 g. protein, 0.5 g. fiber* without added fat.

---

*Fiber values will be higher than those given if skins are eaten as suggested.

Potatoes cooked in a small amount of water are especially good served with the water in which they were cooked seasoned with a small amount of table fat. Each individual may mash his/her serving slightly and use the water as a sauce, or the whole pot full may be mashed slightly in the water before serving. 1 teaspoon table fat will add flavor to 3 or 4 servings this way (1 pound potatoes) while adding about 9 Calories per serving. Those who can afford it may add more fat to their serving at the rate of 35 Calories per teaspoonful.

If the potatoes are drained, save the water for soups or bread baking or for reheating leftover potatoes.

If the potatoes become darkened from overcooking or the nature of the cooking water, add a bit of cream of tartar, vinegar, or lemon juice to restore whiteness.

Mashed potatoes, midwestern style—Boil potatoes as above. Drain, reserving the water. Mash thoroughly or whip in an electric mixer. Combine ⅓ c. dry milk and 1 tsp. table fat with each cup potato water to be used to moisten the potatoes, or use whole milk. Nutrients will vary with the richness of the milk and the amount of table fat used. On the average, a ½ cup serving provides 100 Calories, 2.2 g. protein, 0.4 g. fiber.

Potatoes and parsley or kale (also green beans)—Prepare and boil potatoes as for boiled potatoes except add ¼ c. chopped onion to 1 pound potatoes. Just before the potatoes are tender, add ½ pound chopped kale or parsley or green beans (more or less, according to taste and supply). Cook with the lid off until the green vegetable is bright green. Cover and cook longer if desired. Do not let the bright green color fade. Season with 1 tsp. table fat (or more if desired) and salt to taste. Serve liquid and all. Yields 4 servings, about 125 Calories, 4.4 g. protein, 2.2 g. fiber each with ½ lb. green vegetable and 1 tsp. fat. (Serve with a cheese plate, apple-celery-nut salad, whole wheat bread and butter for a delightful summer meal.)

Potato and kale or parsley soup—Prepare and cook potatoes, onions, and kale or parsley as above, but dice the potatoes and use enough water to cover them for cooking. When potatoes are tender and the green vegetable cooked, add an equal amount of milk, and salt to taste. Heat but *do not boil.* If it boils it will curdle. (Curdling hurts only the appearance, so don't throw it away if it does boil.) Each cup of soup provides about 155 Calories, 7.4 g. protein, 1.47 g. fiber when made with whole milk, 115 Calories when made with skim.

One pound potatoes, ½ pound kale or parsley, and 1 quart milk yields 8 cups soup. Allow more than one cup for hearty eaters in the family.

This is a good way to use leftover potatoes, even baked ones. Just dice them, skin and all, add onion and water, and proceed as above.

Serve with cheese, crackers, or whole wheat toast, carrot sticks, and fruit for a hearty nutritious lunch.

Potato soup—Omit green vegetable. You still have a tasty soup.

Baked potatoes—Scrub thoroughly. Remove blemishes, green spots, sprouts, etc. If there are no blemishes to remove, prick the skin in several places to allow steam to escape. Brush skins with table fat or wrap in aluminum foil. Arrange on baking sheet or rack and bake in a hot oven (400 F.) until the potatoes feel soft when pinched, about 1 hour for medium large potatoes. 1 potato (3 to a pound as purchased) provides about 100 Calories, 3 g. protein, 0.6 g. fiber without fat. 1 tsp. table fat adds 35 Calories, 1 Tbsp. commercial sour cream adds about 25 Calories.

For attractive service, cut a cross in the top of each potato. Hold the potato with a towel or hot pad and squeeze to break up the inside of the potato without disturbing the shell. Top with 1 tsp. table fat and a dash of paprika. Garnish with a sprig of parsley. Nutrients are as for baked potato with 1 tsp. fat.

Twice baked potatoes—Choose large potatoes. Prepare and bake as above. Split each potato in two down the middle lengthwise. Scoop out the potato leaving 2 half shells intact. Mash and season the potato as for mashed potatoes, midwestern style, and return them to the shells. Return to the oven and heat until the top is lightly browned. Garnish with paprika and parsley and serve. (You may sprinkle with grated cheese before returning potato to the oven and bake until the cheese melts.) Calories and other nutrients are a little more than for mashed potatoes.

Scalloped potatoes (old-fashioned)

1. Grease a baking dish 7½x12x2 inches or a 2-quart casserole.
2. Prepare by scrubbing, etc., then slice very thin:
   6 medium (2 lb.) potatoes
3. Place half the potato slices in the baking dish. Sprinkle with
   ½ tsp. salt
   2 Tbsp. flour
   Dash of pepper, if desired
   1 Tbsp. minced onion
4. Spread the rest of the potato slices on top and sprinkle with
   ½ tsp. salt
5. Heat together and pour over the potatoes in the baking dish:
   3 c. whole milk
   1 Tbsp. table fat
6. Cover and bake at 375 F. for 50 minutes. Uncover and complete baking until potatoes are tender and a delicately brown crust forms on top. Yields 8 servings, 122 Calories, 4.6 g. protein, 0.69 g. fiber each.

Scalloped potatoes (method II)—Use precooked or fresh sliced potatoes as above. Increase the table fat to 3 Tbsp. and make a thin white sauce of the fat, flour, milk and salt (see Sauces for Vegetables). Arrange half the potato slices in the baking dish. Sprinkle with onion and spread with half the sauce. Top with the rest of the potatoes and the rest of the sauce. Bake as above, except if precooked potatoes are used total baking time will be about 30 minutes. Calories are increased to 147 per serving for 8 servings.

Scalloped potatoes and ham (for a main dish)
Use either method for making scalloped potatoes. Add 1 pound chopped lean ham, one-half of it scattered over each layer of potatoes. Ham drippings may be substituted for table fat. Yields 8 servings, 210 Calories, 16.1 g. protein, 0.69 g. fiber each made the old-fashioned way, 235 Calories made with sauce.

Potatoes au gratin—Substitute 2 cups (½ lb.) grated cheddar cheese for lean ham. Yields 8 servings, 235 Calories, 11.8 g. protein, 0.69 g. fiber made the old-fashioned way, 260 Calories made with sauce.

Potato Salad—Prepare and cook potatoes in their jackets or use leftover potatoes. Flavors blend more perfectly if the potatoes are warm when mixed.
Combine and toss lightly:

   6 c. diced potatoes (2 pounds - 6 medium potatoes)
   4 hard-cooked eggs, diced
  ¼ c. pickle relish *or* chopped sweet pickle
  ½ c. celery (optional)
  ¼ c. minced onion
   2 tsp. salt (omit if potatoes are salted)
  ¼ c. French dressing
   1 c. mayonnaise type *or* boiled dressing (see following recipe)

Refrigerate for several hours for best blending of flavors, but it may be served warm. Garnish with slices of hard-cooked egg, stuffed olives, parsley, and paprika for attractive service. Yields 16 one-half cup servings, 143 Calories, 2.5 g. protein, 0.3 g. fiber each made with mayonnaise type dressing; 94 Calories, 3.2 g. protein made with homemade boiled dressing.

Boiled Dressing (1 cup - 20 Calories, 0.6 g. protein per tablespoon)

Combine and mix well in a heavy saucepan:

1 Tbsp. flour
¾ tsp. salt
¼ tsp. dry mustard
1½ tsp. sugar *or* 1 tsp. honey
Dash paprika
1 egg yolk, well beaten

Gradually stir in:

⅔ c. milk

Cook over low heat, stirring constantly until thick. Remove from heat.

Add and allow to melt:

1 Tbsp. table fat

Blend in:

2 Tbsp. vinegar (more if desired)

Note: Boiled dressing may be used wherever mayonnaise or mayonnaise type dressings are. It may be diluted with fruit juices or milk for fruit salads or combined with whipped or sour cream as desired.

Boiled Vegetable Dinner
A meatless stew with variations

(Quantities and variety of vegetables may vary with taste and supply.)

Combine and cook until nearly tender in a small amount of lightly salted water:

3 medium (1 lb.) potatoes, scrubbed and chunked
3 medium (½ lb.) carrots, scrubbed or peeled, sliced or chunked
1 large or several small (1 lb.) onion wedges

When nearly tender, add and continue to cook

2 cups, more or less, green beans, peas, green soybeans, or similar vegetable

210

Next add and tend until bright green
½ pound of green cabbage wedges, parsley, kale, or
other green
Finally add:
1 quart (2 lb.) whole tomatoes, fresh or canned
2 Tbsp. table fat or more

Other vegetables such as rutabaga, turnips, kohlrabi, cauliflower, broccoli, corn, celery, whatever you have available may be added at appropriate times. In the winter it may all be put into a hearty beef or turkey broth, thickened slightly, and meat returned to it for serving as stew. Omit the table fat if meat is used. Bits of leftover lasagna or other casseroles make good additions.

Serve in bowls with cheese, pickles, whole wheat bread, butter, and milk as accompaniments.

This quantity makes about 12 cups, 100 Calories, 3 g. protein, 1.24 g. fiber each. Allow more than 1 cup per serving for most adults.

Vegetable Soup

For a hearty vegetable soup, dilute the meatless stew above to the desired consistency with liquids drained from vegetables, noodles, etc., that have been retained in the soup jar, with water seasoned at the rate of 1 tsp. salt and 1 Tbsp. table fat per quart (4 cups), *or* with meat or poultry stock made from cooking the bones or from boullion cubes. Nutrients will vary with liquid used.

Borscht Soup

Use grated or diced beets for one of the vegetables in the vegetable soup. Add 1 tablespoon lemon juice or vinegar just before serving if the beets fade or if you prefer the flavor. Top each serving with sour cream if you wish to be authentic and can afford the Calories. Each tablespoon sour cream adds 25 Calories. Borscht is usually made with beef stock.

SOUPS AND SALADS

SOUPS

(See standard recipe books for meat stocks and soups made with them—also many soups not suggested here. See potato variations for potato soups and bean variations for bean soup and chili. See quick breads for noodles to be used in soup.)

Cream of Vegetable Soups

Combine, heat, and serve:
- 2 c. thin white sauce (see Sauces for Vegetables)
- 2 c. vegetables with cooking water, chopped, blended, or sieved, as you choose. Include 1 onion slice with whatever vegetable is chosen. Some suggested ones are celery, green peas or beans, spinach, carrots, onions, corn.

Season as desired, e.g. parsley, fresh chopped or flaked, bay leaf, celery leaves or seed, spices—use your imagination. Yields 4 cups, Calories varying but around 125, protein about 6 grams, fiber near 0.14 g. per cup when sauce is made with skim milk, 165 Calories if whole milk is used.

Cream of Tomato Soup

Combine and heat to boiling:
- 2 c. tomatoes, fresh or canned
- 1 Tbsp. chopped onion or onion flakes

Blend or sieve if you want a smooth soup.
Prepare and have boiling hot
    2 c. thin white sauce*
Just before serving, slowly pour the tomatoes *into the sauce* or milk, stirring constantly. (If you pour the sauce or milk into the tomatoes, it will curdle.) Yields 4 cups soup, about 114 Calories, 5.5 g. protein, 0.33 g. fiber each when sauce made with skim milk is used, 154 Calories when sauce with whole milk is used, 30 Calories less per cup if plain milk and only 1 Tbsp. fat is used.

Salsify Soup
(mock oyster soup)

Select salsify that has been stored or left in the ground after maturity, preferably through a frost. (Freshly grown salsify has its carbohydrates as inulin which is of doubtful value as food. During storage the inulin turns to sugar producing a more valuable and more tasty food.) Scrub the salsify and remove blemishes. Slice. Cook in water to cover, salted lightly, until tender. For ½ lb. (3 medium roots) add and heat but do not boil:
    4 cups milk
    1 Tbsp. table fat
    Salt and pepper to taste
Yields 4 servings, 145 Calories, 10.4 g. protein, 1 g. fiber each when made with skim milk, 220 Calories when made with whole milk.

Real Oyster Stew (Soup)

Heat to sizzling in a heavy three-quart pot
    4 Tbsp. butter
Pick over (no shells or pearls) and add:
    1 pint (2 c.) fresh oysters with their liquor
    1 tsp. onion juice or finely minced onion (optional)

---

*You may use plain milk and only 1 Tbsp. fat or less, but it is harder to keep the soup from curdling.

213

Heat gently just until the edges of the oysters curl. Do not overcook or they will be tough!
Combine and scald but do not boil:

  1 c. table cream
  2½ c. whole milk
  ½ c. chicken, turkey, *or* clam broth
  1 tsp. salt, or to taste
  Pepper to taste

Combine oysters and milk mixture and heat but do not boil. Boiling produces tough oysters and curdled soup. Yields 6 cups, 270 Calories, 12 g. protein each. (Using half-and-half cream would reduce Calories to 240, using only whole milk, no cream, would reduce them to 213, *or* using skim milk would reduce Calories to 170 per cup, each change adding a bit of protein and reducing the richness of the soup. Or you may increase the proportion of milk to oysters for a less expensive and still delicious dish.)

Chunky Tomato-Onion Soup

Combine:

  4 cups whole tomatoes, fresh peeled or canned
  1 medium onion cut into wedges
  1 tsp. salt
  1 tsp. celery seed (optional)
  1 Tbsp. table fat (or more)

Simmer until onions are clear and tender. Serve. Yields 4 servings, 94 Calories, 3.1 g. protein, 1.2 g. fiber each when made with 1 Tbsp. fat. Add 100 Calories for each additional tablespoon fat used.

SALADS

Standard cookbooks and materials from Government Extension Services provide recipes and suggestions for salads and dressings of nearly unlimited variety. Only a few can be included here.

Garden Salad

Wash 1 pound leaf lettuce or other green (e.g. dandelions) carefully, using several waters (salt if worms may be present) lifting the leaves from the water, not pouring the water off the greens. Drain and blot thoroughly. Chop or tear into sizes easily handled with a fork.* Toss lightly with dressing made by combining:

2 Tbsp. sugar *or* 1⅓ Tbsp. honey or less

1 Tbsp. vinegar *or* lemon juice

4 Tbsp. sour cream *or* light whipping cream *or* mayonnaise type salad dressing *or* real mayonnaise.

Beat until smooth. If cream is used, it may be whipped before being combined with other ingredients.

Yields 6 servings, 49 Calories, 2.2 g. protein, 0.5 g. fiber each made with commercial sour cream, 61 Calories with light whipping cream, 78 Calories, 1 g. protein made with mayonnaise type salad dressing, 98 Calories made with real mayonnaise.

Coleslaw

Substitute 1 pound finely shredded cabbage for the lettuce or greens of the garden salad. Other vegetables such as chopped onion, slivers of green or red sweet pepper, red cabbage, shredded carrots, or tomato chunks may be substituted for some of the cabbage. Yield will be about the same as for garden salad with maybe 4 or 5 extra Calories for the cabbage.

Cabbage-Pineapple Salad

Add to the coleslaw

1 cup pineapple (diced or crushed, juice pack, drained)

Pineapple juice may be substituted for vinegar or lemon juice in the dressing. Adds 10 Calories per serving to coleslaw yields.

---

*Other garden vegetables as radishes, green onions, parsley may be substituted for some of the lettuce.

Tossed Salad

(Any of a variety of combinations of fresh, crisp vegetables and fruits are suitable. Here are suggested proportions for only one such combination.)

Wash, drain, or blot dry and tear into easily handled pieces
    2 large leaves crisp lettuce (3½ oz.)

Add:
    ½ of a medium tomato, washed and chunked *or* 3 cherry tomatoes halved
    2 sweet pepper rings (2 oz.) whole or chunked
    1 slice of a medium onion separated into rings *or* 2 green onions in ½-inch pieces *or* onion powder
    1 Tbsp. chopped parsley

Just before serving toss with
    salt (to taste) and
    dash of garlic powder

Yields 2 large servings, 35 Calories, 2 g. protein, 1.1 g. fiber each without dressing. Oil and vinegar type dressings (French, Italian, etc.) add 65 Calories per tablespoon, bleu cheese dressing adds 75 Calories, thousand island 80, real mayonnaise 100, and mayonnaise type commercial dressings 70 Calories per tablespoon. With salt, onion, and garlic seasoning, dressings are not necessary.

Other vegetables and fruits suitable for tossed salads are grated carrots, radish slices, celery slices or chunks, avocado pieces, broccoli stems (peeled and chunked), cabbage hearts or wedges, cauliflowerettes, diced apples, cucumbers with fluted skins* sliced or diced, and greens such as water cress, endive, tender spinach, dandelion leaves and a variety of lettuces.

Chef's Salad

To the basic tossed salad add slivers of cheese, ham, sliced or quartered hard-cooked eggs, crisp bacon or soya bacon, cooked and drained green soybeans, peas, or other legumes,

---

*Flute cucumbers by repeatedly drawing a fork down the unpeeled cucumber lengthwise until the entire skin area is fluted. Slice crosswise and arrange on a relish tray or use in tossed salad.

chunks of tuna, salmon, smoked fish, chicken, or turkey or any other protein foods to make it a main dish salad. Calories and protein will vary with foods chosen and salad dressing used. Dressings are as listed with the tossed salad. In general, 1 oz. cheese provides 100 to 113 Calories, 7.1 g. protein; 1 oz. lean ham about 50 Calories, 5.6 g. protein; 1 oz. chicken (roasted and skinned) about 55 Calories, 9.2 g. protein; 1 oz. tuna 36 Calories (water packed), 56 (oil packed), 8 g. protein; ½ cup cooked peas 57 Calories, 4.5 g. protein; ½ cup cooked soybeans 95 Calories, 7.8 g. protein; 1 large egg 80 Calories, 6 g. protein; 1 Tbsp. soya bacon 40 Calories, 3 g. protein.

Carrot Raisin Salad

Combine and toss lightly:
- 3 c. carrots peeled,* grated, and piled lightly (about 1 lb. as purchased)
- 3 Tbsp. raisins (more or less)
- 3 Tbsp. mayonnaise type salad dressing *or* 3 Tbsp. lemon juice

Dash of salt

Yields 6 servings, 77 Calories, 0.8 g. protein, 0.7 g. fiber each with salad dressing, 44 Calories with lemon juice. 1 tsp. honey added to lemon juice adds 4 Calories per serving.

---

*Unpeeled carrots may turn dark and often have an earthy flavor. Use them unpeeled if you like. Peeling carrots does not destroy nutritive values as peeling potatoes does.

Apple-Celery-Nut-Salad
(Waldorf Salad)

Combine and toss lightly:

2 c. tart apples (2 medium), cored (but not peeled) and chopped*

1 c. celery chopped (2 large sticks)

3 Tbsp. mayonnaise type salad dressing

3 Tbsp. chopped walnuts (more or less—optional)

Yields 6 servings, 90 Calories, 1.1 g. protein, 0.40 g. fiber each with nuts, 65 Calories, .2 g. protein, 0.33 g. fiber each without nuts. Calories may be reduced 10 per serving by using 2 Tbsp. salad dressing and 1 Tbsp. milk.

Variations of this salad include the addition of other fruits such as seeded tokay grapes, avocado, pineapple, pears, and other nuts such as pecans and black walnuts, the addition of marshmallows, etc. Use your imagination. You may substitute sweetened whipped cream for the salad dressing. There will actually be fewer Calories if an equal amount of cream is used, still fewer if whipped topping is used.

Guacamole Salad
(may also be used as a dip)

Mash together or blend:

2 large peeled and diced avocados (1¼ lb.)

1 large ripe, peeled, and diced tomato (½ lb.)

Salt to taste

2 Tbsp. minced onion

1 tsp. lemon juice

Serve on lettuce bed, inside a red sweet pepper ring if available.

Yields 4 servings, 200 Calories, 3.1 g. protein, 2.7 g. fiber each without pepper, or 6 servings, 132 Calories, 2.1 g. protein, 1.8 g. fiber each. (Avocado is a high-Calorie food. Values calculated on California mid- and late-winter fruit.)

---

*If apples that darken easily are used, dip into salted water as they are chopped, drain immediately, and use in the salad.

MAIN DISH SALADS

Kidney Bean Salad

Combine and toss lightly:
  1½ c. cooked, drained kidney beans (1 14-oz. can)
  1 c. shredded cabbage
  ½ c. shredded carrots
  1 Tbsp. minced onion
  2 Tbsp. diced green pepper
  Salt and pepper to taste
  French dressing to moisten (see following recipe)
Yields 4 servings, 101 Calories, 6.3 g. protein, 1.3 g. fiber
each without dressing. Add 65 Calories for each tablespoon
commercial French dressing used (16 Calories per serving) or
see recipe below for homemade dressing values.

Homemade French dressing

Combine in a bottle or jar:
  1 clove garlic, sliced (optional)
  ¼ c. vinegar or lemon juice
  2 Tbsp. catsup (optional)*
  ½ c. salad oil
  ¼ tsp. dry mustard
  ½ tsp. paprika
  ⅛ tsp. or less pepper
  ¾ tsp. salt
  1 to 3 tsp. sugar or honey as desired
Shake vigorously each time dressing is used. Yields 15 Tbsp.
dressing, 60 Calories per tablespoon

---

*Use 2 extra tablespoons lemon juice if no catsup.

Green Peas, Cheese, and Pickle Salad

(Also green beans, soybeans, and limas, fresh or leftover)
Combine and toss lightly:

2 c. cooked, drained, and chilled peas or other vegetables

1 oz. cheddar cheese chunked

2 Tbsp. sweet pickle relish *or* chopped sweet pickles

2 tsp. minced onion

½ c. diced celery (optional)

2 Tbsp. mayonnaise type salad dressing

Yields 4 servings, 130 Calories, 6.8 g. protein, 1 g. fiber each when made with peas; 168 Calories, 12.8 g. protein, 2.53 g. fiber with green limas; 174 Calories, 14.7 g. protein, 2.19 g. fiber made with green soybeans; and 89 Calories, 2.8 g. protein, 0.72 g. fiber each when made with green snap beans. Homemade boiled dressing (see potato salad recipe) would reduce Calories by 25 and increase protein by 0.6 g. per serving.

Serve in a lettuce cup, garnished with parsley and tomato wedges with corn on the cob or scalloped potatoes for the major portion of a good meal. Baked custard would be a good choice for dessert.

Chicken (Turkey, Fish, or Meat) Salad

Combine and toss lightly:

1½ c. diced cooked chicken (about ½ lb.), *or* turkey, *or* tuna, etc.

2 Tbsp. French dressing

1 Tbsp. vinegar, lemon juice, or sweet pickle vinegar

Allow the meat to marinate while preparing other ingredients (for an hour if possible).
Add and toss lightly:

2 hard-cooked eggs, diced

¼ c. sweet pickle relish *or* chopped sweet pickles

1 Tbsp. minced onion

1 c. diced celery

¼ c. mayonnaise type salad dressing *or* boiled dressing
—may be half dressing and half sour cream.

2 Tbsp. sweet pepper or pimiento, chopped (optional)

Serve in a lettuce cup or on tomato petals* on a lettuce leaf. Garnish with parsley and paprika. With cooked green peas, whole wheat bread or bun, butter and cheese apple crisp it makes a lunch fit for a celebration. Yields 4 servings, 270 Calories, 19.2 g. protein, 0.15 g. fiber each made with chicken and mayonnaise type dressing; 252 Calories, 15.4 g. protein made with 1 can (6½ oz.) oil-packed, drained tuna; 230 Calories, 17.1 g. protein when made with water-packed tuna. Calories may be reduced by 50 per serving if boiled dressing is used.

Cottage Cheese-Green Pepper Salad

Combine and mix:

    2 cups creamed cottage cheese
    ½ cup chopped sweet pepper (1 medium pod) more or
       less
    1 Tbsp. minced onion
    2 Tbsp. mayonnaise type dressing

Serve in a lettuce cup or on tomato petals on a lettuce leaf. Garnish with parsley and paprika. Serve with a green vegetable, whole wheat bread and butter, milk, and a fruit dessert for a quick and excellent lunch. Yields 4 servings, 170 Calories, 17 g. protein, 1 g. fiber each without lettuce or tomato.

Fruit Plate

(Use your imagination. Here is one suggestion.)

Arrange lettuce leaves to cover dinner plate.

Place ⅓ c. cottage cheese in the center of the plate. Top it with

---

*Tomato petals are made by removing the stem scar and cutting the tomato nearly through into 6 or 8 sections. Be sure that the bottom remains whole so the petals are attached to each other when they open up. Salt lightly and fill with salad mixture.

½ tsp. mayonnaise type salad dressing topped with
½ a maraschino cherry, drained and blotted.

Around the cheese arrange any fruits available. Here is a suggestion:

1 banana, split lengthwise, placed cut side down, circling the cheese
1 pineapple ring centered with
1 moisturized prune. Two more prunes placed for accents on the plate.
1 half sphere of alternating red apple wedges and grapefruit sections placed between the tips of the banana slices.
1 cluster of grapes placed at the other tip of the banana or alongside.

Serve with peanut butter and whole wheat crackers or bread and milk for a complete meal. Provide extra fruit and cheese for hearty eaters. As described, each plate offers about 344 Calories, 15.5 g. protein, 2.9 g. fiber without accompaniments.

GELATIN SALADS

Cranberry Relish Salad

Grind together:

4 c. cranberries (1 lb.) rinsed and stemmed
2 medium oranges, skin and all, seeds removed
¼ c. walnuts (optional)

Add and mix

⅔ c. honey

Allow the fruit and honey mixture to stand while preparing the gelatin. For best blending of flavors, it should stand several hours.

Combine:

3 oz. raspberry flavored gelatin (½ c.)
3 oz. cherry flavored gelatin (½ c.)
1 pkg. unflavored gelatin softened in
¼ c. water

Add and stir until dissolved:
  2 c. boiling water
Add and mix:
  2 c. cold water or ice and water

Add the fruit and honey mixture. Mix thoroughly. Place in serving dish, mold or molds. Chill until set. If molded, submerge molds quickly in hot water. Turn upside down in hands for individual molds or on a plate for a large mold. Place on a cold tray, return to refrigerator and allow to firm up before placing on lettuce bed and garnishing with mayonnaise type salad dressing for serving. Yields 22 servings, 76 Calories, 1.2 g. protein, 0.37 g. fiber each without salad dressing, lettuce, or nuts. Add 10 Calories, 0.2 g. protein, 0.03 g. fiber if nuts are used, 5 Calories, .3 g. protein, .2 g. fiber for lettuce, 20 to 25 Calories per tsp. salad dressing.

Carrot Pineapple Salad

Combine and stir until dissolved:
  6 oz. (1 c.) orange flavored gelatin*
  2 c. boiling water
Drain into a measuring cup, juice from:
  1 19-oz. can crushed pineapple *or* pineapple chunks
Add ice water or ice to the pineapple juice to make 2 cups. Add the juice and ice to the gelatin mixture. Stir until thoroughly mixed. Add the drained pineapple. Mix. Add:
  1 pound carrots (3 large) peeled and grated

Pour into serving dish or mold(s) and chill until set. (I mix mine in a baking dish 9x13x2 inches.) If in molds, unmold as for cranberry relish salad. If made in a baking dish, cut and serve on beds of lettuce, with or without salad dressing. Serves 18, 63 Calories, 1.3 g. protein, 0.34 g. fiber each without dressing or lettuce.

---

*For more nutrition and fewer Calories substitute unflavored gelatin and real orange juice. Soften 2 packages (2 Tbsp.) unflavored gelatin in 2 Tbsp. cold water. Dissolve in 1 c. boiling water. Add ¾ c. (6 oz.) frozen concentrated orange juice mixed with juice drained from pineapple and water to make 3 cups liquid. Calories are reduced by 12 per serving, protein increased slightly. Costs less.

Perfection Salad

Soften:
- 2 Tbsp. plain gelatin in
- ¼ c. cold water

Add and stir until dissolved:
- 2 c. boiling water
- 3 Tbsp. honey *or* ¼ c. sugar
- 1 tsp. salt

Add, mix, and allow to thicken slightly:
- 1½ c. pineapple juice
- Dash of pepper
- Dash of garlic powder

Prepare and combine:
- 2 c. shredded cabbage
- 1½ c. diced celery
- ¼ c. chopped sweet pepper (green or red)
- ½ c. sliced stuffed olives
- ½ c. vinegar (or a combination of vinegar and lemon juice)
- 1 tsp. salt

When gelatin has thickened slightly, fold in vegetables. Pour into molds or a 9x13x2-inch pan. Chill until set. Unmold as for cranberry relish salad or cut and serve on lettuce bed with or without salad dressing. Yields 18 servings, 35 Calories, 1.1 g. protein, 0.43 g. fiber each without dressing or lettuce. (See cranberry relish salad for dressing and lettuce values.)

Tomato Aspic

Measure out 3½ c. tomato juice. Heat 1 cup to boiling. Use the rest cold.

Soften:
- 2 Tbsp. plain gelatin in
- ¼ c. tomato juice

Add and stir until dissolved
- 1 c. boiling tomato juice

Add to dissolved gelatin mix:
- 2¼ c. cold tomato juice
- 2 tsp. minced onion *or* onion juice
- ½ tsp. salt or to taste
- ¼ tsp. celery salt
- Dash of pepper if desired
- 1 Tbsp. Vinegar *or* lemon juice

Pour into 1 quart mold, 9 individual molds, or an 8x8x2-inch pan. Chill until set. Unmold as for cranberry relish salad or cut and serve on lettuce beds with or without dressing. Serves 9, 24 Calories, 2.2 g. protein, 0.19 g. fiber each without lettuce or dressing. (See cranberry relish salad for lettuce and dressing values.) May be made into a ring mold and the center filled with cottage cheese or a meat or fish salad.

BEVERAGES

There are several beverages on the present market designed to replace coffee and tea which contain caffeine. Some are packaged for instant, convenient use. Some are made of cereals, some of cereals with fruit or molasses, some of soya and some of herbs. The cereal with fruit drinks generally average 1 Calorie per ounce and the cereal with molasses ones about 2 Calories per ounce. (Coffee, tea, and some diet drinks average about 1 Calorie per ounce.)

Be cautious with herb teas. Some are dangerous when used indiscriminately. Sassafras, for example, contains saffrole which has been banned as a flavoring agent because it is carcinogenic (causes cancer). Some, like maté and guarana, contain caffeine themselves. Herb teas are frequently medicinal in content. They must be used with skill to be used safely.*

Vegetable juices, including the liquid sometimes drained

Resource Material

R. K. Siegel, "Herbal Intoxication, Psychoactive Effects from Herbal Cigarettes, Tea and Capsules," *Journal of the American Medical Association*, Vol. 236, Aug. 2, 1976, p. 473, abstracted in the *Journal of the American Dietetic Association*, Vol. 69, Nov. 1976, p. 576.

A. B. Segelman, F. P. Segelman, J. Karliner, and R. D. Sofia, "Sassafras and Herb Tea," *ibid.*, p. 477, extracted in JADA, *ibid.*

from cooked or canned vegetables, make interesting beverages. Many of these become especially attractive when combined with tomato juice in the manner of commercial V8 juice. Vegetable juices prepared from most raw vegetables with enzymes undeterred lose vitamins C and E rapidly. They need to be used immediately after preparation or heated to stop enzyme activity. Calories and nutrients vary with the food and its dilution.

Fruit juices are nutritious and delicious. They do, however, often carry a lot of Calories even when not sweetened with honey or sugar. Be aware of the number of Calories involved before you use large amounts if you need to watch your weight. Most fruit punches have far more Calories from sugar than from fruit, and fruit flavored crystals are practically all sugar with just a little flavoring, coloring matter, and sometimes about 30 milligrams vitamin C per glass.

Milk is a beverage with a bonus. Skim or buttermilk has fewer Calories than fruit drinks; it blends with many foods; and its supply of protein is so great that it is classified as a solid food in dietary planning. It is a repository of many needed nutrients.

Water is, after all, the one beverage that is necessary for life and the only one I know that has absolutely no Calories. Use it generously for daily consumption and for entertaining.

Warm Barley Drink

Scatter a thin layer of whole barley in a shallow baking pan. Roast in a 350° F. oven, shaking or stirring frequently, until it is browned to the degree that you like it. Experiment to determine the flavor you prefer. One to 1½ hours of roasting develops a full flavored, amber colored drink.

Cool the roasted grain and grind fine in grinder or blender. Combine 1 tablespoon of the ground grain with each 8 oz. cup of water in a large pot. (The liquid boils up several times its volume. You can put in some oil to stop the foaming, but that adds Calories and changes the flavor.) Bring to a boil. Turn heat low and simmer 10 to 15 minutes. Drain and serve plain or with honey or brown sugar and milk.

One tablespoon barley contains 35 Calories, 0.96 g. protein, 0.09 g. fiber. Varying amounts of these nutrients are in the beverage, depending on the fineness of the grind and the proportion of the solids consumed. It is not likely that the Calorie, protein, or fiber content will be high. Honey adds 22 Calories per teaspoonful, sugar 17. (Solids from lightly browned grain may be used in soups and cereals. Dark browned grain may impart a burned flavor to those foods.)

Small amounts of whole wheat flour, cornmeal, bran, rolled oats, or rye flour may be added when the barley is just browning for a variety of flavors. The finely ground flours will burn if roasted the full time.

Rose Hips

Rose hip teas are popular in some areas. Most commercial ones are combined with other ingredients, sometimes caffeine-containing tea. Watch what you buy. Do not depend on the salesperson for information. Read the label yourself.

The University of Alberta, Edmonton, Alberta, has found that 3 average rose hips contain vitamin C approximately equivalent to that of one medium orange. This nutrient is best retained when the entire fruit is used. The University of Alberta Extension Service has instructions for harvesting, preserving, and using the fruits.

Grape Juice (Communion Wine)

Wash grapes (Concord type preferred). Remove from stems. Crush slightly. Add water to almost cover the grapes.* Simmer until pulp is soft. Strain juice through a cloth pulled tight over a crock or pot. Restrain if you want it perfectly clear. To each gallon of juice add 1 cup sugar or ⅔ cup mild honey *or*

---

*The grapes may be simmered without the addition of water or sugar, but the juice will be quite concentrated in flavor, and the Calories will be as high or higher than with the sweetening suggested.

less, depending on the tartness of the grapes. Reheat to dissolve the sweetener. Cool and serve if the juice is to be used immediately.

The juice may be canned or frozen for preservation.

To freeze—Place in appropriate containers, leaving headspace for expansion, label, and freeze.

To can—Heat the sweetened juice to simmering. Pour into sterilized jars, leaving ⅛ to ¼ inch headspace. Adjust lids. Place in water bath with a rack or cloth beneath the jars and separating them and water to cover them. Bring water to a boil and boil 10 minutes. Remove from water. Complete the seal if the lids are not self-sealing. Cool. Store in a dark, cool place.

Each gallon of juice yields 16 eight-ounce glasses, 130 to 160 Calories, 0.5 g. protein, negligible fiber each. (Calories vary with proportion of water to fruit and amount of sweetening used. Juice without water or sweetening has about 165 Calories per 8-ounce serving.)

A second extraction of juice may be made by covering the grape pulp with water and repeating the process described above.

The pulp may be used to make grape butter. Remove the seeds with a sieve or food mill. Add ¾ to 1 cup sugar to each cup of pulp. Boil until thick and glossy. Pour into hot jelly glasses or jars. If there is more than will be used in a few weeks, seal the jars with regular sealing lids or with melted paraffin. Each tablespoon of the "butter" contains about 55 Calories, 0.1 g. protein, 0.2 g. fiber.

Tomato Juice

Wash ripe tomatoes. Remove blemishes and cores. Cut into pieces and heat to boiling. Simmer just enough to soften tissues. Press through a sieve or food mill to remove skins and seeds. (They may be blended instead, but bits of skins may be objectionable.) Cool and serve or can or freeze for later use. (See USDA or Canadian Extension Service bulletins for instructions.) One teaspoon salt per quart of juice enhances the flavor.

For immediate use, clean tomatoes with blemishes and probably skins removed may be reduced to juice in a blender without heating. With or without heating, nutrients are protected by natural components of the fruit.

Tomato juice averages 45 to 50 Calories, about 2.2 g. protein, 0.48 g. fiber per 8-oz. cup.

Other Fruit Juices

Orange, pineapple, grapefruit, apple, and other fruit juices are generally available frozen, canned, or fresh, or may easily be extracted from fresh fruit. They average 1 to 2 g. protein, 0.25 g. fiber each 8-oz. glass. Grapefruit has 95 Calories, orange juice 110 Calories, apple juice 120 Calories, and pineapple juice 135 Calories per 8 ounces. (Note that some beverage glasses hold twice that much, especially in Texas.) Lemon and lime juices have only 60 to 65 Calories per 8 ounces, but most people want them diluted and sweetened. Undiluted they contain enough acid to damage teeth.

Lemonade or Limeade

May be made in varying dilutions and with varying amount of sweetener. Here is one suggestion.

Boil together:

    1 c. sugar *or* ⅔ c. *mild* flavored honey

    1 c. water

Chill

Prepare 1 cup lemon or lime juice. If from fresh fruit, roll the fruit vigorously until soft before cutting. Cut through the center halfway between the stem and blossom end. Extract the juice with a juicer, or squeeze hard. Most large lemons yield 2 Tbsp. juice. Limes vary with size. Combine the syrup and juice. Dilute with water to make 2 quarts—8 glasses of lemonade, each with 8 ounces of fluid plus extra ice. Drop the skins into the ade for a time before serving to add flavor and use all the juice.

Each glass provides about 105 Calories made with sugar, 94 Calories made with honey, 0.12 g. protein, and a trace of fiber. Only about 8 of these Calories are from the fruit.

(Back on the farm we used to use 1 lemon to a gallon of water, and the men insisted it helped them withstand the heat.)

*Spiced Cider (Nonalcoholic)**
(Special for Hallowe'en or winter evenings)

Served freshly pressed or pasteurized and chilled, cider needs no spices to make it enjoyable. For a cold day when warmth is welcome, spicing may increase the enjoyment, and if the juice is fresh, heating may increase the time that it may be enjoyed.

In a 6- or 8-quart container, gently heat for 20 to 30 minutes:
- 1 gallon sweet cider with a spice bag containing:
- 12 whole cloves
- 3 or 4 sticks of cinnamon bark, each 3 inches long
- ⅛ tsp. nutmeg

Discontinue heating when the spices have flavored the cider to your liking. Brown sugar or honey may be added to taste but is generally not needed. Serves 16 mugs (8 oz.), 113 Calories, 0.2 g. protein, 0.2 g. fiber each without added sweetening.

---

*Cider is juice pressed from uncooked apples. It ferments easily unless pasteurized or otherwise preserved. In Canada it is regularly served in alcoholic form. If fermentation is allowed to proceed undeterred, vinegar results.

Orange Smoothie
(An eggnog for Christmas)

Separate 6 eggs
Beat until frothy:
　6　egg whites
　½ tsp. salt
Gradually beat in:
　½ c. sugar *or* ⅓ c. honey
Beat until stiff and light yellow:
　6　egg yolks
　½ c. sugar *or* ⅓ c. honey
Add and mix well:
　5　c. milk
　6　oz. frozen concentrated orange juice
　2　tsp. lemon juice

When meringue forms shiny peaks, fold into the egg yolk mixture. Blend thoroughly. Pour into punch bowl. Sprinkle with nutmeg and/or grated orange peel. Yields 16 4-oz. punch cups, 106 Calories, 5.4 g. protein, 0.02 g. fiber each when made with skim milk and honey, 136 Calories when made with whole milk and sugar. (High in nutrition but also in Calories, this is more of a food than a beverage. Concentrated orange and lemon juice help to "cook" the egg protein.)

Easy Christmas Punch

Dilute according to directions
　3　6-oz. cans of frozen lemonade
Stir in
　1　15-oz. package frozen strawberries
Just before serving add
　1　quart (32 oz.) ginger ale
Add ice to chill thoroughly.

Yields 24 8-oz. glasses, 85 Calories, negligible protein and fiber per glass, 48 punch cups, 43 Calories per cup.

Carrousel Fruit Punch

Soften
  1 Tbsp. (package) unflavored gelatin in
  2 Tbsp. cold water
Add 1 c. boiling water and stir until gelatin is dissolved
Add:
  1 15-oz. package frozen strawberries*
  1 48-oz. can pineapple juice
  1 6-oz. can frozen orange juice
  1 6-oz. can frozen lime juice
  Water and ice to make 20 cups
Just before serving add
  1 quart ginger ale
Yields 24 8-oz. glasses, 90 Calories, 0.75 g. protein, 0.33 g. fiber each; 48 punch cups, 45 Calories, 0.4 g. protein each.

Rhubarb Thirst Quencher

Select a crock or other nonmetal container that holds 1½ gallons. In it
Combine:
  5 pounds rhubarb (20 cups) cut into 1-inch pieces
  2 sliced lemons
  2 c. sugar *or* 1⅓ c. honey
  Boiling water to cover (about 3 quarts—12 cups)**
Let stand 24 hours, stirring occasionally. Strain and chill. Serve. Yields 16 8-oz. glasses, 32 punch cups, 100 Calories per glass, 50 Calories per cup with sugar; 90 Calories per glass, 45 per punch cup made with honey. Negligible protein and fiber. Only 4 Calories per glass are from fruit.

---

*1 3-oz. package strawberry gelatin mix may be substituted for gelatin and berries—a few less calories and less costly, but also less nutritious.

**You may speed the process by bringing all ingredients to a boil. Strain, chill, and serve. Product will not be the same but will be delicious.

Pineapple Punch

Boil together and cool:
    4 c. sugar *or* 3 c. honey
    6 c. water
Combine:
    4½ c. orange juice
    6 c. lemon juice
    10 c. pineapple juice
Combine syrup, fruit juices, ice, and water to make 5 gallons. Serve with 1 gallon pineapple sherbet floating in balls on the surface.

Yields 192 4-oz. punch cups, 48 Calories, 0.3 g. protein, 0.02 g. fiber each with sherbet; 28 Calories, 0.1 g. protein without sherbet, but made with sugar, 5 Calories per cup less made with honey. Each cup contains about the equivalent of 1 teaspoon sugar above the sugar of the fruit and sherbet.

Warm Fruit Punch

Bring 12 cups water to a boil with a spice bag suspended in it made with:
    8 to 12 whole cloves
    2 to 3 3-inch pieces of cinnamon bark
Allow to simmer until water begins to color and taste spicy. Add
    1½ c. sugar *or* 1 c. honey (more or less to taste)
Return to boiling, stirring until sweetener is dissolved.
Just before serving time add:
    ¾ c. orange juice
    ¾ c. lemon juice
    ½ c. pineapple juice

Yields 28 4-oz. punch cups, 49 Calories, 0.1 g. protein, negligible fiber each made with sugar, 44 Calories made with honey. Only 7½ of those Calories are from fruit. The rest are from sugar or honey. Use only occasionally and in moderation.

Lime Punch

Combine and boil together:
- 1⅓ c. honey *or* 2 c. sugar
- 2 c. water

Cool

Combine:
- 2 c. lime juice *or* 3 packages lime flavored drink mix
- 48 oz. pineapple juice

Combine fruit or mix and syrup. Add water and ice to make 20 cups.

Just before serving add
- 1 quart ginger ale

Yields 24 8-oz. glasses or 48 4-oz. punch cups, 115 Calories, 0.3 g. protein, 0.19 g. fiber per glass; 58 Calories, 0.15 g. protein, 0.1 g. fiber per punch cup with lime juice.

CONFECTIONS

Stuffed Dates or Prunes or Other Dried Fruits

Dates and Prunes—Replace the seed with pecan, English walnut half, almond, or other nutmeats. Yield varies with the nut. With pecans or walnuts each stuffed fruit averages about 20 Calories, 0.2 g. protein, 0.13 g. fiber.

Replace the seed with cheese, or a cheese and nut mixture. Yield varies with the filling. Here is a suggested one:

Combine and beat until smooth:
    3 oz. cream cheese
    2 Tbsp. light cream, evaporated milk, or sweetened condensed milk.
    Dash of salt

Add and mix well
    ¼ c. chopped nuts

If this mixture is used to fill 45 dates (about ½ pound) or 35 large prunes (also about ½ pound)* each filled fruit will offer approximately 27 Calories, 0.4 g. protein, 0.13 g. fiber.

---

*Unfilled dates of this size provide about 14 Calories, 0.1 g. protein, 0.02 g. fiber each, unfilled prunes about 16 Calories, 0.1 g. protein, 0.10 g. fiber.

Apricots or portions of other dried fruits—Place nut or filling on fruit open-faced sandwich style. Yield varies with weight of fruit and filling.

Honey-Fruit Balls

Grind in a food grinder* or blender 1½ c. dried fruits. A suggested mixture is:

- ¼ c. pitted dried prunes
- ¼ c. dried apricots
- ¼ c. dried figs
- ½ c. dried dates (pitted)
- ¼ c. raisins

Add and mix thoroughly
- 3 Tbsp. honey *or less*

With buttered hands, form into balls. Roll in
- ½ c. chopped nuts or coconut

Yields 30 balls, 43 Calories, 0.4 g. protein, 0.33 g. fiber each when rolled in coconut, a few more Calories and a bit more protein when rolled in other nuts.

Apricot Patties
(Or crescents, balls, whatever shape you like)

Chop finely in blender or on chopping board *or* grind:*
- ¾ c. dried apricots (4½ oz.)
- ¾ c. shredded coconut (2½ oz.)

Add:
- ½ tsp. grated orange rind
- ½ tsp. grated lemon rind
- 1 Tbsp. orange juice

*Dried apricots, prunes, and raisins may go through the grinder more easily if they stand in boiling water about 5 minutes first. Blot to remove excess moisture if soaked. Drain well and use the water in cooking cereal or making syrup.

Knead mixture until blended, and it will form balls when pressed together. If the mixture is too dry, add a bit more orange juice. If it is too wet, add more dry chopped apricots or a bit of powdered sugar.

Scoop up the mixture by the tablespoonful and mold into the desired shape. Roll in ½ oz. finely chopped nuts or coconut.

Yields 12 patties, 54 Calories, 0.9 g. protein, 0.57 g. fiber each.

Coconut Macaroons

Combine and mix:
- ⅔ c. sweetened condensed milk
- 3 c. shredded coconut (8 oz.)
- 1 tsp. vanilla
- ¾ tsp. almond flavoring

Drop by teaspoonfuls onto brown paper on a cookie sheet. Bake at 350° F. 8 to 10 minutes or until delicately browned around the edges. Carefully lift the brown paper bearing the macaroons from the cookie sheet. Cover the hot pan with a wet towel. Replace the brown paper with the macaroons. Steam from the towel will loosen the confections and permit them to be removed easily. Yields 30 macaroons, 47 Calories, 0.9 g. protein, 0.41 g. fiber each.

Pam's Instant Fudge

Combine in a saucepan, melt, and blend:
1 c. each:

peanut butter	sunflower seeds	carob powder
honey	chopped nuts	
coconut	sesame seed	

Pour into a greased pan, 9x13 inches. Chill. Yields 54 1½-inch squares, 105 Calories, 2.8 g. protein, 0.49 g. fiber each. Watch those Calories!

Cream Cheese Fudge
(Uncooked and easy)

Combine and whip until creamy:
   3 oz. cream cheese
   2 c. sifted powdered sugar
   ½ tsp. vanilla
   Dash of salt

Melt and add:
   2 oz. (squares) baking chocolate (unsweetened)*

Add and mix thoroughly
   ½ c. chopped nuts

Spread in a greased pan, 8 inches square. Cool in the refrigerator. Cut into squares. Yields 25 1½-inch squares, 78 Calories, 0.9 g. protein, 0.06 g. fiber each. Watch those Calories! It's hard to stop with one or two or even three squares!

---

*⅓ c. cocoa or carob and 2 Tbsp. melted table fat may be substituted for chocolate. Sift cocoa or carob with powdered sugar to use.

RECIPE INDEX

Bread and Rolls, Whole Wheat (Straight Dough Method)	61
Cinnamon Bread	71
Cinnamon Rolls	70
Fruit Bread	72
Raisin Bread	71
Bread and Rolls, Whole Wheat (Sponge Method)	72
Breakfasts	74
Cornmeal Mush	75
Cracked Wheat	74
Granola	77
Leftover Cereals	76
Rice	74
Rolled Oats	74
Wheat Nuts	76
Whole Wheat Grains	75
Quick Breads	78
Biscuits with Variations	88
Cobbler	90
Corn Bread	94
Doughnuts, Facts About	84
Doughnuts, Cake and Yeast	86
French Toast	82
Muffins	91

Noodles	95
Pancake Accompaniments	82, 83
Pancakes	78
Shortcake	90
Waffles	79, 80

Cakes ... 96

Angel Food	96
Apple	100
Applesauce with Icing	101, 102
Banana Loaf or Cupcakes	102
Carrot Loaf, Cake, and Pudding	104, 111
Chocolate with Icing	99
Date Nut Loaf	108
Devil's Food with Icing	105
Fruit Cobbler (Cake Type)	110
Gingerbread	98
Nut Torte with Date Cheese Topping	97, 98
Oatmeal Cake	107
Pumpkin Loaf	103
Shortcake	108
Spice	99
Upside-Down, Pineapple, Cherry	109, 110
Zucchini Loaf	104

Cookies ... 113

Applesauce-Nut	114
Carrot Cookies	120
Coco-Mints with Mint Filling or Frosting	117, 118
Coconut Kisses	122
Cowboy Cookies	113
Date Balls	120
Fudge Brownies	116
German Love Cookies	116
Gingersnaps	118
Oatmeal Cookies	114
Oatmeal Date Bars	115
Oatmeal Nut Crisps	121
Peanut Butter Bars	121

Peanut Butter Cookies 119
Tea Cookies (pressed) 119

Pastries 123
Apple Pie 131
Butter Tarts 125
Cream Puffs or Eclairs 126
Cottage Cheese Cake (pie) 127
Custard Pie with Carrot Variation 134
Dutch Apple Pie 135
Fruit Pies, Fresh, Canned 130
Graham Cracker Crusts 126
Meringues 133
Mince Pie (Mock Mincemeat) 131
Mincemeat (real) 132
One-Crust Pies 124
Pecan Pie 129
Pumpkin Pie or Custard 128
Rhubarb Pie, Plain, Custard 133, 134
Whole Wheat Pie Crust 123

Fruit Desserts 136
Ambrosia 142
Apples, Baked 137
Apple Crisp 140
Apple (or Rhubarb) Crumble 138
Applesauce with Variations 136
Bride's Salad 142
Cranberry Ice 144
Cranberry Sauce 141
Fruit Betty 139
Fruit Compote 141
Fruit Gelatin Desserts 146, 147
Heavenly Hash 147
Lemon Chiffon Ring with Fresh Fruit 144
Pineapple Chiffon 145
Prune (or Apricot) Whip 143
Rhubarb, Stewed 138
Scandinavian Sweet Soup 141

Milk Desserts 149
    Baked Custard 150
    Custard, Stirred 153
    Haupia 155
    Homemade Ice Cream 153
    Lemon Fluff 154
    Pudding, Bread, Rice, or Whole Wheat 150
    Pudding, Butterscotch, Chocolate, Meringue,
        Raisin, Vanilla 151, 152
    Whipped Topping, Low Calorie 149
Meats and Meat Substitutes 157
    Beans, Dried, Peas, and Lentils 171
    Beef, Curry, Pot Roast 187, 188
    Beef Stroganoff 190
    Cheese, Pimiento Spread, Quiche Lorraine
       . . . . 160, 161, 185
    Chicken, Pie, Creamed 158, 159
    Dressing, Whole Wheat Bread and Celery 165
    Eggs, Creamed, Deviled, Foo Yung, Hard-cooked,
        Green Rice, Fried Rice, Omelet, Poached
       179-184
    Egg Salad Sandwich 185
    Eggplant Parmesan 186
    Fish, Fried, Baked, Stuffed, Broiled, Barbecued
       . . . . 162, 164, 166, 167
    Goulash, Whole Wheat 169
    Ham, Sweet-Sour 170
    Lasagna 169
    Liver, with Onions, Sour Sauce 191, 192
    Macaroni, Cheese, and Egg Casserole 168
    Mackerel, Patties, Loaf 161, 162
    Meat Loaf 189
    Pizza 177, 178
    Quiche Lorraine with Variations 160
    Salmon, Pie, Creamed 159
    Shrimp, Creamed 159
    Steak, Teriyaki 190

Tuna, Chopstick, Casserole, Sandwich Spread, Pie
.... 157, 158, 159, 185
Turkey, Pie, Creamed 158, 159
Vegetables 193
Asparagus................................ 197
Beets with Variations 202
Broccoli 195
Brussel Sprouts 197
Cabbage 196
Carrots with Variations 203
Cauliflower 198
Green Beans, Snap, Wax 200
Greens, Wild............................ 200
Kale 195
Lima Beans............................. 200
Mustard 195
Parsley or Mint Carrots................... 203
Parsnips 204
Peas 201
Potatoes with Variations.................. 205
Potatoes, Sweet, with Variations 204
Sauces, Basic White, Cheese, Mushroom,
Lemon-Butter 193, 194
Soybeans............................... 200
Spinach 195
Turnips................................ 195
Vegetable Dinner, Boiled 210
Soups 212
Bean 175
Borscht 211
Chili 174
Oyster, Mock, Real 213
Parsley 206
Potato................................. 207
Potato and Kale 206
Tomato, Cream, Chunky-Onion 214
Vegetable 211

  Vegetable, Cream of 212
Salads 214
  Apple-Celery-Nut (Waldorf) 218
  Cabbage-Pineapple Salad 215
  Carrot Raisin 217
  Chef's Salad 216
  Chicken (Turkey, Fish, or Meat) Salad 220
  Coleslaw 215
  Cottage Cheese-Green Pepper Salad 221
  Fruit Plate 221
  Garden Salad with Vinegar and Cream Dressing . 215
  Gelatin Salads, Cranberry, Carrot-Pineapple,
    Perfection, Tomato Aspic 222, 223, 224
  Guacamole Salad (or Dip) 218
  Kidney Bean Salad with French Dressing 219
  Peas, Cheese, and Pickle Salad 220
  Tossed Salad 216
Beverages 226
  Barley Drink, Warm 227
  Cider, Spiced (Nonalcoholic) 231
  General Suggestions 226
  Juice, Grape, Tomato, Other 228, 229, 230
  Lemonade, or Limeade 230
  Orange Smoothie (A Christmas Eggnog) 232
  Punch, Carrousel, Warm Fruit, Christmas, Lime,
    Pineapple 232, 233, 234, 235
  Rhubarb Thirst Quencher 233
  Rose Hips 228
Confections 236
  Apricot Patties 237
  Coconut Macaroons 238
  Dates, Prunes, or Other Dried Fruits, Stuffed . . . 236
  Honey-Fruit Balls 237
  Fudge, Instant, Cream Cheese 238, 239

NOTES

NOTES

NOTES